FREE Study Skills Videos

Dear Customer,

Thank you for your purchase from Mometrix! We consider it an honor and a privilege that you have purchased our product and we want to ensure your satisfaction.

As a way of showing our appreciation and to help us better serve you, we have developed Study Skills Videos that we would like to give you for <u>FREE</u>. These videos cover our *best practices* for getting ready for your exam, from how to use our study materials to how to best prepare for the day of the test.

All that we ask is that you email us with feedback that would describe your experience so far with our product. Good, bad, or indifferent, we want to know what you think!

To get your FREE Study Skills Videos, you can use the **QR code** below, or send us an **email** at <u>studyvideos@mometrix.com</u> with *FREE VIDEOS* in the subject line and the following information in the body of the email:

- The name of the product you purchased.
- Your product rating on a scale of 1-5, with 5 being the highest rating.
- Your feedback. It can be long, short, or anything in between. We just want to know your impressions and experience so far with our product. (Good feedback might include how our study material met your needs and ways we might be able to make it even better. You could highlight features that you found helpful or features that you think we should add.)

If you have any questions or concerns, please don't hesitate to contact me directly.

Thanks again!

Sincerely,

Jay Willis
Vice President
<u>jay.willis@mometrix.com</u>
1-800-673-8175

SCAN HERE

Mometrix
TEST PREPARATION
The World's #1 Test Preparation Company

MPRE

Study Guide
Secrets Prep

for the Multistate Professional
Responsibility Examination

2 Full-Length Practice Tests

Detailed Answer
Explanations

2nd Edition

Written and edited by Matthew Bowling

Printed in the United States of America

This paper meets the requirements of ANSI/NISO Z39.48-1992 (Permanence of Paper).

Mometrix offers volume discount pricing to institutions. For more information or a price quote, please contact our sales department at sales@mometrix.com or 888-248-1219.

Mometrix Media LLC is not affiliated with or endorsed by any official testing organization. All organizational and test names are trademarks of their respective owners.

Paperback
ISBN 13: 978-1-5167-1807-8
ISBN 10: 1-5167-1807-0

DEAR FUTURE EXAM SUCCESS STORY

First of all, **THANK YOU** for purchasing Mometrix study materials!

Second, congratulations! You are one of the few determined test-takers who are committed to doing whatever it takes to excel on your exam. **You have come to the right place.** We developed these study materials with one goal in mind: to deliver you the information you need in a format that's concise and easy to use.

In addition to optimizing your guide for the content of the test, we've outlined our recommended steps for breaking down the preparation process into small, attainable goals so you can make sure you stay on track.

We've also analyzed the entire test-taking process, identifying the most common pitfalls and showing how you can overcome them and be ready for any curveball the test throws you.

Standardized testing is one of the biggest obstacles on your road to success, which only increases the importance of doing well in the high-pressure, high-stakes environment of test day. Your results on this test could have a significant impact on your future, and this guide provides the information and practical advice to help you achieve your full potential on test day.

Your success is our success

We would love to hear from you! If you would like to share the story of your exam success or if you have any questions or comments in regard to our products, please contact us at **800-673-8175** or **support@mometrix.com**.

Thanks again for your business and we wish you continued success!

Sincerely,
The Mometrix Test Preparation Team

> **Need more help? Check out our flashcards at:**
> **http://mometrixflashcards.com/MPRE**

TABLE OF CONTENTS

Introduction

Thank you for purchasing this resource! You have made the choice to prepare yourself for a test that could have a huge impact on your future, and this guide is designed to help you be fully ready for test day. Obviously, it's important to have a solid understanding of the test material, but you also need to be prepared for the unique environment and stressors of the test, so that you can perform to the best of your abilities.

For this purpose, the first section that appears in this guide is the **Secret Keys**. We've devoted countless hours to meticulously researching what works and what doesn't, and we've boiled down our findings to the five most impactful steps you can take to improve your performance on the test. We start at the beginning with study planning and move through the preparation process, all the way to the testing strategies that will help you get the most out of what you know when you're finally sitting in front of the test.

We recommend that you start preparing for your test as far in advance as possible. However, if you've bought this guide as a last-minute study resource and only have a few days before your test, we recommend that you skip over the first two Secret Keys since they address a long-term study plan.

If you struggle with **test anxiety**, we strongly encourage you to check out our recommendations for how you can overcome it. Test anxiety is a formidable foe, but it can be beaten, and we want to make sure you have the tools you need to defeat it.

Secret Key #1 – Plan Big, Study Small

There's a lot riding on your performance. If you want to ace this test, you're going to need to keep your skills sharp and the material fresh in your mind. You need a plan that lets you review everything you need to know while still fitting in your schedule. We'll break this strategy down into three categories.

Information Organization

Start with the information you already have: the official test outline. From this, you can make a complete list of all the concepts you need to cover before the test. Organize these concepts into groups that can be studied together, and create a list of any related vocabulary you need to learn so you can brush up on any difficult terms. You'll want to keep this vocabulary list handy once you actually start studying since you may need to add to it along the way.

Time Management

Once you have your set of study concepts, decide how to spread them out over the time you have left before the test. Break your study plan into small, clear goals so you have a manageable task for each day and know exactly what you're doing. Then just focus on one small step at a time. When you manage your time this way, you don't need to spend hours at a time studying. Studying a small block of content for a short period each day helps you retain information better and avoid stressing over how much you have left to do. You can relax knowing that you have a plan to cover everything in time. In order for this strategy to be effective though, you have to start studying early and stick to your schedule. Avoid the exhaustion and futility that comes from last-minute cramming!

Study Environment

The environment you study in has a big impact on your learning. Studying in a coffee shop, while probably more enjoyable, is not likely to be as fruitful as studying in a quiet room. It's important to keep distractions to a minimum. You're only planning to study for a short block of time, so make the most of it. Don't pause to check your phone or get up to find a snack. It's also important to **avoid multitasking**. Research has consistently shown that multitasking will make your studying dramatically less effective. Your study area should also be comfortable and well-lit so you don't have the distraction of straining your eyes or sitting on an uncomfortable chair.

 The time of day you study is also important. You want to be rested and alert. Don't wait until just before bedtime. Study when you'll be most likely to comprehend and remember. Even better, if you know what time of day your test will be, set that time aside for study. That way your brain will be used to working on that subject at that specific time and you'll have a better chance of recalling information.

Finally, it can be helpful to team up with others who are studying for the same test. Your actual studying should be done in as isolated an environment as possible, but the work of organizing the information and setting up the study plan can be divided up. In between study sessions, you can discuss with your teammates the concepts that you're all studying and quiz each other on the details. Just be sure that your teammates are as serious about the test as you are. If you find that your study time is being replaced with social time, you might need to find a new team.

2

Secret Key #2 – Make Your Studying Count

You're devoting a lot of time and effort to preparing for this test, so you want to be absolutely certain it will pay off. This means doing more than just reading the content and hoping you can remember it on test day. It's important to make every minute of study count. There are two main areas you can focus on to make your studying count.

Retention

It doesn't matter how much time you study if you can't remember the material. You need to make sure you are retaining the concepts. To check your retention of the information you're learning, try recalling it at later times with minimal prompting. Try carrying around flashcards and glance at one or two from time to time or ask a friend who's also studying for the test to quiz you.

To enhance your retention, look for ways to put the information into practice so that you can apply it rather than simply recalling it. If you're using the information in practical ways, it will be much easier to remember. Similarly, it helps to solidify a concept in your mind if you're not only reading it to yourself but also explaining it to someone else. Ask a friend to let you teach them about a concept you're a little shaky on (or speak aloud to an imaginary audience if necessary). As you try to summarize, define, give examples, and answer your friend's questions, you'll understand the concepts better and they will stay with you longer. Finally, step back for a big picture view and ask yourself how each piece of information fits with the whole subject. When you link the different concepts together and see them working together as a whole, it's easier to remember the individual components.

Finally, practice showing your work on any multi-step problems, even if you're just studying. Writing out each step you take to solve a problem will help solidify the process in your mind, and you'll be more likely to remember it during the test.

Modality

Modality simply refers to the means or method by which you study. Choosing a study modality that fits your own individual learning style is crucial. No two people learn best in exactly the same way, so it's important to know your strengths and use them to your advantage.

For example, if you learn best by visualization, focus on visualizing a concept in your mind and draw an image or a diagram. Try color-coding your notes, illustrating them, or creating symbols that will trigger your mind to recall a learned concept. If you learn best by hearing or discussing information, find a study partner who learns the same way or read aloud to yourself. Think about how to put the information in your own words. Imagine that you are giving a lecture on the topic and record yourself so you can listen to it later.

For any learning style, flashcards can be helpful. Organize the information so you can take advantage of spare moments to review. Underline key words or phrases. Use different colors for different categories. Mnemonic devices (such as creating a short list in which every item starts with the same letter) can also help with retention. Find what works best for you and use it to store the information in your mind most effectively and easily.

3

Secret Key #3 – Practice the Right Way

Your success on test day depends not only on how many hours you put into preparing, but also on whether you prepared the right way. It's good to check along the way to see if your studying is paying off. One of the most effective ways to do this is by taking practice tests to evaluate your progress. Practice tests are useful because they show exactly where you need to improve. Every time you take a practice test, pay special attention to these three groups of questions:

- The questions you got wrong
- The questions you had to guess on, even if you guessed right
- The questions you found difficult or slow to work through

This will show you exactly what your weak areas are, and where you need to devote more study time. Ask yourself why each of these questions gave you trouble. Was it because you didn't understand the material? Was it because you didn't remember the vocabulary? Do you need more repetitions on this type of question to build speed and confidence? Dig into those questions and figure out how you can strengthen your weak areas as you go back to review the material.

 Additionally, many practice tests have a section explaining the answer choices. It can be tempting to read the explanation and think that you now have a good understanding of the concept. However, an explanation likely only covers part of the question's broader context. Even if the explanation makes perfect sense, **go back and investigate** every concept related to the question until you're positive you have a thorough understanding.

As you go along, keep in mind that the practice test is just that: practice. Memorizing these questions and answers will not be very helpful on the actual test because it is unlikely to have any of the same exact questions. If you only know the right answers to the sample questions, you won't be prepared for the real thing. **Study the concepts** until you understand them fully, and then you'll be able to answer any question that shows up on the test.

It's important to wait on the practice tests until you're ready. If you take a test on your first day of study, you may be overwhelmed by the amount of material covered and how much you need to learn. Work up to it gradually.

On test day, you'll need to be prepared for answering questions, managing your time, and using the test-taking strategies you've learned. It's a lot to balance, like a mental marathon that will have a big impact on your future. Like training for a marathon, you'll need to start slowly and work your way up. When test day arrives, you'll be ready.

Start with the strategies you've read in the first two Secret Keys—plan your course and study in the way that works best for you. If you have time, consider using multiple study resources to get different approaches to the same concepts. It can be helpful to see difficult concepts from more than one angle. Then find a good source for practice tests. Many times, the test website will suggest potential study resources or provide sample tests.

Practice Test Strategy

If you're able to find at least three practice tests, we recommend this strategy:

UNTIMED AND OPEN-BOOK PRACTICE

Take the first test with no time constraints and with your notes and study guide handy. Take your time and focus on applying the strategies you've learned.

TIMED AND OPEN-BOOK PRACTICE

Take the second practice test open-book as well, but set a timer and practice pacing yourself to finish in time.

TIMED AND CLOSED-BOOK PRACTICE

Take any other practice tests as if it were test day. Set a timer and put away your study materials. Sit at a table or desk in a quiet room, imagine yourself at the testing center, and answer questions as quickly and accurately as possible.

Keep repeating timed and closed-book tests on a regular basis until you run out of practice tests or it's time for the actual test. Your mind will be ready for the schedule and stress of test day, and you'll be able to focus on recalling the material you've learned.

Secret Key #4 – Pace Yourself

Once you're fully prepared for the material on the test, your biggest challenge on test day will be managing your time. Just knowing that the clock is ticking can make you panic even if you have plenty of time left. Work on pacing yourself so you can build confidence against the time constraints of the exam. Pacing is a difficult skill to master, especially in a high-pressure environment, so **practice is vital**.

Set time expectations for your pace based on how much time is available. For example, if a section has 60 questions and the time limit is 30 minutes, you know you have to average 30 seconds or less per question in order to answer them all. Although 30 seconds is the hard limit, set 25 seconds per question as your goal, so you reserve extra time to spend on harder questions. When you budget extra time for the harder questions, you no longer have any reason to stress when those questions take longer to answer.

Don't let this time expectation distract you from working through the test at a calm, steady pace, but keep it in mind so you don't spend too much time on any one question. Recognize that taking extra time on one question you don't understand may keep you from answering two that you do understand later in the test. If your time limit for a question is up and you're still not sure of the answer, mark it and move on, and come back to it later if the time and the test format allow. If the testing format doesn't allow you to return to earlier questions, just make an educated guess; then put it out of your mind and move on.

On the easier questions, be careful not to rush. It may seem wise to hurry through them so you have more time for the challenging ones, but it's not worth missing one if you know the concept and just didn't take the time to read the question fully. Work efficiently but make sure you understand the question and have looked at all of the answer choices, since more than one may seem right at first.

Even if you're paying attention to the time, you may find yourself a little behind at some point. You should speed up to get back on track, but do so wisely. Don't panic; just take a few seconds less on each question until you're caught up. Don't guess without thinking, but do look through the answer choices and eliminate any you know are wrong. If you can get down to two choices, it is often worthwhile to guess from those. Once you've chosen an answer, move on and don't dwell on any that you skipped or had to hurry through. If a question was taking too long, chances are it was one of the harder ones, so you weren't as likely to get it right anyway.

On the other hand, if you find yourself getting ahead of schedule, it may be beneficial to slow down a little. The more quickly you work, the more likely you are to make a careless mistake that will affect your score. You've budgeted time for each question, so don't be afraid to spend that time. Practice an efficient but careful pace to get the most out of the time you have.

Secret Key #5 – Have a Plan for Guessing

When you're taking the test, you may find yourself stuck on a question. Some of the answer choices seem better than others, but you don't see the one answer choice that is obviously correct. What do you do?

The scenario described above is very common, yet most test takers have not effectively prepared for it. Developing and practicing a plan for guessing may be one of the single most effective uses of your time as you get ready for the exam.

In developing your plan for guessing, there are three questions to address:

- When should you start the guessing process?
- How should you narrow down the choices?
- Which answer should you choose?

When to Start the Guessing Process

Unless your plan for guessing is to select C every time (which, despite its merits, is not what we recommend), you need to leave yourself enough time to apply your answer elimination strategies. Since you have a limited amount of time for each question, that means that if you're going to give yourself the best shot at guessing correctly, you have to decide quickly whether or not you will guess.

Of course, the best-case scenario is that you don't have to guess at all, so first, see if you can answer the question based on your knowledge of the subject and basic reasoning skills. Focus on the key words in the question and try to jog your memory of related topics. Give yourself a chance to bring the knowledge to mind, but once you realize that you don't have (or you can't access) the knowledge you need to answer the question, it's time to start the guessing process.

It's almost always better to start the guessing process too early than too late. It only takes a few seconds to remember something and answer the question from knowledge. Carefully eliminating wrong answer choices takes longer. Plus, going through the process of eliminating answer choices can actually help jog your memory.

Summary: Start the guessing process as soon as you decide that you can't answer the question based on your knowledge.

7

How to Narrow Down the Choices

The next chapter in this book (**Test-Taking Strategies**) includes a wide range of strategies for how to approach questions and how to look for answer choices to eliminate. You will definitely want to read those carefully, practice them, and figure out which ones work best for you. Here though, we're going to address a mindset rather than a particular strategy.

Your odds of guessing an answer correctly depend on how many options you are choosing from.

Number of options left	5	4	3	2	1
Odds of guessing correctly	20%	25%	33%	50%	100%

You can see from this chart just how valuable it is to be able to eliminate incorrect answers and make an educated guess, but there are two things that many test takers do that cause them to miss out on the benefits of guessing:

- Accidentally eliminating the correct answer
- Selecting an answer based on an impression

We'll look at the first one here, and the second one in the next section.

To avoid accidentally eliminating the correct answer, we recommend a thought exercise called **the $5 challenge**. In this challenge, you only eliminate an answer choice from contention if you are willing to bet $5 on it being wrong. Why $5? Five dollars is a small but not insignificant amount of money. It's an amount you could afford to lose but wouldn't want to throw away. And while losing

$5 once might not hurt too much, doing it twenty times will set you back $100. In the same way, each small decision you make—eliminating a choice here, guessing on a question there—won't by itself impact your score very much, but when you put them all together, they can make a big difference. By holding each answer choice elimination decision to a higher standard, you can reduce the risk of accidentally eliminating the correct answer.

The $5 challenge can also be applied in a positive sense: If you are willing to bet $5 that an answer choice *is* correct, go ahead and mark it as correct.

Summary: Only eliminate an answer choice if you are willing to bet $5 that it is wrong.

8

Which Answer to Choose

You're taking the test. You've run into a hard question and decided you'll have to guess. You've eliminated all the answer choices you're willing to bet $5 on. Now you have to pick an answer. Why do we even need to talk about this? Why can't you just pick whichever one you feel like when the time comes?

The answer to these questions is that if you don't come into the test with a plan, you'll rely on your impression to select an answer choice, and if you do that, you risk falling into a trap. The test writers know that everyone who takes their test will be guessing on some of the questions, so they intentionally write wrong answer choices to seem plausible. You still have to pick an answer though, and if the wrong answer choices are designed to look right, how can you ever be sure that you're not falling for their trap? The best solution we've found to this dilemma is to take the decision out of your hands entirely. Here is the process we recommend:

Once you've eliminated any choices that you are confident (willing to bet $5) are wrong, select the first remaining choice as your answer.

Whether you choose to select the first remaining choice, the second, or the last, the important thing is that you use some preselected standard. Using this approach guarantees that you will not be enticed into selecting an answer choice that looks right, because you are not basing your decision on how the answer choices look.

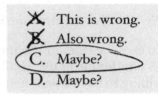

This is not meant to make you question your knowledge. Instead, it is to help you recognize the difference between your knowledge and your impressions. There's a huge difference between thinking an answer is right because of what you know, and thinking an answer is right because it looks or sounds like it should be right.

Summary: To ensure that your selection is appropriately random, make a predetermined selection from among all answer choices you have not eliminated.

Test-Taking Strategies

This section contains a list of test-taking strategies that you may find helpful as you work through the test. By taking what you know and applying logical thought, you can maximize your chances of answering any question correctly!

It is very important to realize that every question is different and every person is different: no single strategy will work on every question, and no single strategy will work for every person. That's why we've included all of them here, so you can try them out and determine which ones work best for different types of questions and which ones work best for you.

Question Strategies

☑ READ CAREFULLY

Read the question and the answer choices carefully. Don't miss the question because you misread the terms. You have plenty of time to read each question thoroughly and make sure you understand what is being asked. Yet a happy medium must be attained, so don't waste too much time. You must read carefully and efficiently.

☑ CONTEXTUAL CLUES

Look for contextual clues. If the question includes a word you are not familiar with, look at the immediate context for some indication of what the word might mean. Contextual clues can often give you all the information you need to decipher the meaning of an unfamiliar word. Even if you can't determine the meaning, you may be able to narrow down the possibilities enough to make a solid guess at the answer to the question.

☑ PREFIXES

If you're having trouble with a word in the question or answer choices, try dissecting it. Take advantage of every clue that the word might include. Prefixes and suffixes can be a huge help. Usually, they allow you to determine a basic meaning. *Pre-* means before, *post-* means after, *pro-* is positive, *de-* is negative. From prefixes and suffixes, you can get an idea of the general meaning of the word and try to put it into context.

☑ HEDGE WORDS

Watch out for critical hedge words, such as *likely, may, can, sometimes, often, almost, mostly, usually, generally, rarely,* and *sometimes.* Question writers insert these hedge phrases to cover every possibility. Often an answer choice will be wrong simply because it leaves no room for exception. Be on guard for answer choices that have definitive words such as *exactly* and *always.*

☑ SWITCHBACK WORDS

Stay alert for *switchbacks.* These are the words and phrases frequently used to alert you to shifts in thought. The most common switchback words are *but, although,* and *however.* Others include *nevertheless, on the other hand, even though, while, in spite of, despite,* and *regardless of.* Switchback words are important to catch because they can change the direction of the question or an answer choice.

10

⊘ FACE VALUE

When in doubt, use common sense. Accept the situation in the problem at face value. Don't read too much into it. These problems will not require you to make wild assumptions. If you have to go beyond creativity and warp time or space in order to have an answer choice fit the question, then you should move on and consider the other answer choices. These are normal problems rooted in reality. The applicable relationship or explanation may not be readily apparent, but it is there for you to figure out. Use your common sense to interpret anything that isn't clear.

Answer Choice Strategies

⊘ ANSWER SELECTION

The most thorough way to pick an answer choice is to identify and eliminate wrong answers until only one is left, then confirm it is the correct answer. Sometimes an answer choice may immediately seem right, but be careful. The test writers will usually put more than one reasonable answer choice on each question, so take a second to read all of them and make sure that the other choices are not equally obvious. As long as you have time left, it is better to read every answer choice than to pick the first one that looks right without checking the others.

⊘ ANSWER CHOICE FAMILIES

An answer choice family consists of two (in rare cases, three) answer choices that are very similar in construction and cannot all be true at the same time. If you see two answer choices that are direct opposites or parallels, one of them is usually the correct answer. For instance, if one answer choice says that quantity x increases and another either says that quantity x decreases (opposite) or says that quantity y increases (parallel), then those answer choices would fall into the same family. An answer choice that doesn't match the construction of the answer choice family is more likely to be incorrect. Most questions will not have answer choice families, but when they do appear, you should be prepared to recognize them.

⊘ ELIMINATE ANSWERS

Eliminate answer choices as soon as you realize they are wrong, but make sure you consider all possibilities. If you are eliminating answer choices and realize that the last one you are left with is also wrong, don't panic. Start over and consider each choice again. There may be something you missed the first time that you will realize on the second pass.

⊘ AVOID FACT TRAPS

Don't be distracted by an answer choice that is factually true but doesn't answer the question. You are looking for the choice that answers the question. Stay focused on what the question is asking for so you don't accidentally pick an answer that is true but incorrect. Always go back to the question and make sure the answer choice you've selected actually answers the question and is not merely a true statement.

⊘ EXTREME STATEMENTS

In general, you should avoid answers that put forth extreme actions as standard practice or proclaim controversial ideas as established fact. An answer choice that states the "process should be used in certain situations, if…" is much more likely to be correct than one that states the "process should be discontinued completely." The first is a calm rational statement and doesn't even make a definitive, uncompromising stance, using a hedge word *if* to provide wiggle room, whereas the second choice is far more extreme.

⊘ BENCHMARK

As you read through the answer choices and you come across one that seems to answer the question well, mentally select that answer choice. This is not your final answer, but it's the one that will help you evaluate the other answer choices. The one that you selected is your benchmark or standard for judging each of the other answer choices. Every other answer choice must be compared to your benchmark. That choice is correct until proven otherwise by another answer choice beating it. If you find a better answer, then that one becomes your new benchmark. Once you've decided that no other choice answers the question as well as your benchmark, you have your final answer.

⊘ PREDICT THE ANSWER

Before you even start looking at the answer choices, it is often best to try to predict the answer. When you come up with the answer on your own, it is easier to avoid distractions and traps because you will know exactly what to look for. The right answer choice is unlikely to be word-for-word what you came up with, but it should be a close match. Even if you are confident that you have the right answer, you should still take the time to read each option before moving on.

General Strategies

⊘ TOUGH QUESTIONS

If you are stumped on a problem or it appears too hard or too difficult, don't waste time. Move on! Remember though, if you can quickly check for obviously incorrect answer choices, your chances of guessing correctly are greatly improved. Before you completely give up, at least try to knock out a couple of possible answers. Eliminate what you can and then guess at the remaining answer choices before moving on.

⊘ CHECK YOUR WORK

Since you will probably not know every term listed and the answer to every question, it is important that you get credit for the ones that you do know. Don't miss any questions through careless mistakes. If at all possible, try to take a second to look back over your answer selection and make sure you've selected the correct answer choice and haven't made a costly careless mistake (such as marking an answer choice that you didn't mean to mark). This quick double check should more than pay for itself in caught mistakes for the time it costs.

⊘ PACE YOURSELF

It's easy to be overwhelmed when you're looking at a page full of questions; your mind is confused and full of random thoughts, and the clock is ticking down faster than you would like. Calm down and maintain the pace that you have set for yourself. Especially as you get down to the last few minutes of the test, don't let the small numbers on the clock make you panic. As long as you are on track by monitoring your pace, you are guaranteed to have time for each question.

⊘ DON'T RUSH

It is very easy to make errors when you are in a hurry. Maintaining a fast pace in answering questions is pointless if it makes you miss questions that you would have gotten right otherwise. Test writers like to include distracting information and wrong answers that seem right. Taking a little extra time to avoid careless mistakes can make all the difference in your test score. Find a pace that allows you to be confident in the answers that you select.

⊘ KEEP MOVING

Panicking will not help you pass the test, so do your best to stay calm and keep moving. Taking deep breaths and going through the answer elimination steps you practiced can help to break through a stress barrier and keep your pace.

Final Notes

The combination of a solid foundation of content knowledge and the confidence that comes from practicing your plan for applying that knowledge is the key to maximizing your performance on test day. As your foundation of content knowledge is built up and strengthened, you'll find that the strategies included in this chapter become more and more effective in helping you quickly sift through the distractions and traps of the test to isolate the correct answer.

Now that you're preparing to move forward into the test content chapters of this book, be sure to keep your goal in mind. As you read, think about how you will be able to apply this information on the test. If you've already seen sample questions for the test and you have an idea of the question format and style, try to come up with questions of your own that you can answer based on what you're reading. This will give you valuable practice applying your knowledge in the same ways you can expect to on test day.

Good luck and good studying!

Regulation of the Legal Profession

Powers of Courts and Other Bodies to Regulate Lawyers

While several different regulatory bodies may impact every attorney, the most prevalent source of professional regulation for legal professionals is the state in which they practice.

Legal professionals are entrusted with the ability and licensure to practice law in the particular state(s) in which they have been admitted. Within a state, the practice of law is largely self-policing. As such, a tremendous amount of trust is placed in legal professionals to carry out their duties in an effective and efficient manner to ensure that both their clients and the public at large are best served. For this reason, a state is particularly concerned with ensuring that its legal professionals carry out the practice of law in a competent and ethical manner.

Other sources of regulation include the rules of federal courts or agencies. An attorney who practices exclusively in federal court is still subject to regulation by every state in which that attorney is admitted to practice.

GOVERNING BODIES WITHIN STATES

In general, there are three different governing bodies that regulate the legal profession within each state. These include state courts, the state bar association, and the state legislature.

The state courts have an inherent power over the legal profession because of the connection between the practice of law and the administration of justice. In fact, because of this connection, the highest court in the state has the most power with respect to the establishment of professional standards. The influence of the state courts is felt primarily through:

- adoption of ethical rules (which are typically modeled after the ABA Model Rules of Professional Conduct);
- case law decided by the state courts that impacts the legal profession; and
- rules of court established or adopted by a given state court to govern conduct within that court.

Every state in the United States has a bar association. State bar associations play an integral role in both establishing and enforcing legal professional standards. Additionally, the majority of state bar associations are now integrated. This means that attorneys who wish to practice law in a state with an integrated bar association must first become a member of that bar association. The general duties of a state bar association include:

- conducting the state's bar examination;
- overseeing the state's continuing legal education programs; and
- providing support to the state courts both in implementing the legal profession's ethical standards and in applying them to specific cases of alleged misconduct.

The state legislature usually plays a less direct role in regulating legal professionals, typically through enacting or modifying statutes that govern specific aspects of practicing law.

Admission to the Profession

GENERAL ISSUES

The applicant usually must graduate from an accredited law school. Additionally, the applicant must provide the state—usually the bar admission committee—with an application for admission. Finally, the applicant must sit for and pass the state's bar examination, which is administered by that state's bar association. Once the applicant meets these requirements, he or she is admitted to practice law in that state and is sworn in before the state's highest court. The state's bar association typically impacts every step of the admissions process. Admission to practice within one state does not automatically grant the ability to practice in another state. Some states require that all applicants pass the state bar examination. Some groups of states have reciprocity agreements such that any attorney licensed to practice in one state in the group can be admitted to practice in another state in the group, provided that certain conditions are met.

CANDOR

ABA Model Rule 8.1 requires candor from bar applicants, as set forth below. Specifically, a candidate for bar membership shall not:

(a) knowingly make a false statement of material fact; or
(b) fail to disclose a fact necessary to correct a misapprehension known by the person to have arisen in the matter, or knowingly fail to respond to a lawful demand for information from an admissions or disciplinary authority, except that this rule does not require disclosure of information otherwise protected by Rule 1.6.

With respect to the first requirement, the key concept is that the applicant cannot have **knowingly** made the false statement; accidental false statements are not covered by the rule. The second requirement is different in that it requires active disclosure of relevant information.

MORAL CHARACTER

States have deemed moral character to be highly important to the practice of law. Therefore, good moral character is a requirement for admission to practice law. State bar associations will usually require that applicants complete various forms and surveys. Frequently, these surveys will require the applicants to disclose all accusations of misconduct, criminal or otherwise, rather than just convictions or punishments for misconduct. Additionally, applicants are typically required to provide the bar association with a list of personal references. Bar admissions committees then contact these references to determine the moral character of the applicant. If, through the application process, a question arises concerning the moral fitness of an applicant, he or she may be asked to appear before the bar admissions committee to clarify any issues. It is important to understand that the applicant bears the burden of proof for establishing good moral character.

Due to the importance of good moral character on the overall fitness of an applicant, bar admissions committees may review virtually all of an applicant's past or ongoing conduct. Perhaps the most obvious example of this is an applicant's criminal conduct. However, an applicant will not be denied admission to practice law as a result of committing just any crime. Rather, it must be shown that the crime committed was a crime of moral turpitude; these are generally crimes that involve dishonesty and/or violence. Bar admissions committees may also consider crimes of which the applicant was accused but acquitted. Accusations of academic misconduct, bad credit, failure to pay financial obligations, and substance abuse are also considered. Applicants with potentially

16

disqualifying conduct may present evidence of rehabilitation. The committee may also consider any litigation to which the candidate was a party.

Regulation After Admission – Lawyer Discipline

The process by which attorneys are investigated and disciplined for ethics violations takes place in several stages. This process begins with a complaint of attorney misconduct to the appropriate authority in the relevant jurisdiction. This is most often the applicable state bar association. The next step in the disciplinary process is the review of the complaint. Reports of misconduct that have no merit are dismissed. If a report of misconduct is found to have merit, the reviewing authority will usually contact the attorney, usually in writing, and ask the attorney to comment on the potential misconduct. Based upon the attorney's response (or refusal to respond) and the facts available, the authority may pursue the complaint through a hearing. Depending on the outcome of the hearing, the attorney may be sanctioned. At any stage in this process, the authority may offer the attorney an informal resolution, such as a required ethics class.

COMPLAINT STAGE

The process of disciplining an attorney for violating the ethics rules begins with the filing of a complaint with that attorney's disciplining authority. In the vast majority of cases, this authority is the accused attorney's state bar association. Most state bar associations have specific committees that field and respond to filed complaints. In the typical case, a complaint is filed against an attorney by a dissatisfied client. The client's grievance could involve anything from claimed misrepresentation to the mishandling of funds. Anyone who has knowledge of an attorney's violation of the ethics rules may file a complaint. Further, ABA Model Rule 8.3 requires attorneys with knowledge of certain violations to report misconduct on the part of fellow attorneys. Any complaint filed against an attorney is considered privileged information. If the complaint is determined to have merit, the accused attorney will be asked by the disciplinary authority to respond in writing

HEARING STAGE

If the attorney's response (or lack thereof) fails to resolve the complaint, a hearing may be ordered by the disciplinary authority. Disciplinary hearings have the following characteristics:

- The accused attorney is entitled to due process which includes the right to an attorney, right to proper notice, the right to present evidence at the hearing, and the right to question all witnesses for the other party.
- If applicable, the charged attorney may invoke their rights under the Fifth Amendment of the U.S. Constitution and may not be disciplined for doing so. However, many of the criminal evidentiary exclusion rules are inapplicable.
- The burden of proof is placed on the complaining party and most states impose a "preponderance of the evidence" standard.

If sanctions are recommended at the conclusion of the hearing, the attorney may appeal the decision to the state's highest court. The appealing attorney carries the burden of showing the wrongdoing of the disciplinary authority.

POTENTIAL SANCTIONS

Disciplinary authorities have at their disposal a variety of potential sanctions. Typically the sanction chosen is commensurate with the misconduct and surrounding circumstances. The three most commonly-imposed sanctions are:

- **Reprimand:** This official recognition of misconduct is issued by the disciplinary authority governing the attorney and may either be public or private. In either case, the reprimand will be placed on file with the disciplinary authority.
- **Suspension:** A suspension inhibits the offending attorney's ability to practice law by suspending the attorney's license for some prescribed period. Typically, the offending attorney's license is restored automatically at the expiration of such time.
- **Disbarment:** Disbarment is the permanent termination of an attorney's license to practice law. Often attorneys may apply for readmission upon demonstration of rehabilitation.

RULES GOVERNING PROCEEDINGS
WHEN A DISCIPLINARY PROCEEDING HAS COMMENCED

ABA Model Rule 8.5(a) states that an attorney's actions are governed by their licensing jurisdiction. The same attorney, however, could simultaneously be governed by another jurisdiction if the offending conduct occurred in that jurisdiction. ABA Model Rule 8.5(b)(1) dictates that a disciplinary authority will apply "the rules of the jurisdiction in which the tribunal sits, unless the rules of the tribunal provide otherwise."

WHEN A DISCIPLINARY PROCEEDING HAS NOT COMMENCED

Where there is overlapping jurisdiction in a disciplinary matter and no proceeding has commenced, ABA Model Rule 8.5(b)(2) controls, stating:

> "[F]or any other conduct, the rules of the jurisdiction in which the lawyer's conduct occurred, or, if the predominant effect of the conduct is in a different jurisdiction, the rules of that jurisdiction shall be applied to the conduct. A lawyer shall not be subject to discipline if the lawyer's conduct conforms to the rules of a jurisdiction in which the lawyer reasonably believes the predominant effect of the lawyer's conduct will occur."

Note the exoneration of an attorney who violates the ethics rules of their home jurisdiction when the attorney reasonably believes the predominant effect of their actions will occur in another jurisdiction that tolerates their actions.

STATE DECISIONS

One state's decision to discipline an attorney does not bind another state. Instead, most states break the disciplinary process into two distinct components:

- determination of misconduct; and
- imposition of sanctions.

Most states accept the determination of misconduct made by another state. The accepting state is not bound to apply the sanctions imposed by the sanctioning state. In fact, most states will accept another state's determination of misconduct and then apply their own rules to determine if, and to what extent, sanctions are to be imposed. This practice can result in two or more states recognizing that misconduct occurred but imposing (or electing not to impose) different sanctions.

FEDERAL COURT DECISIONS

It is fairly settled that a state will honor the determination of attorney misconduct by another state. It is up to each state, however, to determine the sanctions that are appropriate for such misconduct. Federal courts utilize a different approach. Each federal court in which an attorney is licensed to practice is required to make its own independent determination of an attorney's alleged misconduct. While a federal court is not bound by the determination of a state disciplinary authority, such determination is relevant evidence that may be sufficient in and of itself for the federal court to find that the attorney violated the ethics rules.

SARBANES-OXLEY ACT
EFFECT ON SECURITIES LAWYERS

As a result of corporate corruption that led to the demise of several infamous corporations in the early 2000s (e.g. Enron), the United States Congress passed the Sarbanes-Oxley Act. While this piece of legislation is very large and reaches a broad spectrum of issues, there are applications of the law that directly affect securities lawyers. Generally, the Sarbanes-Oxley Act seeks to establish rules that encourage and even require securities lawyers to report instances where the clients they represent violate federal or state securities laws or similar laws. Securities lawyers are specifically addressed by the Sarbanes-Oxley Act because of such lawyers' unique ability to see and identify potential abuses; such wrongdoing can negatively impact—sometimes to an alarming degree— individual companies, their shareholders, and financial markets in general.

"SECURITIES LAWYER"

Simply stated, the term "securities lawyer" as used in the Sarbanes-Oxley Act refers to any attorney who represents an issuer of securities or who practices before the SEC. This includes attorneys who engage in business transactions with the SEC, communicate with the SEC, or represent clients before the SEC. Generally, the Sarbanes-Oxley Act seeks to cover all attorneys who may be in a position to detect any securities law violation by a client without casting the net so wide as to dilute the intended meaning of the Act.

REQUIRED REPRESENTATIONS

Under the Sarbanes-Oxley Act, a securities lawyer who becomes aware that a client or some individual or individuals within a client's organization have materially violated a state or federal securities law must report the evidence supporting such a violation to the chief legal officer or the chief executive officer of the client. This reporting duty arises whenever the securities lawyer becomes aware of credible evidence of such a violation. From this point, the Sarbanes-Oxley Act requires the chief legal/executive officer to conduct an investigation of the allegation(s). By dictating these responsibilities, the Sarbanes-Oxley Act seeks to assign the discovery obligations to the attorney and the investigative responsibilities to the high-ranking officer of the organization.

OBLIGATIONS AFTER VIOLATION NOTIFICATION

The Sarbanes-Oxley Act seeks to ensure that securities law violations are avoided by companies subject to both state and federal securities laws. Once a securities attorney has informed a chief legal officer of a potential violation, the chief legal officer must conduct an investigation into the attorney's claims. Additionally, the chief legal officer must report the results of the investigation to the reporting attorney and take all reasonable steps to get the client to address any violations. If the attorney believes the proper steps have not been taken by the company, the attorney must convey the evidence to the company's board of directors and the audit committee of the company's board of directors or a committee of external directors.

IMPACT ON CLIENT CONFIDENTIALITY

Sarbanes-Oxley can create tension between the interest in avoiding securities law violations and the general concerns associated with confidentiality. To alleviate this tension, the Sarbanes-Oxley Act limits a securities lawyer's ability to disclose confidential client information. Specifically, an attorney may disclose confidential information to the Securities and Exchange Commission *only* if doing so is reasonably necessary to:

- keep the client from engaging in conduct that will result in substantial financial injury to itself or its shareholders;
- to mitigate the damage caused by any illegal acts that the attorney's representation furthered; or
- to prevent the client from committing perjury before the SEC or any other branch of the federal government.

PROTECTIONS EXPOSING WRONGDOING

The Sarbanes-Oxley Act is intended to compel attorneys to disclose client actions that violate state and/or federal securities laws. Predictably, companies whose actions are reported by their attorneys may seek retaliation against their attorneys. As an initial layer of protection, the Sarbanes-Oxley Act shields any attorney who complies with the act from any civil liability and also shields them from any discipline sought under a contrasting state law. Additionally, if an attorney is fired by their company after reporting a violation as required under the Sarbanes-Oxley Act, the attorney may report the firing to the company's board of directors. This is a precursor to a wrongful termination suit that could create civil liability and negative publicity for the company.

Mandatory and Permissive Reporting of Professional Misconduct

MORAL TURPITUDE

Moral turpitude typically involves conduct where a person engages in dishonesty for his or her personal gain. Embezzlement and fraud are specific examples of crimes that involve moral turpitude, though they are certainly not the only such crimes. Crimes of moral turpitude are not, in and of themselves, fatal to a bar application. If an applicant can affirmatively demonstrate that he or she has rehabilitated his or her character such that he or she is now fit for the practice of law, then admission may still be granted. In addition to crimes of moral turpitude, any false statements to, or the hiding of information from, the admissions committee constitutes moral turpitude.

CONDUCT NOT PRECLUDING ADMISSION

Bar admissions committees have the very important responsibility of admitting or denying admission to applicants who wish to practice law within their state. However, bar admissions committees may not base admissions decisions on unlawful criteria. For example, a state may not prohibit an attorney from practicing in that state because he or she is not a United States citizen. This has been held to violate the United States Constitution's Equal Protection Clause. Further, courts have held that states cannot deny admission due to lack of residency within the target state. This has been found to violate the United States Constitution's Privileges and Immunities Clause. Likewise, political activity—such as membership in the Communist Party—is generally not considered moral turpitude unless the activity rises to the level of engaging in or supporting the overthrow of the government by force.

MISCONDUCT

When an attorney is admitted to a state bar association, he or she is still subject to oversight by that bar association. The attorney must abide by the rules of professional conduct that exist in that jurisdiction. Specifically, ABA Model Rule 8.4(a) states that it is professional misconduct for a lawyer to "violate or attempt to violate the Rules of Professional Conduct, knowingly assist or induce another to do so, or do so through the acts of another."

Rule 8.4(b) states that it is professional misconduct for a lawyer to "commit a criminal act that reflects adversely on the lawyer's honesty, trustworthiness or fitness as a lawyer in other respects." While crimes involving fraud or deceit are clearly within the purview of this rule, crimes like solicitation of prostitution and isolated citations for driving under the influence generally are not.

DISHONESTY, FRAUD, DECEIT, OR MISREPRESENTATION

It is clear from ABA Model Rule 8.4(b) that any crime that includes an attorney act of dishonesty is professional misconduct. In fact, such actions are deemed so detrimental that ABA Model Rule 8.4(c) expands this concept, stating that it is professional misconduct for a lawyer to "engage in conduct involving dishonesty, fraud, deceit or misrepresentation."

It is important to note that the above rule does not require the conduct involving dishonesty, fraud, deceit, or misrepresentation to rise to the level of a criminal act. Therefore, mere acts with the above traits constitute professional misconduct. Such acts include, but are not limited to, plagiarism and misappropriation of funds.

PREJUDICIAL CONDUCT

Perhaps the most fundamental role of any attorney is to assist in the process of administering justice. This duty exists irrespective of the scope and subject matter of the attorney's representation. As stated by ABA Model Rule 8.4(d), "[i]t is professional misconduct for a lawyer to . . . engage in conduct that is prejudicial to the administration of justice."

Comment 3 to Rule 8.4(d) gives further guidance:

> "A lawyer who, in the course of representing a client, knowingly manifests by words or conduct, bias or prejudice based upon race, sex, religion, national origin, disability, age, sexual orientation or socioeconomic status, violates paragraph (d) when such actions are prejudicial to the administration of justice. Legitimate advocacy respecting the foregoing factors does not violate paragraph (d). A trial judge's finding that peremptory challenges were exercised on a discriminatory basis does not alone establish a violation of this rule."

INFLUENCING PUBLIC OFFICIALS

The mere statement or implication of the ability to improperly influence a government agency or official is professional misconduct. ABA Model Rule 8.4(e) declares that "[i]t is professional misconduct for a lawyer to . . . state or imply an ability to influence improperly a government agency or official or to achieve results by means that violate the Rules of Professional Conduct or other law."

Note that this rule only applies to *improper* influence and/or achieving results by unethical or unlawful means; it does NOT proscribe otherwise lawful advocacy. Any statements, implications, or actions that do not cross this threshold will generally not subject the attorney to professional misconduct. Thus, a statement such as "I'll get the judge to see it our way," followed only by effective oral arguments, would not be professional misconduct, provided there were no additional circumstances violating the Rules or other applicable law.

CONTACT WITH A JUDGE

Because of the critical role played by courts in administering justice and preserving our system of government, maintaining an honest and unbiased judiciary is of high concern to all states and all bar associations. For this reason ABA Model Rule 8.4(f) states: "It is professional misconduct for a lawyer to . . . knowingly assist a judge or judicial officer in conduct that is a violation of applicable rules of judicial conduct or other law."

Note that merely *assisting* a judge or judicial officer violate the rules or law is considered professional misconduct by the attorney, so long as that attorney provided the assistance *knowingly*. "Assisting" contemplates a variety of behaviors, including but not limited to: concealing, facilitating, planning, conspiring, etc.

WHISTLEBLOWER DUTIES

An attorney is required at times to report misconduct of others within the profession. According to ABA Model Rule 8.3(a) and (b):

(a) A lawyer who knows that another lawyer has committed a violation of the Rules of Professional Conduct that raises a substantial question as to that lawyer's honesty, trustworthiness or fitness as a lawyer in other respects, shall inform the appropriate professional authority.

(b) A lawyer who knows that a judge has committed a violation of applicable rules of judicial conduct that raises a substantial question as to the judge's fitness for office shall inform the appropriate authority.

While the duty to report is mandatory, there are two significant limitations. First, the attorney must know that there has been a violation. Second, as stated by Comment [3]: "This Rule limits the reporting obligation to those offenses that a self-regulating profession must vigorously endeavor to prevent."

"KNOW" AND "SUBSTANTIAL" THRESHOLDS

From a practical standpoint, it would be impossible to enforce a rule requiring attorneys to report any and all violations. Therefore, as an initial threshold, ABA Model Rule 8.3 requires an attorney to report wrongdoing only where the attorney "knows" of another attorney's or judge's misconduct. This knowledge may be drawn from the facts of a given scenario, but must still rise to the level of actual knowledge. Mere suspicion of wrongdoing does not create a *duty* to report; however, an attorney may elect to report such suspicions. Finally, the term "substantial" refers not to the weight of the evidence against the offending attorney or judge, but rather to the seriousness of the alleged offense. (See Comment 3 to ABA Model Rule 8.3)

REPORTING MISCONDUCT EXCEPTIONS

Client confidentiality is of paramount concern to the legal profession. ABA Model Rule 1.6(a) states: "A lawyer shall not reveal information relating to the representation of a client unless the client gives informed consent, the disclosure is impliedly authorized in order to carry out the representation or the disclosure is permitted by paragraph (b)."

An unyielding duty to report misconduct could directly conflict with the above duty of confidentiality, especially for a lawyer representing an accused attorney. Thus, one duty must supersede the other. ABA Model Rule 8.3(c) defers to Rule 1.6(a) by stating: "This Rule does not

22

require disclosure of information otherwise protected by Rule 1.6 or information gained by a lawyer or judge while participating in an approved lawyer's assistance program."

Unauthorized Practice of Law by Lawyers and Non-Lawyers

INCOMPETENCE

Similar to the disciplinary proceedings for attorneys who have violated ethics rules, there are proceedings available to remove from practice attorneys that have a disability that impairs their ability to competently practice law. An all-too-common example of such a disability is a substance dependency problem. The disability process operates in a similar fashion to the disciplinary process and sometimes includes a psychiatric evaluation. In a disability proceeding, if the attorney is found to be incapacitated to practice law, the attorney's license is suspended until such time that the attorney can affirmatively demonstrate that he or she is again fit for practice.

PRACTICES SUBJECT TO DISCIPLINE

An attorney is required to be licensed in the jurisdiction in which the attorney practices law. The ABA Model Rules recognize two primary activities that relate to the unauthorized practice of law for which an attorney may be subject to discipline. First, the Rules prohibit an attorney from practicing law in a jurisdiction in which the attorney is not licensed, except under limited circumstances. Second, the Rules prohibit an attorney from helping a non-attorney practice law except under limited circumstances. See ABA Model Rule 5.5(a). The non-attorney, while not subject to discipline for professional misconduct, could be subject to other civil or criminal penalties. ABA Model Rule 5.5(b) continues by prohibiting an attorney who is not licensed in a particular jurisdiction from making any representations that the attorney is licensed to practice in that jurisdiction and from establishing any type of continuous presence for the purpose of practicing law in that jurisdiction.

Multi-jurisdictional Practice

"ACTIVE PARTICIPATION" EXCEPTION

ABA Model Rules 5.5(a)–(b) contain specific prohibitions relating to the unauthorized practice of law. Rule 5.5, however, does take into consideration the fact that certain practicalities must be accounted for as the modern practice of law continually expands its geographic boundaries. For this reason, ABA Model Rule 5.5(c) allows an attorney to give legal advice in a jurisdiction where they are not licensed as long as:

- The attorney is not disbarred or suspended in any jurisdiction;
- The provision of legal services in the foreign jurisdiction is temporary; and
- The attorney works in association with an attorney who is admitted to practice in the foreign jurisdiction and who actively participates in the matter.

"SPECIAL AUTHORIZATION" EXCEPTION

ABA Model Rule 5.5(c)(2) provides an additional exception to the general rules disallowing the unauthorized practice of law. This rule contemplates a situation where an attorney is granted special authorization to provide legal services in a jurisdiction in which they are not licensed. In these special authorization cases, an attorney is also allowed to provide legal services in the foreign jurisdiction if the attorney reasonably expects to receive authorization in the future. This last provision makes the rule fairly expansive. Recall that to be eligible for this special authorization, the requesting attorney must not be suspended or disbarred in any jurisdiction and the legal services provided must be temporary.

"Alternative Dispute Resolution" Exception

Pursuant to ABA Model Rule 5.5(c)(3), an attorney may provide legal services in a jurisdiction in which the attorney is not licensed if the legal services are in, or are reasonably related to, arbitration, mediation, or some other type of alternative dispute resolution proceeding. However, the legal services provided must be reasonably related to the attorney's practice in a jurisdiction in which that attorney is licensed. This rule does not supersede any requirements of pro hac vice admission a particular jurisdiction may have for such legal services. Once again, the attorney wishing to use this provision must not be disbarred or suspended from practice in any jurisdiction, and the provision of legal services must be temporary.

"Reasonably Related" Exception

ABA Model Rule 5.5 attempts to strike the proper balance between two competing interests. On the one hand, there is the obvious public interest of limiting the otherwise unauthorized practice of law. This interest, however, can be at odds with the interest of an attorney's clients to receive the best and most comprehensive representation possible from that attorney. ABA Model Rule 5.5(c)(4) provides an exception to the general prohibition of the unauthorized practice law in situations where the otherwise unauthorized practice is reasonably related to an attorney's authorized practice. Without some allowance in this respect, attorneys could be forced to limit their practice to the detriment of their clients' interests, or to associate multiple foreign-licensed attorneys at a high cost, in cases where multiple jurisdictions are involved.

Exceptions to Permanent Presence

ABA Model Rule 5.5(d) contains two exceptions to the general rule that an attorney cannot practice law on an ongoing basis in a jurisdiction in which the attorney is not licensed. The first situation is one where the attorney provides only their employer (or its organizational affiliates) with legal services. This exception requires that the attorney maintain their employer as their only client and that the services provided are not services for which that particular jurisdiction requires pro hac vice admission. See ABA Model Rule 5.5(d)(1). The second situation is where the attorney is providing legal services that are authorized by federal law or the law of the jurisdiction in which the legal services are provided. See ABA Model Rule 5.5(d)(2). Both situations require that the practicing attorney not be disbarred or suspended from practice by any jurisdiction.

Requirements If Permitted to Practice

When an attorney is granted permission to practice in a jurisdiction where the attorney is not licensed, that attorney may become subject to the obligations of attorneys licensed in that jurisdiction. For example, if a multi-jurisdictional attorney is permitted to practice under ABA Model Rule 5.5(c) or (d), ABA Model Rule 8.5(a) subjects that attorney to the disciplinary rules of any jurisdictions to which that attorney is admitted, or in which that attorney provides services or offers to provide services. This requirement forces the attorney to have a high level understanding of multiple jurisdictions' ethics rules in order to ensure that the attorney's practice is ethical. Additionally, if an attorney is permitted to practice under ABA Model Rule 5.5(d)(1), the attorney may have to satisfy that state's continuing legal education requirements, in addition to any continuing legal education requirements imposed by jurisdictions in which the attorney is admitted.

Fee Division with a Non-Lawyer

NON-ATTORNEY INVOLVEMENT

A non-attorney is prohibited from practicing law in any jurisdiction in the United States. ABA Model Rule 5.5(a) forbids any attorney from assisting a non-lawyer carrying on the practice of law. The paramount issue in determining whether or not this type of misconduct has occurred lies in determining whether the non-licensed party's actions rise to the level of practicing law. This determination could vary between jurisdictions. This determination is generally made by considering:

- whether the activity involves legal knowledge and skill beyond that which the average layperson possesses;
- whether the activity constitutes advice or services concerning binding legal rights or remedies; and
- whether the activity is one traditionally performed by lawyers.

TAX LAW PARAMETERS

An attorney who assists a non-attorney in providing legal services is in violation of ABA Model Rule 5.5. The main issue in cases dealing with the unauthorized practice of law is usually whether or not the activity engaged in rises to the level of the "practice of law." In the context of providing tax advice, this issue can be muddled by the fact that many non-lawyers (e.g. accountants and return preparers) can be involved with assisting clients in tax-related matters. While this activity can be construed as offering law-related services, it is not considered the "practice of law;" that is, non-lawyers are permitted to prepare tax returns and to advise clients on issues that affect the preparation of their tax returns. Non-lawyers would probably want to avoid giving extensive advice on tax law, however.

DIFFERENCE IN CONSEQUENCES

The ABA Model Rules are ultimately intended to govern the actions of members of the legal community. An attorney who assists a non-lawyer in providing legal services without a license is subject to the full range of discipline provided for in that jurisdiction's rules of ethics. The harshest penalty available to a jurisdiction's attorney discipline authority is disbarment. In the case of a non-lawyer, such a punishment is not relevant because a non-lawyer is not licensed in the first place. Therefore, it is incumbent on each jurisdiction to prescribe laws that address the unauthorized practice of law by non-lawyers. Typically, jurisdictions may impose civil and criminal penalties upon non-lawyers engaged in the unauthorized practice of law. Short of imposing punishment, courts in different jurisdictions may also order non-lawyers to cease their unlicensed practice of law.

EXCEPTIONS ASSISTING NON-LAWYERS

There are several situations in which attorneys may work with non-lawyers without violating ABA Model Rule 5.5. For instance, an attorney may assign work to non-lawyer employees in the attorney's office. This includes legal assistants, paralegals, and law clerks. To comply with the Model Rules, the attorney must supervise the work assigned to the non-lawyer(s) and must ultimately be responsible for the results of the work. Comment 3 to ABA Model Rule 5.5 states that attorneys are allowed to educate non-lawyers on the legal aspects of their duties. Further, an attorney may assist a non-lawyer in preparing the non-lawyer's case if the non-lawyer is appearing pro se in a legal proceeding. In that situation, the non-lawyer would be appearing "pro se." Finally, attorneys may employ suspended or disbarred attorneys as long as they give them work that non-

25

lawyers could perform. Suspended or disbarred attorneys may not use this final exception as a means to circumvent the prohibition on the unlicensed practice of law.

FEE SPLITTING ARRANGEMENTS

The Rules of Professional Conduct seek to protect the independence of attorneys and eliminate as many conflicts of interest as possible. To this end, ABA Model Rule 5.4(a) states that "[a] lawyer or law firm shall not share legal fees with a non-lawyer." As Comment 1 to Rule 5.4 explains:

> "The provisions of this Rule express traditional limitations on sharing fees. These limitations are to protect the lawyer's professional independence of judgment. Where someone other than the client pays the lawyer's fee or salary, or recommends employment of the lawyer, that arrangement does not modify the lawyer's obligation to the client. As stated in paragraph (c), such arrangements should not interfere with the lawyer's professional judgment."

EXCEPTIONS TO FEE SPLITTING

ABA Model Rule 5.4(a) lists situations where lawyers may share fees with non-lawyers:

(1) an agreement by a lawyer with the lawyer's firm, partner, or associate may provide for the payment of money, over a reasonable period of time after the lawyer's death, to the lawyer's estate or to one or more specified persons;

(2) a lawyer who purchases the practice of a deceased, disabled, or disappeared lawyer may, pursuant to the provisions of Rule 1.17, pay to the estate or other representative of that lawyer the agreed-upon purchase price;

(3) a lawyer or law firm may include non-lawyer employees in a compensation or retirement plan, even though the plan is based in whole or in part on a profit-sharing arrangement; and

(4) a lawyer may share court-awarded legal fees with a nonprofit organization that employed, retained or recommended employment of the lawyer in the matter.

"PARTNER" AND "ASSOCIATE"

The term "partner" in the private law firm context refers to a member of a law firm that is listed in the firm's partnership agreement. Typically, partners share in the profits and liabilities of the firm. Many law firms are not structured as partnerships. In such situations, attorneys that run the firm may be referred to as members or shareholders depending on the business structure used by the firm. The term "associate" is often used to refer to an attorney who is a non-managing and/or non-shareholding employee of the firm. The term associate may refer to regular salaried employees as well as independent contractors of the firm.

"OF COUNSEL" AND "GENERAL COUNSEL"

In the broadest sense, the term "of counsel" refers to an attorney who has a relationship with a law firm that cannot otherwise be designated as a partner or associate. The title "of counsel" is often utilized to refer to a former or retired partner who still maintains some relationship with the firm. Additionally, "of counsel" attorneys are often independent contractors regularly utilized by a firm to provide specific services. The term "general counsel" is a title most often given to the highest ranking legal officer of a company's internal legal department. The term is also used to identify the attorney or firm that is acting as the primary legal counsel for a particular organization in a specific matter.

NON-ATTORNEY PARTNERSHIPS

The Rules of Professional Conduct are intended to protect clients. Part of this protection centers on the elimination of conflicts of interests that can impair the judgment of the attorney. With respect to attorneys forming partnerships with non-attorneys, ABA Model Rule 5.4(b) states that "[a] lawyer shall not form a partnership with a non-lawyer if any of the activities of the partnership consist of the practice of law." This rule prohibits such partnerships even where all of the legal work is conducted by the attorney and none of the legal work is undertaken by the non-attorney. However, it does not prevent an attorney from forming some sort of business partnership that does not practice law, such as a financial consulting firm.

In order to prevent conflicts of interest and other impairment to the judgments of attorneys, the Model Rules impose strict duties on attorneys with respect to practicing in a firm or other association in which a non-attorney has significant involvement.

ABA Model Rule 5.4(d) states: "A lawyer shall not practice with or in the form of a professional corporation or association authorized to practice law for a profit, if:

(1) A non-lawyer owns any interest therein, except that a fiduciary representative of the estate of a lawyer may hold the stock or interest of the lawyer for a reasonable time during administration;
(2) A non-lawyer is a corporate director or officer thereof or occupies the position of similar responsibility in any form of association other than a corporation; or
(3) A non-lawyer has the right to direct or control the professional judgment of a lawyer."

SALE/PURCHASE OF LAW PRACTICE

Like other businesses, law practices are bought and sold. Unlike most businesses, the overriding public interests of taking care of the firm's clients require certain conditions to be met before the firm can be sold or purchased. ABA Model Rule 1.17 states that "[a] lawyer for a law firm may sell or purchase a law practice" if the following conditions are met:

(a)   The seller ceases to engage in the private practice of law, or in the area of practice that has been sold, [in the geographic area] [in the jurisdiction] (a jurisdiction may elect either version) in which the practice has been conducted;
(b)   The entire practice, or the entire area of practice, is sold to one or more lawyers or law firms;
(c)   The seller gives written notice to each of the seller's clients regarding: (1) the proposed sale; (2) the client's right to retain other counsel or to take possession of the file; and (3) the fact that the client's consent to the transfer of the client's files will be presumed if the client does not take any action or does not otherwise object within ninety (90) days of receipt of the notice.

The ABA Model Rules seek to protect the interests of clients of a firm that has been sold in several ways. First, ABA Model Rule 1.17(d) states: "[t]he fees charged clients shall not be increased by reason of the sale." Additionally, ABA Model Rule 1.17, Comment 6 states:

"The Rule requires that the seller's entire practice, or an entire area of practice, be sold. The prohibition against sale of less than an entire practice area protects those clients whose matters are less lucrative and who might find it difficult to secure other counsel if a sale could be limited to substantial fee-generating matters. The purchasers are required to undertake all client matters in the practice or practice

27

area, subject to client consent. This requirement is satisfied, however, even if a purchaser is unable to undertake a particular client matter because of a conflict of interest."

PERFORMING LAW-RELATED SERVICES

Some types of services naturally flow from an attorney's general law practice. The identity and nature of these services will often depend on the type of law practice conducted by the attorney. The Rules of Professional Conduct do not forbid an attorney from performing law-related services that are ancillary to their legal functions. ABA Model Rule 5.7(b) defines "law-related services" as: "services that might reasonably be performed in conjunction with and in substance are related to the provision of legal services, and that are not prohibited as unauthorized practice of law when provided by a non-lawyer." Depending on the services and the context in which they are provided, the Model Rules may or may not govern.

Generally, if law-related services are kept separate and distinct from the attorney's law practice, the law-related services are not subject to the Rules of Professional Conduct. However, ABA Model Rule 5.7(a) states:

> "A lawyer shall be subject to the Rules of Professional Conduct with respect to the provision of law-related services, as defined in paragraph (b), if the law-related services are provided: by the lawyer in circumstances that are not distinct from the lawyer's provision of legal services to clients; or in other circumstances by an entity controlled by the lawyer individually or with others if the lawyer fails to take reasonable measures to assure that a person obtaining the law-related services knows that the services are not legal services and that the protections of the client-lawyer relationship do not exist."

PROVIDING NON-LEGAL SERVICES

ABA Model Rule 1.8(a) states that "[a] lawyer shall not enter into a business transaction with a client or knowingly acquire an ownership, possessory, security or other pecuniary interest adverse to a client" unless the following three factors are met:

(1) the transaction and terms on which the lawyer acquires the interest are fair and reasonable to the client and are fully disclosed and transmitted in writing in a manner that can be reasonably understood by the client;

(2) the client is advised in writing of the desirability of seeking and is given a reasonable opportunity to seek the advice of independent legal counsel on the transaction; and

(3) the client gives informed consent, in a writing signed by the client, to the essential terms of the transaction and the lawyer's role in the transaction, including whether the lawyer is representing the client in the transaction.

Responsibilities of Partners, Managers, Supervisory and Subordinate Lawyers

RESPONSIBILITIES

Generally, the partners in a law firm are those responsible for making the necessary decisions with respect to running the law firm. One of these primary responsibilities involves overseeing the actions of associates under their management. ABA Model Rule 5.1(a) states:

> "A partner in a law firm, and a lawyer who individually or together with other lawyers possesses comparable managerial authority in a law firm, shall make reasonable efforts to ensure that the firm has in effect measured giving reasonable assurance that all lawyers in the firm conform to the Rules of Professional Conduct."

Non-partners who directly supervise the work of other attorneys are responsible for taking reasonable steps to make sure those attorneys comply with the Rules of Professional Conduct. ABA Model Rule 5.1, Comment 3 sets up a sliding scale for meeting these obligations:

> "Other measures that may be required to fulfill the responsibility prescribed in paragraph (a) can depend on the firm's structure and the nature of its practice. In a small firm of experienced lawyers, informal supervision and periodic review of compliance with the required systems ordinarily will suffice. In a large firm, or in practice situations in which difficult ethical problems frequently arise, more elaborate measures may be necessary. Some firms, for example, have a procedure whereby junior lawyers can make confidential referral of ethical problems directly to a designated senior partner or special committee. See Rule 5.2. Firms, whether large or small, may also rely on continuing legal education in professional ethics. In any event . . . the partners may not assume that all lawyers associated with the firm will inevitably conform to the Rules."

ACCOUNTABILITY FOR OTHERS' ACTIONS

Generally, attorneys are only responsible for their own actions, but there are exceptions. For example, under ABA Model Rule 5.1(c), a lawyer shall be responsible for another lawyer's violation of the Rule of Professional Conduct if:

(1) the lawyer orders or, with knowledge of the specific conduct, ratifies the conduct involved; or

(2) the lawyer is a partner or has comparable managerial authority in the law firm in which the other lawyer practices, or has direct supervisory authority over the other lawyer, and knows of the conduct at a time when its consequences can be avoided or mitigated but fails to take reasonable remedial action.

DUTY OF CARE

Subordinate attorneys are not excused from violating the Rules of Professional Conduct simply because they are instructed to do so by a superior. Such violations can, however, indicate that the attorney is not acting with knowledge of the pertinent Rule(s). For example, ABA Model Rule 5.2, Comment 1 states:

> "Although a lawyer is not relieved of responsibility for a violation by the fact that the lawyer acted at the direction of a supervisor, that fact may be relevant in determining whether a lawyer had the knowledge required to render conduct a violation of the

29

Rules. For example, if a subordinate filed a frivolous pleading at the direction of a supervisor, the subordinate would not be guilty of a professional violation unless the subordinate knew of the document's frivolous character."

POTENTIAL VIOLATIONS

When a complicated ethical issue arises during a legal matter, supervisory attorneys often make the determination as to the proper course of action. The Rules of Professional Conduct provide allowances for subordinate attorneys who rely on their superior's judgment, even when the determination turns out to be incorrect. For example, ABA Model Rule 5.2(b) states that "[a] subordinate lawyer does not violate the Rules of Professional Conduct if that lawyer acts in accordance with a supervisory lawyer's reasonable resolution of an arguable question of professional duty." The question at issue must relate to a legitimately grey area and cannot be an obvious violation for the subordinate attorney to escape potential discipline.

RULES OF PROFESSIONAL CONDUCT

Attorneys often utilize many employees, particularly for tasks that do not absolutely require an attorney's specific legal expertise or admission to the state bar. Many of these employees are not attorneys. As a result, it is imperative that these non-attorney assistants act in accordance with the Rules of Professional Conduct. ABA Model Rule 5.3, Comment 1 states:

> "A lawyer must give such assistants appropriate instruction and supervision concerning the ethical aspects of their employment, particularly regarding the obligation not to disclose information relating to representation of the client, and should be responsible for their work product. The measures employed in supervising non-lawyers should take account of the fact that they do not have legal training and are not subject to professional discipline."

PARTNERS AND SUPERVISORY ATTORNEYS

Because non-attorney employees are not subject to the Professional Rules of Conduct, ABA Model Rule 5.3 requires the following of partners and supervisory attorneys:

(a) a partner, and a lawyer who individually or together with other lawyers possesses comparable managerial authority in a law firm shall make reasonable efforts to ensure that the firm has in effect measures giving reasonable assurance that the person's conduct is compatible with the professional obligations of the lawyer; [and]

(b) a lawyer having direct supervisory authority over the nonlawyer shall make reasonable efforts to ensure that the person's conduct is compatible with the professional obligations of the lawyer[.]

ATTORNEYS SUBJECT TO DISCIPLINE

Generally, attorneys are not responsible for the unethical actions taken by their non-attorney employees. However, under ABA Model Rule 5.3(c), "a lawyer shall be responsible for conduct of such a person that would be a violation of the Rules of Professional Conduct if engaged in by a lawyer" under either of the following conditions:

(1) the lawyer orders or, with the knowledge of the specific conduct, ratifies the conduct involved; or

(2) the lawyer is a partner or has comparable managerial authority in the law firm in which the person is employed, or has direct supervisory authority over the

person, and knows of the conduct at a time when its consequences can be avoided or mitigated but fails to take reasonable remedial action.

Restrictions on Right to Practice

Agreements entered into by attorneys that purport to restrict an attorney's right to practice law are viewed very negatively by the Rules of Professional Conduct. This is because "[a]n agreement restricting the right of lawyers to practice after leaving a firm not only limits their professional autonomy but also limits the freedom of clients to choose a lawyer." ABA Model Rule 5.6, Comment 1. Rule 5.6(a) forbids an attorney from making or offering:

(a) a partnership, shareholders, operating, employment, or other similar type of agreement that restricts the right of a lawyer to practice after termination of the relationship, except an agreement concerning benefits upon retirement; or

(b) an agreement in which a restriction on the lawyer's right to practice is part of the settlement of a client controversy.

The Client-Lawyer Relationship

Formation of Client-Lawyer Relationship

BASIC TENETS

The relationship that exists between the attorney and the client is unique. Generically speaking, the relationship is contractual. However, in many cases there is no formal contract, so custom or industry standard establishes the norms and benchmarks of the relationship. These traditions, however, can be altered by agreement between the contracting parties. Unlike a typical contractual relationship, the attorney becomes the client's fiduciary. The main consequence of this designation is that any uncertainty in the contractual relationship between the attorney and the client will be decided in favor of the client. The attorney must use a high degree of care when representing the client. These special rules are in addition to, not in lieu of, the typical rules of agency that govern non-fiduciary contractual arrangements.

FORMING RELATIONSHIP

In the United States, an attorney is generally free to accept or reject clients as the attorney sees fit. Against this "free agency" backdrop, Restatement § 14 discusses three situations where a client-lawyer relationship is formed:

- A client expresses a desire for the attorney's representation and the attorney agrees;
- A client expresses a desire for the attorney's representation and the attorney fails to clearly deny such representation where the attorney knows or should know that the client is reasonably relying on the attorney's representation; or
- The attorney is appointed by a tribunal to represent the client.

Thus, despite the general rule that attorneys are free to choose their clientele, there are specific exceptions.

COURT-APPOINTED REPRESENTATION

A court will appoint an attorney to represent a client if the client may otherwise find it difficult to obtain adequate representation. A common example of this is poor clients who cannot afford to retain counsel. Another example is unpopular cases/clients where the client may find it difficult to find an attorney. A court-appointed attorney can only be excused from representing a client for good cause. For example:

- An attorney may refuse a court-appointed assignment in any case where representing the client would require the attorney to violate a law or ethics rule. See ABA Model Rule 6.2(a).
- An attorney may refuse a court-appointed assignment if an unreasonable financial burden would be placed on the attorney. See ABA Model Rule 6.2(b).
- An attorney may refuse a court-appointed assignment if the attorney is so opposed to the client or the case that effective representation would not be possible. See ABA Model Rule 6.2(c).

DECLINING REPRESENTATION

The client-lawyer relationship is guarded carefully to protect the interests of clients. This protection is so strong that an attorney even owes certain duties to a prospective client whose case the attorney elects not to take. Such an attorney has the duty to keep confidential any information

conveyed to the attorney by the prospective client in the initial consultation. Further, the attorney must carefully safeguard any property received from the prospective client. This could include money intended for attorney payment, as well as property that is potential evidence. Additionally, the attorney owes the prospective client reasonable care with respect to any advice as to the status or quality of the case, especially any information regarding potential statutes of limitation.

Scope, Objective, and Means of the Representation

GENERAL PARAMETERS OF REPRESENTATION

Generally, an attorney is charged to represent the best interests of the client utilizing all reasonable and lawful methods. This rule, however, is subject to several exceptions. An attorney and their client may enter into an agreement that specifically sets forth the boundaries of the attorney's representation of the client. For example, an attorney may agree to advise a client as to the best business structure, but have nothing to do with drafting or negotiating contracts for that business. Because attorneys may only use lawful means, ABA Model Rule 1.2(d) prohibits attorneys from advising or assisting clients in committing any crime or act of fraud. An attorney may, however, discuss the legal ramifications of specific activities. ABA Model Rule 1.2(a) also permits an attorney to act on behalf of the client if such act is impliedly authorized to pursue the interests of the client.

LIMITING REPRESENTATION

While clients can make all of the critical decisions affecting their representation, an attorney may also limit the scope of representation if certain circumstances are met. Attorney-imposed limitations must be reasonable under the circumstances, and the client must be informed of and agree to such limitations. For instance, attorneys may engage in these limited-scope agreements to represent a client until and unless a legal matter must be litigated. At that point, the agreement might require the client to seek new representation. Even if a client does not agree to an attorney's limited representation, the attorney may withdraw under ABA Model Rule 1.16 if the attorney and client simply cannot resolve their differences with respect to handling a case.

CLIENT'S ILLEGAL ACTS

ABA Model Rule 1.16(a)(1) requires an attorney to withdraw from representing a client if the representation will result in a violation of law or the rules of ethics. Upon learning that a client expects a course of action that would violate the law or rules of ethics, an attorney must inform the client that such action cannot be taken. The attorney must withdraw if the client insists on taking the unlawful or unethical action. If an attorney becomes aware of a client's continuing illegal or fraudulent conduct, the attorney must withdraw under ABA Model Rule 1.2(d). If the client's actions are particularly egregious, it may be necessary for the attorney to complete a "noisy withdrawal" that gives notice of the withdrawal to third parties and retracts that attorney's prior work product and/or disaffirms prior opinions or documents, etc. [See ABA Model Rule 1.2, Comment 10, and Rule 4.1, Comment 3].

ONGOING COMMUNICATION

Because it is the client who ultimately benefits or is burdened by the outcome of a legal matter, the client is given the ultimate authority on the direction of the case. This includes important decisions regarding the objectives and other matters that directly impact the outcome of the case. To make these determinations prudently, the client must be apprised of the status of the case. To this end, ABA Mode Rule 1.4(a)(3) requires that a lawyer reasonably inform the client about the case, including actions the lawyer has taken on the client's behalf.

Some decisions, including those that must be made in an instant (like trial tactics), do not require the client's informed consent according to ABA Model Rule 1.4, Comment 3.

INFORMATION REQUESTS

By requiring an attorney to keep a client reasonably informed, ABA Model Rule 1.4(a)(3) generally ensures that a client will feel adequately knowledgeable about the disposition of the case. Even when such communication exists, the client may request additional information from the attorney. ABA Model Rule 1.4(a)(4) requires a lawyer to promptly comply with reasonable requests for information. This Rule further opens channels of communication, seeking to remove impediments to the client understanding what is going on in the case. In situations where an attorney cannot promptly comply with a client's request, the attorney should communicate with the client when compliance with the request will be possible.

WITHHOLDING INFORMATION

Generally, an attorney must freely and promptly share relevant information with a client when it concerns that client's case. However, ABA Model Rule 1.4, Comment 7 states:

> "In some circumstances, a lawyer may be justified in delaying transmission of information when the client would be likely to react imprudently to an immediate communication. Thus, a lawyer might withhold a psychiatric diagnosis of a client when the examining psychiatrist indicates that disclosure would harm the client. A lawyer may not withhold information to serve the lawyer's own interest or convenience or the interests or convenience of another person. Rules or court orders governing litigation may provide that information supplied to a lawyer may not be disclosed to the client. Rule 3.4(c) directs compliance with such rules or orders."

CIRCUMSTANCES AFFECTING COMMUNICATION

There are many circumstances that may arise during an attorney's representation of a client that can alter the typical communication expectations between the two. For example, if a client requests that the attorney perform an illegal act, the attorney is required to tell the client why such a request cannot be honored. See ABA Model Rule 1.4(a)(5)

Additionally, the level of communication deemed reasonable under the Rules may change depending on factors specific to the client, such as age, sophistication, competency, etc. Where the client is a corporation or other business entity, the attorney must determine the appropriate officer with whom to communicate. Finally, attorneys and long-standing clients may determine that only limited reporting is required with respect to mundane issues.

Decision-Making Authority—Actual and Apparent

CLIENT DECISIONS

Throughout a client's representation it is the client, not the attorney, who decides the scope and extent of the attorney's representation. The client should make important decisions affecting their legal rights. Decisions to be made by the client include:

- Whether to make or accept an offer of settlement;
- How to plead in a criminal proceeding;
- Whether to waive the right to a jury trial in a criminal proceeding;
- Whether or not to testify on their own behalf in a criminal proceeding; and
- Appealing a decision. See ABA Model Rule 1.2(a); Restatement § 22(1).

EMERGENCY ACTION

Typically, it is improper for an attorney to act on behalf of an individual unless that individual has intentionally established a client-lawyer relationship. This intent is not required, however, where the individual has an extremely reduced level of competency and is subject to imminent and irreparable harm from a health, safety, or financial perspective. In these situations, an attorney may act for the individual despite that individual's inability to establish a client-lawyer relationship or to express their views on such relationship. However, even in these extreme cases, the attorney cannot act until the attorney has consulted with the incapacitated person or someone acting on that person's behalf. Further, the attorney should not act unless the attorney believes that the individual has no other representation. The attorney should limit the scope of their work to actions which directly address the imminent and irreparable harm. ABA Model Rule 1.14, Comment 9.

An attorney acting on behalf of a person in an emergency situation owes that person the same duties as a regular client. This includes, to the extent possible, establishing a normal, consensual client-lawyer relationship with the person. The attorney must maintain confidentiality except where disclosures are required to protect the person. The attorney should also freely disclose the attorney's role as representative of the person to any other attorney or legal authority involved in the matter. Note that attorneys normally do not seek nor receive compensation for emergency representation of an incapacitated person. See ABA Model Rule 1.14, Comment 10.

Counsel and Assistance Within the Bounds of the Law

CLIENTS OF DIMINISHED CAPACITY

A lawyer should seek, as far as reasonably possible, to maintain a normal client-lawyer relationship with a client of diminished capacity. ABA Model Rule 1.14(a). In such circumstances, "the lawyer may take reasonably necessary protective action, including consulting with individuals or entities that have the ability to take action to protect the client and, in appropriate cases, seeking the appointment of a guardian ad litem, conservator or guardian." ABA Model Rule 1.14(b). When taking such protective action, the lawyer may reveal information about the client to the extent reasonably necessary to protect the client's interests. ABA Model Rule 1.14(c).

A client may, for example, possess the capacity to make routine decisions, but not final determinations as to complex matters. This is often the case with clients who are minors. Even if a client cannot ultimately make the final determination in a particular matter, the client may be able to provide valuable input as to what course of action best serves the client's interests.

INFORMED CONSENT

While an attorney is generally bound to seek whatever is in a client's best interest, there are circumstances where the attorney's actions must be preceded by the client's consent. ABA Model Rule 1.4(a)(1) requires that an attorney promptly inform the client of any decision or circumstance that requires the client's informed consent. ABA Model Rule 1.0(e) defines "informed consent" as the agreement by a client as to a course of conduct after the attorney has described and explained the various reasonable alternative courses of conduct and the risks associated with each. For example, the Rules require an attorney to receive the informed consent of two clients with potentially conflicting interests before representing them.

Termination of the Client-Lawyer Relationship

REQUIREMENTS TO CEASE REPRESENTATION

There are situations where the ABA Model Rules *require* an attorney to decline or terminate representation. For example, Rule 4.4(a) requires an attorney refuse a case or to cease representation in a situation where the attorney believes that the client's primary motive is to harass or maliciously injure any person. Additionally, ABA Model Rule 3.1 requires that an attorney not take a position that is either factually or legally frivolous. A case is not considered frivolous if the attorney can, in good faith, assert that the facts are as claimed or that the present law should be applied, changed, extended, or reversed.

In addition to certain case-specific factors that require an attorney to cease representation, there are some situations where an attorney's personal circumstances require the attorney to cease representation. For example, ABA Model Rule 1.1 requires that an attorney be sufficiently competent to adequately represent the client in the matter at hand. For instance, an attorney who practiced tax law exclusively would probably not be able to competently represent a defendant in a capital murder case. But an attorney could become sufficiently competent through sufficient study and research. Additionally, ABA Model Rules 1.16(a)(1) and 1.7(a)(2) require an attorney to cease representation where the attorney's personal feelings about the case or the client are such that they impair the attorney's ability to adequately represent the client. Finally, ABA Model Rule 1.16(a)(2) requires an attorney to cease representation where the attorney's mental or physical condition would materially hinder the attorney's ability to represent the client.

GENERAL SITUATIONS

Generally, once an attorney is retained by a client, the client-lawyer relationship extends until the resolution of the underlying issue on which the relationship was based. Understandably, many things can go awry during representation, leading to the termination of the client-lawyer relationship. Irrespective of what brings on the end of the relationship, there are only three ways that the client-lawyer relationship can actually terminate:

- the client ends the client-lawyer relationship;
- circumstances arise that require the attorney to withdraw from representation of the client (mandatory withdrawal); and
- circumstances arise that permit the attorney to withdraw from representation of the client (permissive withdrawal). Restatement § 32.

RAMIFICATIONS

There are many situations that can lead to a client terminating their relationship with an attorney. Because of overriding public policy concerns, namely that clients receive the best possible legal representation, all client-lawyer relationships are deemed to be terminable at will by the client. Thus, a client does not have to show any reason or just cause whatsoever for terminating the client-lawyer relationship.

Despite this large amount of power placed in the hands of the client, the attorney is still entitled to be compensated for the reasonable value of work done up to that point. This entitlement is based on the theory of quantum meruit (unjust enrichment). The attorney may seek compensation regardless of whether the fee structure was flat or contingent, but the attorney's recovery is capped by the terms of the employment agreement.

ROLE OF THE COURTS

Local court rules often require court permission for the withdrawal or substitution of attorneys in ongoing litigation. Because the client-lawyer relationship is viewed as terminable at the will of the client, courts typically allow a client to fire or replace their attorney with or without showing cause. A court may withhold permission if the judge feels that the termination of an attorney would cause undue delay or disruption to the litigation. From an attorney's perspective, a court is far more likely to deny a motion to withdraw from representation. ABA Model Rule 1.16(c) requires an attorney to continue representing a client upon direction of the court even when the attorney has shown good cause supporting termination of the representation.

NECESSARY WITHDRAWAL

ABA Model Rule 1.16(a) identifies three situations where an attorney must withdraw from representation of the client (mandatory withdrawal). First, Rule 1.16(a)(1) states that the attorney must withdraw if "the representation will result in violation of the rules of professional conduct or other law." According to Comment 2 to Rule 1.16, the attorney is not required to withdraw simply because the client *requests* conduct that would violate a law or rule of ethics. Second, Rule 1.16(a)(2) states that the attorney must withdraw if "the lawyer's physical or mental condition materially impairs the lawyer's ability to represent the client." Third, Rule 1.16(a)(3) states that the attorney must withdraw if "the lawyer is discharged." The latter two situations requiring mandatory withdrawal seek to protect the rights and interests of the client.

ALLOWABLE WITHDRAWAL

While an attorney must comply with any laws or rules requiring notice to and/or permission of a tribunal, ABA Model Rule 1.16(b) allows an attorney to withdraw if:

(1) Withdrawal can be accomplished without material adverse effect on the interests of the client;
(2) The client persists in a course of action involving the lawyer's services that the lawyer reasonably believes is criminal or fraudulent;
(3) The client has used the lawyer's services to perpetrate a crime or fraud;
(4) The client insists upon taking action that the lawyer considers repugnant or with which the lawyer has a fundamental disagreement;
(5) The client fails substantially to fulfill an obligation to the lawyer regarding the lawyer's services and has been given reasonable warning that the lawyer will withdraw unless the obligation is fulfilled;
(6) The representation will result in an unreasonable financial burden on the lawyer or has been rendered unreasonably difficult by the client; or
(7) Other good cause for withdrawal exists.

PROPER PROTOCOL

Pursuant to ABA Model Rule 1.16(c), a withdrawing attorney must "comply with applicable law requiring notice to or permission of a tribunal when terminating a representation." Thus, the attorney may be ordered by a tribunal to continue representing a client, even if that client is unreasonably difficult. Furthermore, in accordance with ABA Model Rule 1.16(d), a withdrawing attorney

> "shall take steps to the extent reasonably practicable to protect a client's interests, such as giving reasonable notice to the client, allowing time for employment of other counsel, surrendering papers and property to which the client is entitled and

37

refunding any advance payment of fee or expense that has not been earned or incurred."

It is common for attorneys to summarize the termination and other important information in a writing delivered to the client.

Attorney-Client Contracts

ACQUIRING MEDIA RIGHTS

There are times when a client's case could give rise to a story that is interesting enough to justify writing an article or book, for example in a publicized criminal trial of a celebrity. An attorney's acquisition of media rights is not flatly prohibited by the ABA Model Rules, but is regulated. ABA Model Rule 1.8(d) states that "[p]rior to the conclusion of representation of a client, a lawyer shall not make or negotiate an agreement giving the lawyer literary or media rights to a portrayal or account based in substantial part on information relating to the representation." Thus, an attorney may not even attempt to seek media rights in a client's case until the case is completed, which includes appeals. Media rights that are not based on information relating to the representation are not under the purview of this Rule.

CONTRACTS LIMITING LIABILITY

ABA Model Rule 1.8(h)(1) states that an attorney must not "make an agreement prospectively limiting the lawyer's liability to a client for malpractice unless the client is independently represented in making the agreement." Nevertheless, Comment 14 of Rule 1.8 allows the following:

- An attorney may practice law within a limited liability entity so long as the attorney maintains personal liability for legal malpractice.
- An attorney may reach an agreement with a client that limits the scope of the attorney's representation.
- An attorney may reach an agreement with a client that all malpractice claims shall be arbitrated.

SETTLING MALPRACTICE CLAIMS

Legal malpractice settlements are only allowed where the client "is advised in writing of the desirability of seeking and is given a reasonable opportunity to seek the advice of independent legal counsel in connection therewith." ABA Model Rule 1.8(h)(2).

Fees

Generally, an agreement between an attorney and the client concerning representation is a legal contract. This includes the agreement reached between the parties for applicable fees. The fee agreement is theoretically viewed as being reached between two independent parties in an arm's length transaction. It is important to understand, however, that despite this theoretical foundation, courts understand that many times clients are not in a favorable negotiating position. This could result from the stress created by the legal circumstances the client encounters, or it could simply be a result of client's lack of experience. Thus, courts often shift the weight of the burden to attorneys in fee dispute cases.

Attorney fees must be reasonable. A bill for legal services must be clear on its face and provide the client with an adequate breakdown of charges so that the client can clearly see the origins of the fees and expenses charged.

ADVANCE PAYMENTS AND RETAINER

Technically, an advance payment for services is made prior to the rendering of such services. An attorney may anticipate that forthcoming legal services will cost at least a specific amount, and may request an up-front payment to cover the costs of those services. The ABA Model Rules permit the attorney to require the client to pay in advance for legal services. Such payments should be deposited in the client's trust account and may not be used toward the representation of other clients. The ABA Model Rules also require that the attorney return any advance payment that is not earned once the client-lawyer relationship has been terminated. By contrast, a retainer fee is charged by an attorney to guarantee that attorney's availability for representation. Because this fee is for the attorney's availability and not for any specific services, no refund of the retainer is required when the attorney is fired or withdraws from representation.

ALTERNATIVE PAYMENT ARRANGEMENTS

In addition to the more traditional approach of charging a client fees and having them pay with cash, several other payment arrangements may be undertaken without running afoul of the ABA Model Rules. For example, the Rules permit an attorney to accept property as payment for services. The attorney, however, may not accept any property or interest in property that is the subject of the case in which the attorney is providing legal services. This type of arrangement could lead to a conflict of interest between the attorney and his client. Additionally, attorneys are permitted to accept payment by credit cards, bank loans, or personal promissory notes from their clients. ABA Model Rule 1.8(i)(1) further states that so long as it is authorized by local law, an attorney may acquire a lien to secure payment on a client obligation.

COLLECTING FEES

An attorney is prohibited from utilizing collection methods that violate applicable law, involve the improper use of confidential information, or harass the client. Restatement §41. However, an attorney may generally use civil claims and/or liens to collect past-due fees. An attorney may file suit in civil court against a client for payment of monies due. Further, many jurisdictions automatically recognize a lien on money recovered by an attorney on behalf of the client in a legal proceeding. This lien may be specifically created by statute or recognized under the common law of the jurisdiction. In jurisdictions where this type of automatic lien does not exist, an attorney may create a lien by express agreement with the client. Some jurisdictions recognize a lien that allows the attorney to maintain property of the client until the money owed is paid; other jurisdictions strongly oppose this final type of lien.

ABA Model Rule 1.15(e) allows attorneys to withhold some funds received on behalf of the client until the matter of fees owed by the client is resolved. However, the attorney *must* retain the amounts received in a client trust account, and may only retain property or money that is genuinely in dispute. Thus, an attorney who asserts that their client owes $500 in legal fees would not be allowed to retain $1000 received on behalf of the client; rather, that attorney could set aside up to $500. As far as resolving the underlying legal fee dispute, many bar associations have established arbitration or mediation procedures that attorneys may use to settle a particular dispute. In fact, ABA Model Rule 1.5, Comment 9 recommends that attorneys utilize such procedures when available and applicable, and requires attorneys to use such procedures when required by law.

FEE STRUCTURE AND UNREASONABLE FEES

ABA Model Rule 1.5(b) addresses the issue of when fee and expense rates should be communicated to a client. Essentially, the rule states that fees and expenses should be discussed with the client prior to, or within a reasonable time following, the commencement of representation. In addition, the Rule states a preference for communicating the fee and expense rates to the client in writing.

An attorney who is found to charge unreasonably high fees faces two potential consequences. First, the court that determines an attorney's fee is excessive will simply refuse to enforce the fee agreement, rendering void the attorney's claim to the fee. Second, ABA Model Rule 1.5(a) states that an attorney who charges unreasonable fees is subject to discipline.

ABA Model Rule 1.5(a) sets forth specific factors to guide both practitioners and disciplinary authorities in determining how to evaluate the reasonableness of attorney's fees. In determining the reasonableness of a fee under Rule 1.5(a), the following factors are to be considered:

(1) the time and labor required, the novelty and difficulty of the questions involved, and the skill requisite to perform the legal service properly;
(2) the likelihood, if apparent to the client, that the acceptance of the particular employment will preclude other employment by the lawyer;
(3) the fee customarily charged in the locality for similar legal services;
(4) the amount involved and the results obtained;
(5) the time limitations imposed by the client or by the circumstances;
(6) the nature and length of the professional relationship with the client;
(7) the experience, reputation, and ability of the lawyer or lawyers performing the services; and
(8) whether the fee is fixed or contingent.

UNBILLABLE ITEMS

An attorney may not charge clients for the general overhead costs associated with the operation of the attorney's law office, such as utilities and health insurance. An attorney may, however, charge clients for specific costs associated with the performance of special services. Such costs may include long-distance fees for phone calls or faxes, photocopying, courier costs, etc. In lieu of this actual cost method, ABA Model Rule 1.5 permits an attorney to charge a reasonable fee for such expenses where the attorney and client have reached an agreement in advance. However, the attorney may never charge a client more than the actual expense. Additionally, attorneys are prohibited from billing the same time to more than one client; that is, an attorney may not be "on the clock" for two clients simultaneously.

FEE AGREEMENT NONCOMPLIANCE

There are several potential examples of attorney fee agreements that do not comply with the ABA Model Rules. One example is an arrangement that seeks to automatically terminate the representation if payment is not tendered by the client. This type of agreement runs contrary to Comment 5 to ABA Model Rule 1.5 and is considered egregious because an attorney terminating representation in the midst of a legal contest can place the client's interests in peril. For example, a client may be forced to walk away from a good claim or to give in to a bad claim because of approaching statutes of limitations or other court-imposed deadlines. Another example, listed in Comment 5, is an agreement that provides for services only up to a stated amount when it is foreseeable that further services will likely be required.

CONTINGENCY FEES

Contingency fees refer to attorney fees that become due only if the attorney resolves a matter in the client's favor. In the typical situation, contingency fees represent a percentage of what the client is awarded through judgment or settlement of a case. Contingency fees do not, however, have to be expressed as a percentage – a contingency fee can be a flat fee. The amount to be due or the method for determining it must be agreed upon at the outset of representation. Within one contingency agreement, different outcomes could trigger different fee structures. Contingency fees are disallowed in many countries. The U.S. allows such fees because they are viewed as providing access to legal representation for those who otherwise do not have the resources to secure legal representation. Still, there are specific cases in which contingency fees are disallowed in the United States. There are also further restrictions on contingency fees.

Some types of legal representation are deemed inappropriate for contingent fee arrangements. For example, ABA Mode Rule 1.5(d)(1) specifically prohibits an attorney from entering into a contingent fee arrangement in a domestic relations matter where the fee is contingent upon obtaining a divorce, or upon the amount of alimony, support, or property settlement obtained. But an attorney can recover a contingent fee to recover past due alimony or support payments. ABA Mode Rule 1.5(d)(2) strictly prohibits an attorney for charging the client a contingent fee in a criminal defense matter.

Contingent fees, like all attorney fees, are subject to the general rule of reasonableness, including eight non-exclusive reasonableness factors. ABA Model Rule 1.5(a). Applicable law may impose limitations, such as the maximum permissible percentage. Additionally, Rule 1.5(c) requires a contingent fee arrangement to be in a writing signed by the client. This writing must state how the fee is determined including:

- percentages that accrue to the attorney in the case of settlement, trial, or appeal;
- any expenses deducted from the recovery; and
- whether such expenses are deducted before or after the calculation of the contingency fee.

The writing must also clearly inform the client of any fees that are due regardless of the outcome of the case.

Fee-Sharing Among Lawyers

Generally, attorneys are forbidden from sharing fees. The policy behind this rule seeks to protect the financial interests of clients. This general prohibition is intended to keep fees down by reducing the number of attorneys associated with a case. It is also designed to prevent lawyers from effectively "selling" off their clients. However, there are exceptions to this general rule that preserve the handling of a case and look out for other client interests. One exception is that attorneys working within the same law firm may share fees. Another exception arises where part of a fee is owed to an attorney who worked on a case and is not part of the firm currently handling the case. Finally, in some situations, attorneys that are not in the same law firm may share fees.

The most obvious exception to the rule against fee sharing occurs between lawyers in the same firm. When a client brings a case to a particular law firm, more than one lawyer within that firm may work on the case; the availability and effort of several skilled attorneys is typically viewed as an advantage. Similarly, a law firm would not run afoul of the ethics rules by paying a former partner or associate for work performed on a case. Such payments are typically made in accordance with a separation or retirement agreement.

In many situations, clients can benefit from having lawyers from different firms working on a case. ABA Model Rule 1.5(e) recognizes these situations by allowing attorneys from different firms to share a client's fee if several requirements are met. First, the client must be issued a single bill. Second, the overall fee must be reasonable. Third, the fee-sharing arrangement must either be proportionate to the services provided by each lawyer, or in some other proportion so long as each lawyer assumes joint responsibility for the case. Finally, the client must agree to the arrangement in writing and the writing must state the amount that each lawyer will be paid.

REFERRAL FEES BETWEEN LAWYERS

Referrals between attorneys are common. Referrals may occur due to the health, schedule, or expertise of the original attorney, as well as for other reasons. While referrals are common, ABA Model Rule 7.2(b) disallows referral fees. An attorney may not pay others for recommendations to potential clients, nor may an attorney pay a fee for clients actually referred. Additionally, ABA Model Rule 1.5(e) prohibits referral fees among lawyers when the referring lawyer does not assume responsibility for the matter or does not complete any work on the matter. Such would amount to forbidden fee-sharing. Comment 8 to ABA Model Rule 7.2 permits reciprocal referral arrangements between an attorney and another attorney or other professional, so long as the arrangement is non-exclusive and the lawyer's clients are notified of the arrangement and its details.

Client Confidentiality

Attorney-Client Privilege

CLIENT INFORMATION

One of the most entrenched duties owed by an attorney to a client is that of confidentiality. Without the assurance of confidentiality, clients would be less likely to seek representation. Therefore, ABA Model Rule 1.6 states the general rule that an attorney must not reveal any information relating to the representation of the client. This duty extends to current clients, former clients, and prospective clients. There are several situations where the disclosure of client information is authorized; for example, if the client grants permission to the attorney. Even this situation is predicated on the client's informed consent. Additionally, attorneys may disclose client information if such disclosure is impliedly authorized for the purposes of carrying out the goals of the representation.

OVERLAPPING CONCEPTS

The attorney-client privilege and the duty of confidentiality possess overlapping concepts and are easily confused. One of the distinguishing characteristics between the two doctrines is the identity of who is governed by each rule. The attorney-client privilege is an evidentiary rule that prohibits admitting into evidence certain communications between an attorney and the client. Thus, the party being governed is the court or other governmental tribunal. On the other hand, the duty of client confidentiality governs attorneys specifically, forbidding attorneys from voluntarily divulging information that relates to the representation of their clients.

DIFFERENCE IN INFORMATION COVERED

An attorney's ethical duty of confidentiality to the client is much broader in scope than the attorney-client privilege. The attorney-client privilege only covers confidential communications that take place between a client and their attorney. By comparison, the duty of client confidentiality covers these confidential communications, but also any other information that is obtained by the attorney that deals with the attorney's representation of the client. Stated another way, an attorney's ethical duty of client confidentiality extends to all information obtained by an attorney relating to the representation of a client, even if that information is not covered by the attorney-client privilege.

DIFFERENCES IN VIOLATIONS

Generally, the duty of confidentiality is broader than the attorney-client privilege. This can be demonstrated by how the two rules may be violated. For example, the attorney-client privilege is only concerned with the disclosure of confidential communications that take place between an attorney and a client. Thus, a court that attempted to compel an attorney to reveal the content of a truly confidential communication would run afoul of the attorney-client privilege. On the other hand, the duty of client confidentiality can be violated by an attorney's disclosure or misuse of a client's information. This covers situations where client information is disclosed without the client's informed consent, or where confidential information is used to the detriment of a past, current, or potential client without such client's informed, written consent.

"CLIENT" DEFINED

When determining whether or not the attorney-client privilege applies, it is important to determine if the person claiming the privilege is a "client" as contemplated by the rule. Generally, a client is anyone who seeks legal advice from an attorney. This definition is broad enough that a person is considered a client at the outset of contact with an attorney. Thus, the initial communications are covered even if no formal representation results.

"CLIENT" IN THE CORPORATE CONTEXT

When an attorney is advising an entity, it may be difficult to determine who the client is for purposes of applying the attorney-client privilege. This is particularly true of corporate clients. The inquiry is complicated by the fact that a corporation is made up of employees, officers, and stakeholders (e.g. shareholders).

Generally, the attorney-client privilege protects communications between an attorney and the corporation's high-level officers. The attorney-client privilege may also cover communications between the attorney and employees of the corporation when:

- The employee communicates with the corporation's attorney at the behest of their superior;
- The employee knows that they are communicating with the attorney to get legal advice for the corporation; and
- The communication relates to a subject for which the employee has the discretion to act on behalf of the corporation.

IDENTIFICATION GUIDELINES

Typically, identifying the attorney in the client-lawyer relationship is easy. However, there are several important nuances. Normally, an attorney must be licensed to practice law in the relevant jurisdiction. However, for the purposes of the attorney-client privilege, communications will be protected where the client reasonably believes that the attorney is licensed in the appropriate jurisdiction, even if the attorney is not. Also, the attorney-client privilege only protects confidential communications that are made when the attorney is acting as the client's attorney and not merely as a friend, family member, or lawyer that the client happens to know.

"COMMUNICATION"

Only communications that are intended to be confidential are protected by the attorney-client privilege. Additionally, the term "communication" is not so narrowly construed as to require direct communication between just the attorney and the actual client. For example, communications between agents of either the attorney and/or the client that relate to the representation are also protected by the attorney-client privilege. Note that the attorney-client privilege does not protect certain fundamental details of the client-lawyer relationship, including the client's name, the type of fee arrangement in place, and the identification of the attorney as the client's attorney. Additionally, the client cannot gain protection under the attorney-client privilege by merely giving to the attorney preexisting items that would not otherwise be privileged in the hands of the client.

PROTECTED COMMUNICATION

For a communication to be protected by the attorney-client privilege, it must be confidential. This means that that the communication must be made in such a way that no outsiders are intended to be privy to the communication. This does not mean, however, that whenever outsiders hear or observe a communication, the communication is automatically deemed non-confidential. Instead, the party making the communication must reasonably believe that no outsiders will hear or observe the communication. Note that some third parties may be present during the communication without destroying the confidentiality required by the privilege. This is the case where the third party is present to assist the client-lawyer relationship (e.g. attorney's secretary or client's bookkeeper) or to provide psychological support to the client (e.g. client's family member).

ASSERTION OF THE ATTORNEY-CLIENT PRIVILEGE

Despite the fact that an attorney may not assert the privilege to protect their own interests, the attorney has the duty to assert the client's privilege if the client has not waived the privilege and the client is not present.

DURATION OF PRIVILEGE

The attorney-client privilege never terminates. It continues indefinitely, even past the point of the client's death. Furthermore, an attorney's duty to assert the attorney-client privilege continues indefinitely.

EXCEPTIONS TO PRIVILEGE

When determining whether the attorney-client privilege applies to a given communication, it is important to keep several exceptions in mind. These exceptions are as follows:

- No attorney-client privilege is created for communications between a client and attorney if the client engaged the attorney to help the client commit a criminal or fraudulent act.
- No attorney-client privilege can be claimed where an issue is raised by the client as to a breach of duties on the part of the attorney within the context of the client-lawyer relationship.
- No attorney-client privilege is applicable where a civil action occurs between two parties who were joint clients of the same attorney.
- The privilege may not apply where an attorney is capable of providing evidence as to the client's competency or intent with respect to the disposition of property either by will or by lifetime transfer.

Work Product Doctrine

In many ways, the work product doctrine is similar to the attorney-client privilege. The premise behind the work product doctrine, like that supporting the attorney-client privilege, is that some information is immune from discovery by the opposing party in a legal dispute. Generally, the work product doctrine applies to work product produced by an attorney in the course of representing a client, either in litigation or in anticipation of litigation. There is an exception to the work product doctrine where the opposing party demonstrates both a substantial need for the produced material and the inability to secure the material without undue hardship. Note: separate from the work product doctrine, an attorney's thoughts or opinions regarding a case are also privileged, and there is no exception to such privilege except waiver of the immunity. Thus, absent waiver, an attorney may not be compelled to disclose mental impressions of a case.

Professional Obligation of Confidentiality – General Rule

DURATION OF CONFIDENTIALITY

Simply put, an attorney's duty of confidentiality owed to a client never ends, even if a client is no longer represented by an attorney. ABA Model Rules 1.6(a) and 1.9(c) forbid attorneys from revealing information relating to the representation of a client. Rule 1.6 governs confidentiality generally, while Rule 1.9 governs duties owed to former clients. Recall, however, that the Rules permit some disclosure under certain circumstances (such as to prevent the client from committing a crime), and that some states require disclosure if necessary to prevent reasonably certain death or substantial bodily harm.

Disclosures Expressly or Impliedly Authorized by the Client

ATTORNEY'S IMPLIED AUTHORITY

The ABA Model Rules closely guard the client's right to confidentiality but recognize that attorneys must have some freedom to operate in order to most effectively advocate. With this in mind, ABA Model Rule 1.6(a) states that every client grants their attorney the implied consent to utilize confidential information to the extent necessary to undertake the representation necessary for that client's best interests. However, this implied consent is narrowly construed. Additionally, ABA Model Rule 1.6(a) specifically prohibits an attorney's use of confidential information where the client has given specific instructions to the attorney not to utilize such information.

Other Exceptions to the Confidentiality Rule

FORFEITING PROTECTION

The duty of confidentiality is intended to protect the client from any disclosures of otherwise confidential information. The client may waive the protections of the duty of confidentiality doctrine by giving informed consent for the attorney to disclose the information. This may take place during the course of representation when an attorney strategically wishes to act in a manner that requires the disclosure of confidential information. This could occur if the attorney feels that the use of the confidential information would help the client's overall case. Therefore, as long as the client had been apprised of the various risks and alternative courses of action available, the client could consent to the use of confidential information.

INVOLVING ATTORNEY'S CONDUCT

Generally, the ABA Model Rules guard the client's right to protect confidential information. This right of the client cannot be unintentionally waived like the attorney-client privilege. There are some instances where the Rules allow disclosure of otherwise confidential information. Rule 1.6(b)(5) allows an attorney to disclose confidential client information in proceedings concerning the attorney's conduct. Such proceedings include any controversy regarding the attorney's representation of the client, as well as criminal charges against the attorney. The Rules limit this ability to disclose such information to: 1) only the information that is necessary; and 2) only such parties that need to be informed to resolve the dispute; the attorney must also take any steps necessary to protect the client from any harm that could result from the disclosure (e.g. protective orders). Similarly, ABA Model Rule 1.6(b)(4) permits an attorney to disclose just enough confidential information as is needed to obtain professional ethics advice.

ORDERED BY COURT

Attorneys may have to choose between obeying a law or court order and protecting their client's confidential information. In these situations, the ABA Model Rules allow for disclosures of confidential information. In the case of a law requiring the disclosure, an attorney should first be sure that the law applies to the circumstances. Then the attorney should notify the client of the law. If no challenge to the validity or applicability of the law can be made, the attorney may disclose the confidential information pursuant to ABA Model Rule 1.6(b)(6). Where a court orders a disclosure of confidential information, the attorney should assert all available non-frivolous objections to the order. Then the attorney should meet with the client to analyze the potential for appealing the order. If the order survives appeal or no appeal is taken, ABA Model Rule 1.6(b)(6) permits the disclosure of confidential information.

Preventing Death or Harm

ABA Model Rule 1.6(b)(1) permits an attorney's disclosure of confidential client information where the attorney reasonably believes that such disclosure will prevent reasonably certain death or substantial bodily injury. There are several requirements for the disclosure to be permissible. First, the attorney must reasonably believe that the disclosure will prevent the death or substantial bodily harm. Second, the attorney must be reasonably certain that the death or substantial bodily harm will occur. There is no requirement that the death or substantial bodily harm be imminent. Further, the cause of the death or substantial bodily harm need not be the result of the client's actions. Finally, the attorney is not *compelled* to disclose such information under the rule. Some states, however, do compel the attorney to make such a disclosure.

Financial Harm

The ABA Model Rules were slow to allow attorneys to disclose their clients' confidential information with "only" substantial financial harm at stake. The permission granted by ABA Model Rule 1.6(b)(2) and (3) is limited to situations where the attorney is or has represented the client whose confidential information is the subject of the disclosure and the actions of the client are reasonably certain to cause substantial financial harm to someone. An attorney's disclosure under this provision may come prior to the client's actions or after the actions in order to mitigate the damage that has already occurred.

Conflicts of Interest

Current Client Conflicts – Multiple Clients and Joint Representation

GENERAL CONCERNS

The entire relationship between the attorney and client is dependent upon trust. The presence of a conflict of interest means that the attorney has, or at least has the appearance of, another interest that may cause the attorney to act in favor of the other interest at the expense of the client. A conflict of interest is present whenever the interests of the attorney, another client, a former client, or any third party give rise to a substantial risk that the attorney's representation of the client will be materially and adversely affected.

AFTER REPRESENTATION HAS COMMENCED

ABA Model Rule 1.7 forbids an attorney from representing a client if such representation involves a concurrent conflict of interest. A concurrent conflict of interest exists if the representation of one client will be directly adverse to another client, or if there is a significant risk that the representation of one or more clients will be materially limited by the lawyer's personal interests or responsibility to another person. This Rule means that an attorney cannot begin representation of a client where a conflict already exists.

Rule 1.16(a)(1) addresses the situation where a conflict becomes apparent after representation has commenced and cannot by cured by informed consent of the client(s) involved. It requires the attorney to withdraw if the representation will violate the rules of professional conduct or other law.

EXCEPTIONS CREATING CONCURRENT CONFLICT

ABA Model Rule 1.7(b) allows an attorney to represent a client despite a concurrent conflict of interest if all of the following are met:

(1) The lawyer reasonably believes that the lawyer will be able to provide competent and diligent representation to each affected client;
(2) The representation is not prohibited by law;
(3) The representation does not involve the assertion of a claim by one client against another client represented by the lawyer in the same litigation or other proceeding before a tribunal; and
(4) Each affected client gives informed consent, confirmed in writing.

REASONABLENESS STANDARD FOR CLIENT CONFLICTS OF INTEREST

ABA Model Rule 1.7(b)(1) applies a reasonableness standard in assessing conflicts of interest. Such a standard asks whether or not a reasonable attorney would believe that they could provide competent and diligent representation to each of the clients affected by the conflict of interest. This standard technically does not permit the attorney to consider any special situations, talents, etc., that may be present which would allow that specific attorney to provide competent and diligent representation where an average reasonable attorney could not. If this "reasonable lawyer" standard is not met, then the conflict cannot be overcome, even with informed consent of all affected clients.

CLIENT'S CONSENT TO WAIVE

Where a lawyer has a conflict of interest with a client, representation is only permitted where the client provides informed, written consent. ABA Model Rule 1.7, Comment 18 discusses informed consent as follows:

> "Informed consent requires that each affected client be aware of the relevant circumstances and of the material and reasonably foreseeable ways that the conflict could have adverse effects on the interests of that client. See Rule 1.0(e)(informed consent). The information required depends on the nature of the conflict and the nature of the risks involved. When representation of multiple clients in a single matter is undertaken, the information must include the implications of the common representation, including possible effects on loyalty, confidentiality and the attorney-client privilege and the advantages and risks involved."

MEMORIALIZING A CLIENT'S WAIVER

ABA Model Rule 1.7(b)(4) specifically requires that "each affected client gives informed consent, confirmed in writing." Thus, an oral waiver of a conflict of interest is not effective in eliminating the conflict. ABA Model Rule 1.7, Comment 20 further states that "[s]uch a writing may consist of a document executed by the client or one that the lawyer promptly records and transmits to the client following an oral consent." Thus, there are two types of writings that meet the requirements of Rule 1.7(b). First, the attorney or client may draft a formal written document that memorializes the waiver, or the attorney may promptly reduce to writing (and transmit) an oral agreement between the attorney and the affected clients waiving the conflict of interest. Both types of writings can be satisfied through electronic means, such as email. The affected clients are *not* required to sign the document memorializing consent.

FUTURE AND EXISTING WAIVERS

An attorney may wish to seek consent from a client to waive future conflicts that may arise. An attorney frequently will seek such consent to avoid putting time and resources into a case where the attorney might otherwise be precluded from providing representation. These future consents are subject to the test of ABA Model Rule 1.7(b); additionally, "[t]he effectiveness of such waivers is generally determined by the extent to which the client reasonably understands the material risks that the waiver entails." ABA Model Rule 1.7, Comment 22. Note that "[a] client who has given consent to a conflict may revoke the consent and, like any other client, may terminate the lawyer's representation at any time." ABA Model Rule 1.7, Comment 21.

DIRECTLY ADVERSE CLIENT REPRESENTATIONS

ABA Model Rule 1.7(a)(1) prohibits an attorney from representing a client if such representation will be directly adverse to another client. However, even where there are directly adverse interests involved, the affected parties may give their informed, written consent to waive the attorney's conflict. The true limitations on the attorney's ability to represent clients with directly adverse interests comes from the four-part test found in ABA Model Rule 1.7(b). More often than not, one of the prongs will preclude an attorney from representing clients with directly adverse legal interests. The actual nature of the adverse interests often plays a significant role; for instance, clients with adverse economic interests could potentially waive a conflict, while clients on opposite sides of a lawsuit could not.

SAFEGUARDS IN NONLITIGATION MATTERS

Where a conflict arises in a nonlitigation context, the following safeguards apply:

- "Representation is prohibited if in the circumstances the lawyer cannot reasonably conclude that the lawyer will be able to provide competent and diligent representation." ABA Model Rule 1.7, Comment 15.
- "Each affected client be [made] aware of the relevant circumstances and of the material and reasonably foreseeable ways that the conflict could have adverse effects on the interests of that client." ABA Model Rule 1.7, Comment 18.
- "Paragraph (b) [of ABA Model Rule 1.7] requires the lawyer to obtain the informed consent of [each affected] client, confirmed in writing." ABA Model Rule 1.7, Comment 20.

If the potential conflict becomes a present conflict, the above steps must be repeated. An attorney must cease representation of one of the clients if a reasonable attorney would advise the client to withhold consent to the conflict.

REPRESENTING MULTIPLE CLIENTS

During the course of an attorney's practice, it is common for the attorney to represent the interests of several clients with aligned interests with respect to a common issue. Such multiple-party representation is permissible even though *all* of the interests of the clients are not aligned. "[C]ommon representation is permissible where the clients are generally aligned in interest even though there is some difference in interest among them." ABA Model Rule 1.7, Comment 28. However, as the lines shift in the relationship between the mutually represented clients, an attorney must be aware of the severity of any conflicts and understand when joint representation is no longer advisable. "[A] lawyer cannot undertake common representation of clients where contentious litigation or negotiations between them are imminent or contemplated." ABA Model Rule 1.7, Comment 29.

One of the most protected of all client rights is the attorney-client privilege. When an attorney undertakes the representation of multiple clients in a single matter, the attorney must make known to the individual clients that any information provided to the attorney is not privileged as to the other clients. "The lawyer should, at the outset of the common representation and as part of the process of obtaining each client's informed consent, advise each client that information will be shared and that the lawyer will have to withdraw if one client decides that some matter material to the representation should be kept from the other." ABA Model Rule 1.7, Comment 31. But "it may be appropriate for the lawyer to proceed with the representation when the clients have agreed, after being properly informed, that the lawyer will keep certain information confidential." *Id.*

LOYALTY

Representing organizations can create unique problems for attorneys. While an organization is respected as its own entity under various laws, the organization is comprised of people who act on behalf of the organization. The organization's attorney must also interact with those people that represent the organization. Throughout the course of these dealings, the attorney owes their loyalty to the organization, *not* the individuals within the organization. ABA Model Rule 1.13(a) states that "[a] lawyer employed or retained by an organization represents the organization acting through its duly authorized constituents."

An organization's attorney owes all duties to the organization and not the individuals within that organization. As such, if the interests of the organization and its individuals become adverse ABA Model Rule 1.13, Comment 10 states:

> "In such circumstances the lawyer should advise any constituent, whose interest the lawyer finds adverse to that of the organization of the conflict or potential conflict of interest that the lawyer cannot represent such constituent, and that such person may wish to obtain independent representation. Care must be taken to assure that the individual understands that, when there is such adversity of interest, the lawyer for the organization cannot provide legal representation for that constituent individual, and that discussions between the lawyer for the organization and the individual may not be privileged."

KNOWLEDGE OF POTENTIAL HARM

ABA Model Rule 1.13(b) states:

> "If a lawyer for an organization knows that an officer, employee or other person associated with the organization is engaged in action, intends to act or refuses to act in a matter related to the representation that is a violation of a legal obligation to the organization, or a violation of law that reasonably might be imputed to the organization, and that is likely to result in substantial injury to the organization, then the lawyer shall proceed as is reasonably necessary in the best interest of the organization. Unless the lawyer reasonably believes that it is not necessary in the best interest of the organization to do so, the lawyer shall refer the matter to higher authority in the organization, including, if warranted by the circumstances to the highest authority that can act on behalf of the organization as determined by applicable law."

ABA Model Rule 1.13(b) requires an attorney to report potentially harmful conduct within the organization to the highest authorities within that organization. ABA Model Rule 1.13(c) allows a lawyer to report violations to persons outside the organization. This rule states:

> "[I]f . . . despite the lawyer's efforts in accordance with paragraph (b) the highest authority that can act on behalf of the organization insists upon or fails to address in a timely and appropriate manner an action, or a refusal to act, that is clearly a violation of law, and the lawyer reasonably believes that the violation is reasonably certain to result in substantial injury to the organization, then the lawyer may reveal information relating to the representation whether or not Rule 1.6 permits such disclosure, but only if and to the extent the lawyer reasonably believes necessary to prevent substantial injury to the organization."

Pursuant to Rule 1.13(d), the ability of an attorney to report organizational misconduct to outside persons does *not* apply to attorneys hired to represent the organization to investigate an alleged violation of law or to attorneys hired to defend the organization or one of the individuals within the organization against a claim arising out of an alleged violation of law.

If an attorney is fired in the course of acting in the best interests of the organization client pursuant to ABA Model Rule 1.13(b) or (c), the attorney must still seek to protect the organization by informing the highest authorities within the organization. ABA Model Rule 1.13(e) states:

> "A lawyer who reasonably believes that he or she has been discharged because of the lawyer's actions taken pursuant to paragraphs (b) or (c), or who withdraws under circumstances that require or permit the lawyer to take action under either of those paragraphs, shall proceed as the lawyer reasonably believes necessary to assure that the organization's highest authority is informed of the lawyer's discharge or withdrawal."

ORGANIZATION VERSUS INDIVIDUAL

Where there is a conflict between the organization and the individuals within it, the organization's attorney owes a duty of loyalty and confidentiality to the organization. However, the attorney may represent an individual within the organization if no conflicts of interest are created. As usual, ABA Model Rule 1.7 (duties to current clients) governs. If the organization's consent is required by Rule 1.7, then Rule 1.13(g) requires that "the consent shall be given by an appropriate official of the organization other than the individual who is to be represented, or by the shareholders."

Current Client Conflicts – Lawyer's Personal Interest or Duties

IMPUTABLE TO OTHER ATTORNEYS

The ABA Model Rules impute conflicts of interest to other attorneys in certain circumstances, even though direct conflicts of interest do not exist between those attorneys and the client. Most commonly, conflicts are imputed to attorneys in the same firm as the attorney with whom the direct conflict exists. ABA Model Rule 1.10(a) reflects this principle:

> "While lawyers are associated in a firm, none of them shall knowingly represent a client when any one of them practicing alone would be prohibited from doing so by Rules 1.7 [duties to current clients] or 1.9 [duties to former clients]."

ATTORNEY'S INTERESTS AND CONFLICTS

Problems may arise where an attorney's personal interests conflict with a client's interests. For instance, the attorney might wish to purchase the same piece of real estate as a potential client. Such a situation creates a concurrent conflict of interest if there is a significant risk that the attorney's interest will materially limit their representation of the client. Because of the concurrent conflict, the default rule is that the attorney must not represent the client. Three such conflicts include:

- Financial: These may occur any time that an attorney stands to gain financially from a scenario that is directly inconsistent with the interests of the client.
- Attorney's relatives: The relationship of two attorneys may create conflicts for both of the attorneys. Assume that Attorney 1 represents Client 1 and that Attorney 2 represents Client 2, Client 1's spouse, in the same divorce proceeding. If Attorney 1 and Attorney 2 are married, then a potential conflict exists and both should obtain informed written consent from their clients.

- <u>Sexual relationship</u>: When a sexual relationship arises between an attorney and client, the attorney's judgment may become impaired. ABA Model Rule 1.8(j) subjects the attorney to discipline regardless of the client's consent or the absence of actual harm to the client. A pre-existing sexual relationship between a lawyer and a person who later seeks to become a client does not subject the attorney to discipline.

As with many other conflicts, such conflicts can be overcome if the attorney complies with the test set forth by ABA Model Rule 1.7(b).

FORMERLY-ASSOCIATED ATTORNEY

An attorney changing jobs creates issues for both the new firm and the old firm. Many questions can arise regarding the old firm's rights and obligations with respect to the clients represented by the attorney while he was associated with the old firm. Generally, according to ABA Model Rule 1.10(b) the old firm may represent clients with interests adverse to the clients of the departing attorney if the firm is no longer representing the former client unless:

(1) the matter is the same or substantially related to that in which the formerly associated lawyer represented the client; and
(2) any lawyer remaining in the firm has information protected by Rules 1.6 and 1.9(c) that is material to the matter.

Former Client Conflicts

SIMILARITY TO FORMER CLIENTS

ABA Model Rule 1.9 governs the use of confidential information where an attorney represents a new client in a matter that is the same or substantially similar to a matter in which the attorney represented a former client; it is designed to protect the former client. Rule 1.9(a) requires a former client's informed consent confirmed in writing before an attorney may represent another person in the same or a substantially related matter in which that person's interests are materially adverse to the former client's. Rule 1.9(b) essentially extends the same protection to clients that were represented by an attorney's former law firm if the attorney had acquired material information protected by Rules 1.6 or 1.9(c).

ABA Model Rule 1.9(a) prohibits an attorney from representing a person in the same or a substantially related matter as a former client if that person has interests that are materially adverse to the former client's, unless the former client gives informed consent, confirmed in writing. This rule does not mention confidentiality and therefore applies even if the attorney does not know any of the former client's confidential information. This rule is often used to protect a former client's confidential information, but the presence of such information is not required to prevent the attorney from representing the new client in the matter at issue.

SUBSTANTIALLY RELATED

The ABA Model Rules prohibit attorneys from representing parties adverse to a former client in substantially related matters. ABA Model Rule 1.9, Comment 3 states:

"Matters are 'substantially related' for purposes of this Rule if they involve the same transaction or legal dispute or if there otherwise is a substantial risk that confidential factual information as would normally have been obtained in the prior representation would materially advance the client's position in the subsequent matter. For example, a lawyer who has represented a businessperson and learned extensive

53

private financial information about that person may not then represent that person's spouse in seeking a divorce."

It is common for a lawyer to leave one firm to work at another. This can result in problems with respect to protecting a client's confidential information. ABA Model Rule 1.9(b) prohibits an attorney from representing a person in a matter that is substantially related to one that was the subject of the attorney's former law firm, if that person's interests are adverse to the former firm's client, *and* if the attorney had acquired material information protected by Rules 1.6 or 1.9(c). The former firm's client can waive the conflict through informed consent confirmed in writing. Note that the attorney must have acquired protected information, and the person must have an interest that is materially adverse to the former firm's client for Rule 1.9(b) to apply.

Prospective Client Conflicts

POTENTIAL CLIENTS OF AN ATTORNEY

The duty of confidentiality extends to prospective clients. A "prospective client" is defined as "[a] person who discusses with a lawyer the possibility of forming a client-lawyer relationship with respect to a matter is a prospective client." ABA Model Rule 1.18(a). A prospective client's confidential communications are protected by both the attorney-client privilege and the attorney's ethical duty to maintain the confidentiality of the client. This effectively puts the prospective client in the same position as an existing client with respect to the confidentiality of communications.

PROSPECTIVE CLIENT CONSIDERATIONS

Dealing with a prospective client could limit that attorney's ability to represent other clients in the future. Because the ABA Model Rules endow prospective clients with many of the same confidentiality protections as current and former clients, the ramifications of an attorney's communications with a prospective client can have far-reaching effects. Specifically, ABA Model Rule 1.18(c) states:

> "A lawyer subject to paragraph (b) [which extends Rule 1.9 to prospective clients] shall not represent a client with interests materially adverse to those of a prospective client in the same or a substantially related matter if the lawyer received information from the prospective client that could be significantly harmful to that person in the matter, except as provided in paragraph (d). If a lawyer is disqualified from representation under this paragraph, no lawyer in a firm with which that lawyer is associated may knowingly undertake or continue representation in such a matter, except as provided in paragraph (d)."

Under ABA Model Rule 1.18(d), an attorney who has received disqualifying information may nevertheless represent the client if either of the following requirements are met:

(1) both the affected client and the prospective client have given informed consent, confirmed in writing, *or*:

(2) the lawyer who received the information took reasonable measures to avoid exposure to more disqualifying information than was reasonably necessary to determine whether to represent the prospective client; and

    (i) the disqualified lawyer is timely screened from any participation in the matter and is apportioned no part of the fee therefrom; and

    (ii) written notice is promptly given to the prospective client.

Imputed Conflicts

"Firm" Defined

The imputation of a conflict of interest among members of the same firm is easy to understand in the case of a traditional law firm that employs lawyers to conduct the firm's work. However, there are many less traditional affiliations that exist between lawyers that can rise to the level of being considered a "firm" despite the lack of traditional law firm organization. ABA Model Rule 1.0(c) defines a firm as follows:

> "'Firm' or 'law firm' denotes a lawyer or lawyers in a law partnership, professional corporation, sole proprietorship or other association authorized to practice law; or lawyers employed in a legal services organization or the legal department of a corporation or other organization."

Exceptions to Conflict Imputation

The ABA Model Rules contemplate circumstances where simple professional affiliation is not enough to impute one attorney's conflict of interest to all of the other members of the firm. ABA Model Rule 1.10(a) states that a conflict is not imputed if "the prohibition is based on a personal interest of the prohibited lawyer and does not present a significant risk of materially limiting the representation of the client by the remaining lawyers in the firm."

ABA Model Rule 1.10(b) allows a firm to represent clients that once created conflicts between a formerly-employed attorney and their other client(s), unless any lawyers still employed with the firm have information relating to the representation of the former attorney's clients *and* the matter to be undertaken on behalf of the new clients is the same or substantially related to the representation of the former attorney's clients.

Liability Insurer and Policyholder

Both a liability insurer and liability policyholder will likely have an interest in the minimization of costs. Other interests of these two parties may conflict as a case proceeds. For example, a liability policyholder may not care if it is found to be liable for a claim up to the amount reimbursed by the insurance policy. Similarly, liability insurers sometimes consider external factors in determining the intensity with which they choose to defend a claim, regardless of the wishes of the policyholder. An insurance provider might want to take an issue to trial, while the policyholder might not wish to go to trial. Liability providers often seek to minimize costs. Additionally, a liability insurer may not want to pursue certain arguments because of the possibility of certain business disclosures.

Representing Insurance Policyholders

The Rules of Professional Conduct govern the attorney's representation, not contractual provisions of the insurance policy. Some states identify the policyholder as the sole client, while other states identify the insurance company and the client as joint clients.

Imputed Disqualification

If a former government attorney is disqualified under ABA Model Rule 1.11 there is a distinct possibility that the remainder of the attorney's firm will also be disqualified from the matter. But under ABA Model Rule 1.11(b), the other attorneys at a disqualified attorney's firm may continue representation if:

(1) The disqualified lawyer is timely screened from any participation in the matter and is apportioned no part of the fee therefrom; and

(2) Written notice is promptly given to the appropriate government agency to enable it to ascertain compliance with the provisions of this rule.

Acquiring an Interest in Litigation

REPRESENTING CO-PARTIES IN LITIGATION

Clients may have or appear to have the same interests, such as with co-plaintiffs or co-defendants. Concurrent conflicts of interest can still exist in such situations. Rule 1.7(a)(2) addresses these (and other) situations, stating that there is a concurrent conflict of interest if "there is a significant risk that the representation of one or more clients will be materially limited by the lawyer's responsibilities to another client, a former client or a third person or by a personal interest of the lawyer." This rule is in place in part to protect co-parties from conflicts that may arise as the litigation proceeds. Even if co-parties are amiable toward one another in their personal lives, it may be the case that the entities actually driving the litigation, such as insurance companies, have diverging legal interests.

REPRESENTING CO-DEFENDANTS

CRIMINAL CASES

As with all co-parties to litigation, the representation of criminal co-defendants is subject to the test in ABA Model Rule 1.7(b). With co-defendants in criminal proceedings, however, an even greater level of scrutiny is added. The added scrutiny comes from the Sixth Amendment, which guarantees a criminal defendant's right to effective assistance of counsel. ABA Model Rule 1.7, Comment 23 states:

> "The potential for conflict of interest in representing multiple defendants in a criminal case is so grave that ordinarily a lawyer should decline to represent more than one codefendant. On the other hand, common representation of persons having similar interests in civil litigation is proper if the requirements of paragraph (b) are met."

In other words, absent extreme circumstances, an attorney should not represent criminal co-defendants.

CIVIL CASES

The ABA Model Rules are generally designed to protect the rights and interests of clients even when doing so is detrimental to attorneys. Obviously, attorneys are interested in representing as many clients as possible. ABA Model Rule 1.7 limits such representation, where conflicts of interest may arise. The rules related to conflicts in civil cases are less stringent that those in criminal cases. ABA Model Rule 1.7, Comment 23 states: "common representation of persons having similar interests in civil litigation is proper if the requirements of paragraph (b) are met." This generally means that attorneys may represent co-defendants or co-plaintiffs in civil matters if the proper steps are taken.

CO-PARTIES IN CIVIL CASES

Attorneys wishing to represent co-parties in a civil case must comply with the test set forth in ABA Model Rule 1.7(b). Additionally, with respect to securing truly "informed" consent, "each affected client [must] be [made] aware of the relevant circumstances and of the material and reasonably foreseeable ways that the conflict could have adverse effects on the interests of that client." ABA Model Rule 1.7, Comment 18. If the potential conflict becomes an actual conflict, the test in Rule 1.7(b) must be repeated. An attorney must cease representation of one of the clients if a reasonable attorney would advise the client to withhold consent to the conflict. An attorney in such a situation

56

would have to comply with the usual requirements related to withdrawal, such as those contained in Rule 1.16.

REPRESENTATION IN UNRELATED PROCEEDINGS

On the surface, it may appear that an attorney creates a conflict by representing two distinct clients with inconsistent legal positions in separate proceedings. However, ABA Model Rule 1.7, Comment 24 states that "[o]rdinarily a lawyer may take inconsistent legal positions in different tribunals at different times on behalf of different clients." The issue becomes more complicated if the two proceedings are happening in the same jurisdiction or the results of one proceeding could impact the tribunal's decision in the other matter (e.g. an appellate court with jurisdiction over the second court). In such a situation, an attorney is required to seek the informed, written consent of both clients before proceeding with representation.

CLASS-ACTION LAWSUITS

For class-action lawsuits, the general rule, as stated in ABA Model Rule 1.7, Comment 25 is:

> "When a lawyer represents or seeks to represent a class of plaintiffs or defendants in a class-action lawsuit, unnamed members of the class are ordinarily not considered to be clients of the lawyer for purposes of applying paragraph (a)(1) of this Rule. Thus, the lawyer does not typically need to get the consent of such a person before representing a client suing the person in an unrelated matter. Similarly, a lawyer seeking to represent an opponent in a class action does not typically need the consent of an unnamed member of the class whom the lawyer represents in an unrelated matter."

This rule is necessary because many class action suits involve so many parties that to identify each individual member and all possible conflicts would be unduly burdensome.

SETTLEMENT FOR SEVERAL CLIENTS

As in any case where a single attorney represents multiple clients in a single action, the process of reaching a lump-sum settlement can lead to conflicts of interest between the various clients. For example, suppose an attorney represents five individual parties who are all plaintiffs in a lawsuit against a company. If the defendant company was to approach the plaintiffs' attorney with a settlement offer, questions would arise as to whether or not to accept the offer, how the offer would be divided, etc. All of these questions would inevitably lead to the development of conflicts of interests between the plaintiffs. One client might want to take the settlement because of a dire financial situation, another might wish to reject the settlement and continue to trial, a third client might insist on the money being split into fifths, etc. The same situation could also arise on the defendant's side.

AGGREGATE SETTLEMENTS

Because of the high potential for conflicts in cases where a single attorney participates in an aggregate settlement negotiation on behalf of more than one client, the ABA Model Rules take great care in outlining the circumstances in which such participation is acceptable. Specifically, ABA Model rule 1.8(g) states that a lawyer must not participate in an aggregate settlement "unless each client gives informed consent, in a writing signed by the client." The Rule continues by stating that "[t]he lawyer's disclosure shall include the existence and nature of all the claims or pleas involved and of the participation of each person in the settlement." This rule applies both to civil settlements and criminal plea agreements. Recall that it is quite unlikely that an attorney would represent co-defendants in a criminal case.

CLASS ACTION SETTLEMENTS

Class action settlements are often distinguishable from multi-party representation because an attorney representing a class of litigants usually does not have the full client-lawyer relationship that tends to exist in a multiple representation scenario. Even with this class action relationship in place, attorneys must "comply with applicable rules regulating notification of class members and other procedural requirements designed to ensure adequate protection of the entire class." ABA Model Rule 1.8, Comment 13.

ACQUIRING INTEREST IN A CLIENT'S CAUSE OF ACTION

Several ABA Model Rules seek to limit an attorney's financial stake in litigation. This principle is balanced with the desire to provide access to the courts to persons who would otherwise be unable to pay. Rule 1.8(e) forbids an attorney from financially assisting a client in pending or contemplated litigation, with the following exceptions:

(1)   a lawyer may advance court costs and expenses of litigation, the repayment of which may be contingent on the outcome of the matter; and

(2)   a lawyer representing an indigent client may pay court costs and expenses of litigation on behalf of the client.

The second exception does not contemplate repayment by the indigent client.

ABA Model Rule 1.8(i) states that "[a] lawyer shall not acquire a proprietary interest in the cause of action or subject matter of litigation the lawyer is conducting for a client." This Rule seeks to avoid conflicts of interest that may arise if the attorney's interests were to diverge from those of the client.

There are two exceptions. First, "the lawyer may acquire a lien authorized by law to secure the lawyer's fee or expenses." ABA Model Rule 1.8(i)(1). Second, ABA Model Rule 1.8(i)(2) states that "the lawyer may contract with a client for a reasonable contingent fee in a civil case." These exceptions are intended to enable legal representation by making sure that attorneys will be paid for their services.

Obtaining Substantial Gifts from Clients

ABA Model Rule 1.8(c) makes it clear that an attorney is not permitted to solicit substantial gifts from clients who are not related to the attorney. Comment 6 to Rule 1.8 states "due to concerns about overreaching and imposition on clients, a lawyer may not suggest that a substantial gift be made to the lawyer or for the lawyer's benefit, except where the lawyer is related to the client as set forth in paragraph (c)." Related persons, for purposes of this rule, include persons with whom the attorney or client shares a close familial relationship as well as children, grandparents, spouses, etc. Rule 1.8 does not mean that a lawyer must reject a substantial gift from a client if the attorney did not suggest the gift. However, receipt of a substantial gift "may be voidable by the client under the doctrine of undue influence . . . ." ABA Model Rule 1.8, Comment 6.

In addition to prohibiting attorneys from soliciting substantial gifts from clients who are not relatives, the ABA Model Rules also prohibit an attorney from creating a legal instrument that vests a substantial gift in the attorney. ABA Model Rule 1.8(c) states "[a] lawyer shall not . . . prepare on behalf of a client an instrument giving the lawyer or a person related to the lawyer any substantial gift unless the lawyer or other recipient of the gift is related to the client." This means that an attorney could not draft a will that included a substantial bequest to the attorney if the client was not a related person. However, attorneys are not prohibited from seeking fee-paying positions that relate to the drafting of testamentary documents and the like (e.g. executor of the estate).

The ABA Model Rules Seek to Protect Clients from Being Taken Advantage of by Their Business Transactions with Clients

ATTORNEY'S BUSINESS DEALINGS WITH CLIENT

The ABA Model Rules seek to protect clients from being taken advantage of by their attorneys. For example, ABA Model Rule 1.8(a) forbids an attorney from entering into a business transaction with, or knowingly acquiring any pecuniary interest adverse to, a client unless all the following are met:

(1) the transaction and terms on which the lawyer acquires the interest are fair and reasonable to the client and are fully disclosed and transmitted in writing in a manner that can be reasonably understood by the client;

(2) the client is advised in writing of the desirability of seeking and is given a reasonable opportunity to seek the advice of independent legal counsel on the transaction; and

(3) the client gives informed consent, in a writing signed by the client, to the essential terms of the transaction and the lawyer's role in the transaction, including whether the lawyer is representing the client in the transaction.

Third-Party Compensation and Influence

THIRD-PARTY PAYMENTS

Allowing clients to have legal expenses paid by third parties enables clients with limited resources to access legal representation. This scenario, however, can lead to conflicts of interest and impair a client's ability to get fully unbiased representation. Therefore, ABA Model Rule 1.8(f) forbids a lawyer from representing a client while accepting compensation from a third person unless all of the following are met:

(1) the client gives informed consent;

(2) there is no interference with the lawyer's independence of professional judgment or with the client-lawyer relationship; and

(3) information relating to representation of a client is protected as required by Rule 1.6.

CONFLICTS FROM THIRD PARTIES

Third parties may create conflicts of interest between an attorney and client, as acknowledged by ABA Model Rule 1.7(a)(2). As with many other concurrent conflicts, an attorney may represent a client in spite of a third-party conflict if the test in Rule 1.7(b) is met.

Lawyers Currently or Formerly in Government Service

GOVERNMENTAL SERVICE TO PRIVATE PRACTICE

As with a client's confidentiality interests when an attorney transitions between private firms, the government has its own confidentiality concerns when an attorney leaves government service to practice in the private sector. Unless expressly permitted by law, ABA Model Rule 1.11 states that an attorney formerly employed by the government:

(1)   is subject to Rule 1.9(c); and

(2)   shall not otherwise represent a client in connection with a matter in which the lawyer participated personally and substantially as a public officer or employee, unless the appropriate government agency gives its informed consent, confirmed in writing, to the representation.

"MATTER" DEFINED

ABA Model Rule 1.11(e) defines the term "matter" as:

(1)   any judicial or other proceeding, application, request for a ruling or other determination, contract, claim, controversy, investigation, charge, accusation, arrest or other particular matter involving a specific party or parties, and

(2)   any other matter covered by the conflict of interest rules of the appropriate government agency. As stated in Rule 1.11(e)(2), attorneys departing government service may also be subject to separate and additional confidentiality rules imposed by the particular government agency they are departing.

"PERSONALLY AND SUBSTANTIALLY"

The words "personally and substantially" as used in ABA Model Rule 1.11(a) effectively limit the applicability of Rule 1.11(a), which is already limited due to the narrow meaning of "matter." The first term, "personally," requires that the attorney worked on the matter while representing the government. This does not include only small interactions with the matter or oversight in a managerial capacity. Furthermore, the term "substantial" requires that the attorney's work on the matter was more than just tangentially addressing the issue during the course of working on another matter.

FORMER GOVERNMENT ATTORNEY'S LIMITATIONS

ABA Model Rule 1.11(c) states:

> "Except as law may otherwise expressly permit, a lawyer having information that the lawyer knows is confidential government information about a person acquired when the lawyer was a public officer or employee, may not represent a private client whose interests are adverse to that person in a matter in which the information could be used to the material disadvantage of that person."

Keep in mind that the individual whose information was obtained does not have to be a government employee or agent.

PRIVATE PRACTICE TO GOVERNMENT PRACTICE

With respect to confidentiality owed former clients, the Rules are essentially the same – current government attorneys owe a duty of confidentiality to former clients and current clients. Under ABA Model Rule 1.11(d)(1), a lawyer currently serving as a public officer or employee is subject to Rules 1.7 and 1.9, except as law may otherwise expressly permit.

FORMER PRIVATE ATTORNEYS

The standard for attorneys transitioning into government service is the same for attorneys leaving government service. ABA Model Rule 1.11(d)(2) states that a government attorney shall not:

(i) participate in a matter in which the lawyer participated personally and substantially while in private practice or nongovernmental employment, unless the appropriate government agency gives its informed consent, confirmed in writing; or

(ii) negotiate for private employment with any person who is involved as a party or as lawyer for a party in a matter in which the lawyer is participating personally and substantially, except that a lawyer serving as a law clerk to a judge, other adjudicative officer or arbitrator may negotiate for private employment as permitted by Rule 1.12(b) and subject to the conditions stated in Rule 1.12(b).

The latter part of this rule seeks to prevent improper influence in judicial or administrative processes.

Former Judge, Arbitrator, Mediator or Other Third-Party Neutral

FORMER JUDGE, LAW CLERK, OR ADJUDICATIVE OFFICER ENTERING PRIVATE PRACTICE

It is fairly common for judges, law clerks, and adjudicative officers to leave the bench and enter private practice. In these instances, the departing individual may possess a great deal of knowledge about certain entities and/or individuals that is confidential. In order to protect such parties, ABA Model Rule 1.12(a) states:

"Except as stated in paragraph (d), a lawyer shall not represent anyone in connection with a matter in which the lawyer participated personally and substantially as a judge or other adjudicative officer or law clerk to such a person or as an arbitrator, mediator or other third-party neutral, unless all parties to the proceeding give informed consent, confirmed in writing."

DISQUALIFICATION OF A FORMER JUDGE, LAW CLERK, OR ADJUDICATIVE OFFICER ENTERING PRIVATE PRACTICE

While the need to protect against conflicts of interest and confidentiality breaches is critical, imputing a former judge's entire firm with the conflict could be unnecessary, particularly for large and/or multi-jurisdiction firms. Therefore, the ABA Model Rules contemplate a screening process that shields the remaining attorneys in the firm from the former judge's conflict.

If a firm has an attorney who is disqualified from a matter due to prior involvement as a judge, law clerk, or adjudicative official, the following must occur before other members of the firm may undertake or continue representation in the matter:

- the disqualified lawyer is timely screened from any participation in the matter and is apportioned no part of the fee therefrom; and
- written notice is promptly given to the parties and any appropriate tribunal to enable them to ascertain compliance with the provisions of this rule.

JUDICIAL LAW CLERK LIMITATIONS

Judicial law clerks often work intimately with cases assigned to their judges. Such clerks often must be familiar with the facts of a case to conduct effective research. ABA Model rule 1.12(b) sets out specific parameters governing a law clerk's ability to negotiate employment: "A lawyer serving as a law clerk to a judge or other adjudicative officer may negotiate for employment with a party or lawyer involved in a matter in which the clerk is participating personally and substantially, but only after the lawyer has notified the judge or other adjudicative officer." Judicial law clerks are thus treated differently from other attorneys, and the most common rationale is that such clerks are often young attorneys who are embarking on their legal careers.

ADJUDICATIVE OFFICERS' LIMITATIONS

The ABA Model Rules take a lenient approach with respect to clerks of adjudicative officers seeking private employment. The adjudicative officers themselves, however, do not get the benefit of such leniency. ABA Model Rule 1.12(b) states:

> "A lawyer shall not negotiate for employment with any person who is involved as a party or as lawyer for a party in a matter in which the lawyer is participating personally and substantially as a judge or other adjudicative officer or as an arbitrator, mediator or other third-party neutral."

Competence, Legal Malpractice, and Other Civil Liability

Maintaining Competence

KNOWLEDGE AND SKILL LEVEL

ABA Model Rule 1.1 states that "[a] lawyer shall provide competent representation to a client. Competent representation requires the legal knowledge, skill, thoroughness and preparation reasonably necessary for the representation." To determine whether an attorney has the required knowledge and skill to properly represent a client in a particular matter, several relevant factors are utilized. These factors, as listed in Comment 1 of ABA Rule 1.1, include:

- The complexity and specialized nature of the matter;
- The attorney's general experience;
- The attorney's education and experience in the relevant subject matter;
- The level of preparation and study the attorney is able to devote to the matter; and
- Whether it is feasible to refer the matter to or consult with an attorney with established competence in the field in question.

EXCEPTIONS TO SKILL LEVEL

Generally, ABA Model Rule 1.1 explicitly requires that an attorney possess the requisite skill to represent a client in a given matter. There is, however, one small exception to this rule. ABA Mode Rule 1.1, Comment 3 states:

> "In an emergency a lawyer may give advice or assistance in a matter in which the lawyer does not have the skill ordinarily required where referral to or consultation or association with another lawyer would be impractical. Even in an emergency, however, assistance should be limited to that reasonably necessary in the circumstances, for ill-considered action under emergency conditions can jeopardize the client's interest."

These cases may arise where the client's usual attorney is unavailable and the client needs urgent assistance.

PREPARATION AND PROFESSIONAL COMPETENCY

ABA Model Rule 1.1, Comment 5 sets out guidelines that attorneys must follow in order to be considered to have appropriately prepared to represent the client. Generally, the attorney must determine the facts and best resolution of the case from the client's perspective by applying appropriate legal methods. The appropriateness of the legal methods employed is generally determined by looking to what reasonably competent practitioners would use. The level of preparation required depends in part upon the complexity of the matter and what is at stake. Additionally, ABA Model Rule1.1, Comment 6 says that attorneys should maintain their competency by paying attention to changes in the law and through the continuing legal education requirements set by the bar associations of their jurisdiction(s).

Competence Necessary to Undertake Representation

NO PRIOR EXPERIENCE OPTIONS

An attorney may be approached by prospective or existing clients that have legal matters with which the attorney is unfamiliar. At this initial stage, the attorney must determine if they will be a poor advocate due to the technicality of the matter and/or the lack of adequate time to properly prepare. If the attorney can through preparation become sufficiently competent to represent the client, then the attorney may represent the client. ABA Model Rule 1.1, Comment 4 states: "A lawyer may accept representation where the requisite level of competence can be achieved by reasonable preparation. This applies as well to a lawyer who is appointed as counsel for an unrepresented person."

Exercising Diligence and Care

DILIGENCE

ABA Model Rule 1.3 states that an attorney must act with reasonable diligence and promptness when representing a client. ABA Model Rule 1.3, Comment 1 explains diligence, here a term of art, as the pursuit of the client's interests despite opposition, obstacles, and personal inconvenience. This includes demonstrating dedication and commitment to the client's interests and advocating zealously on behalf of the client. An attorney may use any means necessary to pursue a client's interests so long as the means are legal and ethical. "Diligence" does not require an attorney to act in an uncivil manner.

PROMPTNESS

A lack of promptness by an attorney can have a variety of negative effects on a client. At its most benign, a lack of promptness may cause a client to lose confidence in the attorney. The client may also feel that the attorney does not take the case seriously. A lack of promptness can cause a client a great amount of otherwise unnecessary stress and anxiety. At its worst, an attorney's lack of promptness may jeopardize a client's case. For example, if an attorney misses court-imposed deadlines, a client's interests could be harmed. The case could even be dismissed. A procrastinating attorney could leave themselves with insufficient time to research helpful case law, thereby harming a client's case. Note that attorneys may agree to reasonable delays, such as opposing counsel's request for a continuance, if the interests of the client will not be hurt.

IMPORTANCE OF RESOLUTION

ABA Model Rule 1.3 states that "[a] lawyer shall act with reasonable diligence and promptness in representing a client." This rule applies from the initial contact between an attorney and client until the final resolution of the matter. Until the client's matter is resolved, "a lawyer should carry through to conclusion all matters undertaken for a client." ABA Model Rule 1.3, Comment 4. An attorney may terminate the relationship prior to the resolution of the client's matter in instances where the attorney must, or is permitted to, withdraw from the case. However, "[d]oubt about whether a client-lawyer relationship still exists should be clarified by the lawyer, preferably in writing, so that the client will not mistakenly suppose the lawyer is looking after the client's affairs when the lawyer has ceased to do so." Attorneys who perform services that may need updating, like will drafting, are wise to carefully explain the relationship to clients.

SUCCESSION PLANNING

ABA Model Rule 1.3, which requires attorneys to exercise diligence when representing clients, is broad and far-reaching. It extends to solo practitioners who are no longer capable of adequately representing their clients because of death or disability. ABA Model Rule 1.3, Comment 5 states:

> "To prevent neglect of client matters in the event of a sole practitioner's death or disability, the duty of diligence may require that each sole practitioner prepare a plan, in conformity with applicable rules, that designates another competent lawyer to review client files, notify each client of the lawyer's death or disability, and determine whether there is a need for immediate protective action."

Civil Liability to Client, Including Malpractice

DUTY OF CARE REQUIRED

Generally, the duty owed to clients by attorneys is established as an industry standard. In other words, an attorney is expected to act as competently and diligently as a similarly-situated attorney under the same circumstances. Even if an attorney does not intend to take a person on as a client, the attorney may owe that person the same care as a client if the attorney has neglectfully misled the person into thinking a client-lawyer relationship has been created. Attorneys also owe a duty of care to some non-clients. Restatement §51 states that an attorney owes a duty of care to any party who was intended to benefit from the legal services provided by the attorney (such as the intended beneficiary of a will the attorney drafted), as well as some other non-clients in certain circumstances.

STANDARD OF CARE LIMITATIONS

Attorneys owe their clients the same level of competency and diligence that a similarly-situated attorney would provide. This does *not* mean that an attorney must be infallible, or that an attorney must never make a mistake. There is a critical distinction between diligence and perfection. Where there is no breach of the duty of care, an attorney will not be liable for negligence, even if a client is harmed. An attorney could mistakenly make a well-informed and reasonable decision that results in harm to a client but does not rise to the level of negligence. For example, an attorney could reasonably choose to put an expert on the witness stand, and opposing counsel could elicit damaging testimony on cross-examination. Absent additional facts, the decision to use the expert would not be negligence.

Attorneys are retained by clients primarily for their presumed knowledge of the law that relates to the subject matter of the representation. Because of this, it is important that an attorney be sufficiently knowledgeable of areas of law that impact the client's case. Every attorney need not be an expert on every legal issue. Attorneys must have the legal knowledge of an ordinary, competent, and diligent attorney; this is a sliding standard that depends in part upon the practice area and matter at issue. Additionally, attorneys must use reasonable research techniques to seek knowledge that they do not already possess. Because many issues of law are not definitive, an attorney is only responsible for conducting reasonable research, not for ultimately making the right judgment about an unsettled issue of law. Such would be an unreasonable standard.

Limiting Liability for Malpractice

NO PERMISSIBLE VIOLATIONS

ABA Model Rule 1.1 states that "[a] lawyer shall provide competent representation to a client. Competent representation requires the legal knowledge, skill, thoroughness and preparation reasonably necessary for the representation." Rule 1.3 states that "[a] lawyer shall act with reasonable diligence and promptness in representing a client." Neither of these rules on their face allow for any instances of noncompliance. Most discipline authorities will take into account any special circumstances confronting an attorney prior to levying any sanctions, but this does not change the fact that a violation has occurred. The disciplinary action commences, if at all, with the filing of a complaint against the attorney.

POTENTIAL DISCIPLINARY ACTIONS

The first type of action that can be taken against an incompetent or neglectful attorney is disciplinary action, commenced by complaining to the state bar or other disciplining authority. There is also the civil action of professional malpractice, commenced by a client filing a malpractice lawsuit. There are several distinctions between these two types of actions. First, malpractice cases are brought before and heard by a civil court, whereas disciplinary matters are conducted before a tribunal. Second, the party opposing the attorney in a malpractice suit is the allegedly harmed client, whereas in a disciplinary hearing the opposing party is the state bar or other disciplinary authority. Finally, malpractice suits are brought in order to make the injured client "whole" through some sort of compensation, whereas a disciplinary action is brought to punish the offending attorney and protect the public at large.

PENDING OR FUTURE MALPRACTICE ACTIONS

Ethics violations and professional malpractice actions are two separate and distinct undertakings that require different criteria for the assessment of responsibility and the punishment imposed. Generally speaking, this means that an attorney who has been found to violate the applicable rules of ethics is not automatically guilty, and may ultimately be cleared, of professional malpractice in a civil proceeding involving the same behavior. Furthermore, not only does an ethics violation *not* rise to the level of professional malpractice, it does not even create a legal presumption of professional malpractice. Practically speaking, however, where an attorney's actions are found to violate the rules of ethics, such findings may be persuasive evidence in a later professional malpractice action.

LEGAL THEORIES

In a professional malpractice suit, there are a variety of legal theories that a plaintiff may pursue. Some of the more common theories used in such suits include:

- <u>Intentional Tort</u>: Potential intentional torts include fraud, misrepresentation, malicious prosecution, abuse of process, or misappropriation of funds.
- <u>Breach of Fiduciary Duty</u>: Attorneys, like other fiduciaries, owe clients the highest standard of care. Breaching any fiduciary duties may subject an attorney to liability.
- <u>Breach of Contract</u>: This can arise when an attorney violates some provision of a written or oral agreement with the client. A court may also find that an attorney violated an implied (or unspoken) agreement with the client.
- <u>Negligence</u>: Like any negligence claim, the client must show that the attorney owed a certain duty of care, that the attorney breached the duty, and that the breach caused the client to sustain some kind of damage(s).

PROFESSIONAL NEGLIGENCE CASE

Any tort claim brought by a plaintiff requires a showing of damages and legal causation. Basically, this requires that the plaintiff show that the defendant's actions caused the harm to the plaintiff, and that this harm resulted in damages to the plaintiff. This standard applies to professional negligence claims made against attorneys: the plaintiff must show that, but for the attorney's negligence, the harm would not have befallen the plaintiff, and that it is fair to hold the attorney liable for any such unexpected harm, or for expected harm that occurred in unexpected ways. Perhaps the most pervasive types of attorney malpractice suits result from attorneys missing deadlines, leading to the expiration of the applicable statute of limitations.

LIABLE FOR OTHERS' ACTIONS

Respondeat superior is a general legal doctrine that applies in professional malpractice cases. Essentially, this theory provides that an attorney may be held responsible for the actions of the attorney's subordinates (e.g. a law clerk, secretary, paralegal, etc.) if they are acting within the scope of their employment. Another legal theory implicating attorneys for the actions of others is found in partnership law. Generally, under partnership principles, a partner is held liable for the negligent actions of another partner if such actions are committed in the ordinary course of the partnership's business. This provision is extremely important because a great many law firms operate as partnerships. Additionally, state laws relating to vicarious liability affect the liability of shareholders in incorporated law firms for the actions of their colleagues.

LIMITING MALPRACTICE CLAIMS

Perhaps the most obvious method of limiting malpractice liability is for an attorney to conduct their practice in a prudent and competent manner. However, sometimes unexpected realities can render even the most competent attorney the target of a professional malpractice action. One shield against such claims is professional malpractice insurance. These policies typically shield the attorney from monetary loss, and often the insurance company will provide counsel to defend the attorney against malpractice claims. Additionally, attorneys may limit their exposure to malpractice claims through contractual provisions in their employment agreements. Such contractual limitations are only allowed if the client is independently represented by another attorney during negotiations. Finally, an attorney may settle the malpractice claim with the client, but only after advising the client in writing to seek the advice of independent counsel.

DUTY OF CARE BREACH

Attorneys may be found liable for committing intentional torts, breaching fiduciary duties, breaching contracts, or negligence. These potential causes of action against attorneys are separate claims that can all lead to their own distinct results. Regardless of the outcome of any of these claims in a given situation, the attorney may also face disciplinary action. This is true even where the attorney is not found culpable for any of the client's claims in court. Additionally, if an attorney corrects the wrong by reimbursing the client for any monetary damage, the attorney is still subject to discipline.

Litigation and Other Forms of Advocacy

Meritorious Claims and Contentions

FALSE STATEMENT OF MATERIAL FACT

During the course of negotiations on behalf of a client, attorneys may exaggerate to influence an adverse party's perception of the case. To an extent, this practice does not violate the ABA Model Rules. In making the distinction between acceptable negotiation practices and making false statements of fact, Rule 4.1, Comment 2 states:

> "Whether a particular statement should be regarded as one of fact can depend on the circumstances. Under generally accepted conventions in negotiation, certain types of statements ordinarily are not taken as statements of material fact. Estimates of price or value placed on the subject of a transaction and a party's intentions as to an acceptable settlement of a claim are ordinarily in this category, and so is the existence of an undisclosed principal except where nondisclosure of the principal would constitute fraud. Lawyers should be mindful of their obligations under applicable law to avoid criminal and tortious misrepresentation."

LIMITATIONS ON ARGUMENTS

Attorneys are charged with zealously representing their clients' interests. However, this duty is not without limitation. Attorneys are not free to raise just *any* argument, and this is true whether the attorney is asserting or defending a claim on behalf of a client. ABA Model Rule 3.1 states: "A lawyer shall not bring or defend a proceeding, or assert or controvert an issue therein, unless there is a basis in law and fact for doing so that is not frivolous, which includes a good faith argument for an extension, modification or reversal of existing law." This Rule is not intended to curtail creative thinking on the part of attorneys, but rather to limit frivolous claims.

FRIVOLOUS LEGAL POSITIONS

ABA Model Rule 3.1, Comment 2 discusses frivolous claims as follows:

> "The filing of an action or defense or similar action taken for a client is not frivolous merely because the facts have not first been fully substantiated or because the lawyer expects to develop vital evidence only by discovery. What is required of lawyers, however, is that they inform themselves about the facts of their clients' cases and the applicable law and determine that they can make good faith arguments in support of their clients' positions. Such action is not frivolous even though the lawyer believes that the client's position ultimately will not prevail. The action is frivolous, however, if the lawyer is unable either to make a good faith argument on the merits of the action taken or to support the action taken by a good faith argument for an extension, modification or reversal of existing law."

The sole exception arises in the context of an attorney representing a criminal defendant or a client in a matter that could result in the client's imprisonment. ABA Model Rule 3.1 states: "A lawyer for the defendant in a criminal proceeding, or the respondent in a proceeding that could result in incarceration, may nevertheless so defend the proceeding as to require that every element of the case be established." This exception recognizes a criminal defendants' right to effective assistance of counsel and the importance of making sure that the prosecution fully carries its burden of proof.

Thus, even if an attorney believes their client to be guilty of the crime charged, the attorney may hold the prosecution to its full evidentiary burden.

Expediting Litigation

EXPEDITING LITIGATION PROCEEDINGS

If a speedy resolution of litigation is in the client's best interest, an attorney has the duty to make reasonable efforts to expedite litigation. Comment 1 to ABA Model Rule 3.2 states:

> "Although there will be occasions when a lawyer may properly seek a postponement for personal reasons, it is not proper for a lawyer to routinely fail to expedite litigation solely for the convenience of the advocates. Nor will a failure to expedite be reasonable if done for the purpose of frustrating an opposing party's attempt to obtain rightful redress or repose. It is not a justification that similar conduct is often tolerated by the bench and bar. The question is whether a competent lawyer acting in good faith would regard the course of action as having some substantial purpose other than delay. Realizing financial or other benefit from otherwise improper delay in litigation is not a legitimate interest of the client."

Candor to the Tribunal

DUTY OF CANDOR

Attorneys owe the court a duty of candor with respect to their citations of law before a court or other tribunal. This includes both affirmative statements of law and failure to disclose controlling applicable legal authority that is directly adverse to the client's interests. Under ABA Model Rule 3.3(a), a lawyer shall not knowingly:

(1) make a false statement of fact or law to a tribunal or fail to correct a false statement of material fact or law previously made to the tribunal by the lawyer; [or]

(2) fail to disclose to the tribunal legal authority in the controlling jurisdiction known to the lawyer to be directly adverse to the position of the client and not disclosed by opposing counsel[.]

DUTY PRESENTING FACTS

Similar to representations of law, attorneys owe a court/tribunal a duty of honesty with respect to facts presented. ABA Model Rule 3.3(a)(1) dictates that an attorney must not knowingly "make a false statement of fact or law to a tribunal or fail to correct a false statement of material fact or law previously made to the tribunal by the lawyer." Attorneys are not required to have personal knowledge of all of the facts they present to the court, but ABA Model Rule 3.3, Comment 3 states: "[A]n assertion purporting to be on the lawyer's own knowledge, as in an affidavit by the lawyer or in a statement in open court, may properly be made only when the lawyer knows the assertion is true or believes it to be true on the basis of a reasonably diligent inquiry."

DAMAGING FACTS

The U.S. court system is premised on an adversarial relationship between the parties involved. Because of this, the attorney for one party has no duty to establish facts that are damaging to the client. That is the task of the opposing party. There is an exception where only one side is arguing before the court (e.g. ex parte proceedings). ABA Rule 3.3, Comment 14 states:

> "[I]n any ex parte proceeding, such as an application for a temporary restraining order, there is no balance of presentation by opposing advocates. The object of an ex parte proceeding is nevertheless to yield a substantially just result. The judge has an affirmative responsibility to accord the absent party just consideration. The lawyer for the represented party has the correlative duty to make disclosures of material facts known to the lawyer and that the lawyer reasonably believes is necessary to an informed decision."

FALSE EVIDENCE

ABA Model Rule 3.3(a)(3) prohibits attorneys from "offer[ing] evidence that the lawyer knows to be false." Comment 8 to ABA Model Rule 3.3 states:

> "The prohibition against offering false evidence only applies if the lawyer knows that the evidence is false. A lawyer's reasonable belief that evidence is false does not preclude its presentation to the trier of fact. A lawyer's knowledge that evidence is false, however, can be inferred from the circumstances. See Rule 1.0(f). Thus, although the lawyer should resolve doubts about the veracity of testimony or other evidence in favor of the client, the lawyer cannot ignore an obvious falsehood."

ABA Model Rule 1.0(f) states that "[a] person's knowledge may be inferred from circumstances."

If the attorney discovers that evidence is false after the attorney has presented it to the court, the attorney must take several steps. Comment 10 to ABA Model Rule 3.3, lays out these steps as follows:

> "[T]he advocate's proper course is to remonstrate with the client confidentially, advise the client of the lawyer's duty of candor to the tribunal and seek the client's cooperation with respect to the withdrawal or correction of the false statements or evidence. If that fails, the advocate must take further remedial action. If withdrawal from the representation is not permitted or will not undo the effect of the false evidence, the advocate must make such disclosure to the tribunal as is reasonably necessary to remedy the situation, even if doing so requires the lawyer to reveal information that otherwise would be protected by Rule 1.6. It is for the tribunal then to determine what should be done — making a statement about the matter to the trier of fact, ordering a mistrial or perhaps nothing."

FALSE TESTIMONY

The proper course of conduct when an attorney knows that their criminal client has or will give false testimony to the court is a difficult one. This is a controversial issue because of the tension between an attorney's duty of candor and a criminal defendant's constitutional right to testify on their own behalf. ABA Model Rule 3.3(a)(3) states that an attorney shall not knowingly

> "offer evidence that the lawyer knows to be false. If a lawyer, the lawyer's client, or a witness called by the lawyer, has offered material evidence and the lawyer comes to know of its falsity, the lawyer shall take reasonable remedial measures, including, if necessary, disclosure to the tribunal. A lawyer may refuse to offer evidence, other than the testimony of a defendant in a criminal matter that the lawyer reasonably believes is false."

The attorney should, then, in this order:

- make a concerted effort to dissuade the client from making false testimony;
- if the client refuses, consider withdrawal; and
- if these solutions fail, reveal the situation to the judge.

PROTECTING ADJUDICATIVE PROCEEDINGS

ABA Model Rule 3.3(b) states: "A lawyer who represents a client in an adjudicative proceeding and who knows that a person intends to engage, is engaging or has engaged in criminal or fraudulent conduct related to the proceeding shall take reasonable remedial measures, including, if necessary, disclosure to the tribunal."

Examples of the kinds of conduct contemplated by the rule include activities "such as bribing, intimidating or otherwise unlawfully communicating with a witness, juror, court official or other participant in the proceeding, unlawfully destroying or concealing documents or other evidence or failing to disclose information to the tribunal when required by law to do so." ABA Model Rule 3.3, Comment 12.

Fairness to Opposing Party and Counsel

EVIDENCE AND OPPOSING PARTY

The U.S. court system is based upon fair access to relevant evidence in a matter by both sides in a judicial proceeding. While this does not mean that either side has to gather evidence to undergo research for the opposing side, there exists a need to assure that each side has the opportunity to uncover evidence, regardless of who possesses that evidence. ABA Model Rule 3.4(a) seeks to protect evidence by stating that an attorney must not "unlawfully obstruct another party's access to evidence or unlawfully alter, destroy or conceal a document or other material having potential evidentiary value. A lawyer shall not counsel or assist another person to do any such act." This rule does not supplant pertinent privileged information that would be otherwise relevant evidence.

FALSIFYING EVIDENCE

Attorneys are prohibited from falsifying evidence. The rules against this type of behavior extend beyond the attorney's direct offering of evidence that the attorney knows (or should reasonably know) to be false. ABA Model Rule 3.4(b) states that no attorney shall "falsify evidence, [nor] counsel or assist a witness to testify falsely . . . ." This Rule prohibits attorneys from helping witnesses give false testimony. While it is appropriate to interview witnesses before trial to ascertain what the witness knows, it is inappropriate to counsel the witness as to what they should say in order to offer untrue evidence.

PAYING WITNESSES

Generally, attorneys are disallowed from making payments to witnesses. ABA Model Rule 3.4(b) states that no attorney shall "offer an inducement to a witness that is prohibited by law." The final phrase of the rule does leave some room for certain types of payments. Specifically, there are three common categories of payments that are acceptable. First, witnesses can be paid for their costs (e.g. hotel and meals) for attending a proceeding. Second, witnesses may be reimbursed for wages they lose for participating in the proceeding. Finally, experts may be reasonably compensated for their preparation and delivery of testimony. However, experts' pay may not be contingent or dependent on the results of the case or on the nature of the testimony given by the expert.

INTERFERING WITH WITNESS TESTIMONY

During the investigation phase of a case, an attorney will often discover that testimony of certain witnesses will be damaging to their case. ABA Model Rule 3.4(f) prohibits an attorney from counseling such witnesses to make themselves unavailable for testimony. The attorney may advise a witness not to volunteer information to another party if two qualifications are met:

> (1) the person is a relative or an employee or other agent of a client; and
> (2) the lawyer reasonably believes that the person's interests will not be adversely affected by refraining from giving such information.

APPLICABLE RULES OF PROCEDURE

Rules of evidence and courtroom procedure are in place to assure the orderly progress of cases. Therefore, it is imperative that attorneys do not knowingly disregard these rules in an effort to further their cases. ABA Model Rule 3.4(c) states that no attorney shall "knowingly disobey an obligation under the rules of a tribunal except for an open refusal based on an assertion that no valid obligation exists." This prohibition applies not only to formal rules, but also to orders given by the court in the course of a legal proceeding.

DISCOVERY PHASE

Discovery is a critical component in a legal proceeding. It is during this phase that each party can learn, ascertain, and/or collect pertinent information from the other side. Further, every party to litigation will usually rely, at least in part, upon honesty and professional cooperation of opponents. As a result, ABA Model Rule 3.4(d) states that attorneys shall not "in pretrial procedure, make a frivolous discovery request or fail to make reasonably diligent effort to comply with a legally proper discovery request by an opposing party." Frivolous discovery requests and failure to comply with legitimate discovery requests both have the propensity to be unfairly burdensome and expensive; thus many courts have the ability to impose monetary sanctions for discovery violations. Such sanctions are separate from any attorney discipline for violating Rule 3.4.

PROHIBITED ATTORNEY BEHAVIORS

There are several classifications of attorney behavior that are specifically prohibited at trial. The overall theme of these prohibitions is to ensure that the trier of fact (jury or judge) and law (judge) are presented with the most honest and accurate cases possible. The prohibitions are not intended to stifle otherwise sound advocacy; there is frequently more than one side to a given story. ABA Model Rule 3.4(e) prohibits attorneys from:

- utilizing evidence or information that is inadmissible;
- interjecting the attorney's own personal knowledge of the facts of the case (except in the rare cases where the attorney is called to testify as a witness); and
- interjecting the attorney's own personal opinions about the justness of a cause, the credibility of a witness, the culpability of a civil litigant, or the guilt or innocence of an accused.

THREATENING OPPOSING COUNSEL

There are many types of threats that could theoretically be made between opposing attorneys in a legal action. The two addressed here are threats to bring criminal charges and threats to report disciplinary violations. The Model Rules protect an attorney's right to threaten an adversary with criminal charges so long as the criminal and civil matters are closely related. This is true even if the threatening attorney is utilizing the threat to gain an advantage in a civil case. An attorney is not, however, permitted to threaten an adversary with disciplinary reporting to gain an advantage in a

civil matter. If the adversary's behavior is such that disciplinary reporting is mandatory, then the opposing attorney should report it without any accompanying threats, and irrespective of any perceived advantage.

Impartiality and Decorum of the Tribunal

LEGAL PROCEEDING BEHAVIOR

The whole purpose of legal proceedings is to allow an unbiased third party (tribunal) to resolve a conflict between two or more parties. The relationship between the different sides should facilitate this process and not impede it. Therefore, opposing attorneys are expected to treat each other and all other participants with courtesy and respect, and to respect the seriousness of the proceeding. To do otherwise could hinder the judicial process by confusing the relevant issues and adding additional conflict. ABA Model Rule 3.5(d) states that an attorney shall not "engage in conduct intended to disrupt a tribunal." Comment 5 to Rule 3.5 extends the duty to refrain from disruptive conduct to any proceeding of a tribunal, including depositions. ABA Model Rule 8.4(d) states that it is professional misconduct for an attorney to "engage in conduct that is prejudicial to the administration of justice." Pertinent tribunal rules may impose additional requirements.

PROTECTING IMPARTIALITY AND DECORUM

ABA Model Rule 3.5(a) states that no lawyer shall "seek to influence a judge, juror, prospective juror or other official by means prohibited by law." The breadth of this rule is highlighted by ABA Model Rule 3.5, Comment 1, which states: "Many forms of improper influence upon a tribunal are proscribed by criminal law. Others are specified in the ABA Model Code of Judicial Conduct, with which an advocate should be familiar. A lawyer is required to avoid contributing to a violation of such provisions."

DUTY TOWARD PUBLIC OFFICIALS

An attorney's duty with respect to judges and other candidates for public office is essentially to be honest when rendering evaluations of their fitness, professionalism, or other traits pertinent to legal office. Specifically, ABA Model Rule 8.2(a) states:

> "A lawyer shall not make a statement that the lawyer knows to be false or with reckless disregard as to its truth or falsity concerning the qualifications or integrity of a judge, adjudicatory officer or public legal officer, or of a candidate for election or appointment to judicial or legal office."

If an attorney is running for judicial office, the Code of Judicial Conduct applies to that attorney even *prior* to the attorney's election. ABA Model Rule 8.2(b) states: "A lawyer who is a candidate for judicial office shall comply with the applicable provisions of the Code of Judicial Conduct."

Trial Publicity

TRIAL PUBLICITY – PROHIBITED OUT-OF-COURT STATEMENTS

ABA Model Rule 3.6(a) states:

> "A lawyer who is participating or has participated in the investigation or litigation of a matter shall not make an extrajudicial statement that the lawyer knows or reasonably should know will be disseminated by means of public communication and will have a substantial likelihood of materially prejudicing an adjudicative proceeding in the matter."

The general purpose of this rule is to avoid improper trial publicity that could lead to an unfair hearing. The largest threat these statements pose is prejudicing the potential jury pool.

TRIAL PUBLICITY – PERMISSIBLE OUT-OF-COURT STATEMENTS

For criminal **and** civil cases, ABA Model Rule 3.6(b)(1)–(6) allows an attorney to make the following statements without violating the general prohibition of public statements likely to prejudice an adjudicative proceeding:

(1) the claim, offense or defense involved and, except when prohibited by law, the identity of persons involved;

(2) information contained in a public record;

(3) that an investigation of a matter is in progress;

(4) the scheduling/result of any step in litigation;

(5) a request for assistance in obtaining evidence/information necessary thereto; [and]

(6) a warning of danger concerning the behavior of a person involved, when there is reason to believe that there exists the likelihood of substantial harm to an individual or to the public[.]

Under ABA Rule 3.6(b)(7), **for criminal cases only**, an attorney may publicly make the following statements without violating the general rule prohibiting public statements that are likely to prejudice an adjudicative proceeding:

(i)   the identity, residence, occupation and family status of the accused;

(ii) if the accused has not been apprehended, information necessary to aid in apprehension of that person;

(iii) the fact, time and place of arrest; and

(iv) the identity of investigating/arresting officers/agencies and the length of the investigation.

An attorney can also make public statements about a case to protect a client from prejudice resulting from recent publicity not initiated by the lawyer or their client. ABA Model Rule 3.6(c) states:

> "Notwithstanding [ABA Model Rule 3.6(a)], a lawyer may make a statement that a reasonable lawyer would believe is required to protect a client from the substantial undue prejudicial effect of recent publicity not initiated by the lawyer or the lawyer's client. A statement made pursuant to this paragraph shall be limited to such information as is necessary to mitigate the recent adverse publicity."

This rule essentially allows an attorney to engage in damage control if potentially prejudicial statements have been made about the attorney's client. Additionally, certain factual information, such as information in public records, is not considered prejudicial.

Transactions and Communications with Persons Other than Clients

Truthfulness in Statements to Others

MAKING REPRESENTATIONS OF FACT

In the course of an attorney's practice, there will be many instances where the attorney communicates with third persons. ABA Model Rule 4.1(a) states that an attorney representing a client shall not "make a false statement of material fact or law to a third person." It is important to understand that this duty forbidding misrepresentations does not mean that an attorney must apprise third persons of relevant facts. ABA Model Rule 4.1, Comment 1 states: "[a] lawyer is required to be truthful when dealing with others on a client's behalf, but generally has no affirmative duty to inform an opposing party of relevant facts." Automatically informing an opposing party of relevant facts could operate against a client's best interests.

MISREPRESENTATION

Obviously, an outright lie spoken or written by the attorney to a third person is a misrepresentation that is actionable under the rules of professional ethics. However, there can be other more subtle forms of misrepresentation. For example, ABA Model Rule 4.1, Comment 1 states: "A misrepresentation can occur if the lawyer incorporates or affirms a statement of another person that the lawyer knows is false. Misrepresentations can also occur by partially true but misleading statements or omissions that are the equivalent of affirmative false statements." Therefore, it is imperative that the attorney be aware not only of the validity of statements offered directly, but of the validity of statements that are affirmed by the attorney.

Negotiations typically involve some form of "puffery" to enhance the appearance of one party's position. Comment 2 to ABA Model Rule 4.1 states:

> "Under generally accepted conventions in negotiation, certain types of statements ordinarily are not taken as statements of material fact. Estimates of price or value placed on the subject of a transaction and a party's intentions as to an acceptable settlement of a claim are ordinarily in this category, and so is the existence of an undisclosed principal except where nondisclosure of the principal would constitute fraud. Lawyers should be mindful of their obligations under applicable law to avoid criminal and tortious misrepresentation."

A statement that property is "prime real estate" would likely be puffery, even if many would not consider it particularly valuable. A statement that property (which contained only trace amounts of coal) is "valuable because of extensive mineral deposits" would be a statement of material fact.

DISCLOSING MATERIAL FACTS

An attorney shall not "fail to disclose a material fact to a third person when disclosure is necessary to avoid assisting a criminal or fraudulent act by a client, unless disclosure is prohibited by Rule 1.6." ABA Model Rule 4.1(b). A problem arises when such a disclosure violates the duty of client confidentiality. In these circumstances "a lawyer can avoid assisting a client's crime or fraud by withdrawing from the representation. Sometimes it may be necessary for the lawyer to give notice of the fact of withdrawal and to disaffirm an opinion, document, affirmation or the like." ABA Model

75

Rule 4.1, Comment 3. Withdrawal paired with disaffirming prior statements or filings is an example of a noisy withdrawal.

Communications with Represented Persons

COMMUNICATIONS WITH A REPRESENTED PARTY

When representing a client, especially when approaching the litigation stage, an attorney will deal with parties who are represented by counsel. ABA Model Rule 4.2 states:

> "In representing a client, a lawyer shall not communicate about the subject of the representation with a person the lawyer knows to be represented by another lawyer in the matter, unless the lawyer has the consent of the other lawyer or is authorized to do so by law or a court order."

The purpose of this rule is to protect the contacted party from unintentionally damaging their own or some other party's case without the benefit of their counsel's presence. Otherwise, such communications could be a means to get around lawful discovery objections and privilege assertions.

DIRECT COMMUNICATIONS PROHIBITION

With respect to represented organizations, Comment 7 to ABA Model Rule 4.2 states:

> "In the case of a represented organization, this Rule prohibits communications with a constituent of the organization who supervises, directs or regularly consults with the organization's lawyer concerning the matter or has authority to obligate the organization with respect to the matter or whose act or omission in connection with the matter may be imputed to the organization for purposes of civil or criminal liability. Consent of the organization's lawyer is not required for communication with a former constituent. If a constituent of the organization is represented in the matter by his or her own counsel, the consent by that counsel to a communication will be sufficient for purposes of this Rule."

WHEN COMMUNICATION IS PERMITTED

Comment 4 to ABA Model Rule 4.2 states:

> "This Rule does not prohibit communication with a represented person, or an employee or agent of such a person, concerning matters outside the representation.... Nor does this Rule preclude communication with a represented person who is seeking advice from a lawyer who is not otherwise representing a client in the matter. A lawyer may not make a communication prohibited by this Rule through the acts of another. See Rule 8.4(a). Parties to a matter may communicate directly with each other, and a lawyer is not prohibited from advising a client concerning a communication that the client is legally entitled to make. Also, a lawyer having independent justification or legal authorization for communicating with a represented person is permitted to do so."

Note that attorneys may not circumvent Rule 4.2 by communicating through a surrogate.

Communications with Unrepresented Persons

COMMUNICATING WITH UNREPRESENTED PARTIES

The Model Rules protect parties that are unrepresented by counsel. For example, ABA Model Rule 4.3 states:

> "In dealing on behalf of a client with a person who is not represented by counsel, a lawyer shall not state or imply that the lawyer is disinterested. When the lawyer knows or reasonably should know that the unrepresented person misunderstands the lawyer's role in the matter, the lawyer shall make reasonable efforts to correct the misunderstanding. The lawyer shall not give legal advice to an unrepresented person, other than the advice to secure counsel, if the lawyer knows or reasonably should know that the interests of such a person are or have a reasonable possibility of being in conflict with the interests of the client."

Complying with Rule 4.3 may require an attorney to identify their client and perhaps even explain that the client may have adverse interests to the unrepresented person.

Respect for Rights of Third Persons

GENERAL EXPECTATIONS

Attorneys have a duty to advocate zealously and effectively on behalf of their clients. Still, attorneys must act with a certain level of decorum with respect to third parties. ABA Model Rule 4.4(a) states that an attorney representing a client "shall not use means that have no substantial purpose other than to embarrass, delay, or burden a third person, or use methods of obtaining evidence that violate the legal rights of such a person."

This Rule furthers the civility of legal proceedings and is intended to evoke greater overall efficiency in resolving legal matters by deterring unnecessary activity.

DOCUMENTS SENT BY MISTAKE

It is not uncommon for documents to be mistakenly transferred between parties. In these circumstances, ABA Model Rule 4.4(b) states: "A lawyer who receives a document relating to the representation of the lawyer's client and knows or reasonably should know that the document was inadvertently sent shall promptly notify the sender." The ethics rules are silent, and the states are split, as to whether or not the receiving attorney must return the correspondence or whether the privilege has been waived. But the notification requirement of ABA Model Rule 4.4(b) at least puts the sending attorney on notice of the error so that appropriate mitigation can commence.

Different Roles of the Lawyer

Lawyer as Advisor

ATTORNEY AS ORGANIZATION DIRECTOR

The ABA Model Rules do not forbid an attorney from acting as both the attorney and director of an organization. However, ABA Model Rule 1.7, Comment 35 warns that the attorney

> "should determine whether the responsibilities of the two roles may conflict. The lawyer may be called on to advise the corporation in matters involving actions of the directors. Consideration should be given to the frequency with which such situations may arise, the potential intensity of the conflict, the effect of the lawyer's resignation from the board and the possibility of the corporation's obtaining legal advice from another lawyer in such situations. If there is material risk that the dual role will compromise the lawyer's independence of professional judgment, the lawyer should not serve as a director or should cease to act as the corporation's lawyer when conflicts of interest arise."

GENERAL ADVISORY DUTIES

First and foremost, an attorney has a duty to advise a client based on the attorney's informed judgment. This may require the attorney to advise the client in a manner that is not welcomed by the client. Regardless of the client's hopes, the attorney's duty is render candid legal advice. ABA Model Rule 2.1, Comment 1. Additionally, an attorney may give a client advice that does not pertain to the law, but is relevant to the client's circumstances. This includes advising the client to seek the advice and/or services of other professionals. Rule 2.1, Comment 4. Finally, an attorney may deliver advice to the client prior to being asked if the attorney is aware that the client is considering acting in a manner that will have legal consequences. Rule 2.1, Comment 5.

EVALUATIONS FOR A THIRD PARTY

ABA Model Rule 2.3(a) governs when an attorney may, at a client's request, evaluate that client's situation for use by a third party:

> "A lawyer may provide an evaluation of a matter affecting a client for the use of someone other than the client if the lawyer reasonably believes that making the evaluation is compatible with other aspects of the lawyer's relationship with the client."

An example of this rule in practice is where a client directs an attorney to evaluate the client's creditworthiness for a bank considering a loan for the client.

A lawyer may evaluate a client's situation for use by third parties if the lawyer reasonably believes that making such an evaluation is compatible with other aspects of the client-lawyer relationship. ABA Model Rule 2.3(a). However, such evaluations are prohibited (absent informed consent) when a lawyer knows or should know that such an evaluation will materially harm a client. ABA Model Rule 2.3(b) states: "When the lawyer knows or reasonably should know that the evaluation is likely to affect the client's interests materially and adversely, the lawyer shall not provide the evaluation unless the client gives informed consent."

Pursuant to ABA Model Rule 2.3(c), the ordinary rules regarding confidentiality and disclosure apply to information obtained while preparing such evaluations. Of course, the client is empowered to further limit the scope of the attorney's report and/or to limit the information made available to the attorney for purposes of completing the evaluation. Comment 3 to Rule 2.3 states:

> "When the evaluation is intended for the information or use of a third person, a legal duty to that person may or may not arise. That legal question is beyond the scope of this Rule. However, since such an evaluation involves a departure from the normal client-lawyer relationship, careful analysis of the situation is required. The lawyer must be satisfied as a matter of professional judgment that making the evaluation is compatible with other functions undertaken in behalf of the client."

WIDELY DISPERSED LEGAL OPINIONS

When attorneys provide legal opinions that are expected to be widely dispersed and relied upon, unique obligations arise. Specifically, such an attorney is obligated to be complete, accurate, and honest with respect to the relevant facts and the legal opinion rendered. One common situation where this obligation arises is where the attorney is preparing securities documents to be relied upon by investors. Attorneys rendering opinions in this context are liable for both misstatements and omissions. Additionally, in tax opinions, attorneys must honestly disclose the likely tax treatment of the proposed undertaking even if such opinion is against the interests of the client.

STATEMENTS TO NON-CLIENT THIRD PERSONS

During the course of an attorney's representation of their client, they may find themselves making statements to non-client third persons. This could arise from negotiations, litigation, or another type of interaction with third parties. In this role, the attorney is expected to represent the client to the best of their ability, but owes the third person ethical duties. For example, ABA Model Rule 4.1 requires that the attorney not "make a false statement of material fact or law," nor fail to disclose a material fact if necessary to prevent a client's criminal or fraudulent act, unless disclosure is prohibited by Rule 1.6. This does not mean that the attorney has to disclose all facts harmful to the client's case or that the attorney is obliged to do the other attorney's research for them. An attorney's opinion about a law that turns out to be incorrect is not a false statement of law.

Lawyer as Arbitrator, Mediator, or Other Third-Party Neutral

ATTORNEY AS NEUTRAL

In some circumstances, attorneys must be completely neutral to all parties. ABA Model Rule 2.4(a) states:

> "A lawyer serves as a third-party neutral when the lawyer assists two or more persons who are not clients of the lawyer to reach a resolution of a dispute or other matter that has arisen between them. Service as a third-party neutral may include service as an arbitrator, a mediator or in such other capacity as will enable the lawyer to assist the parties to resolve the matter."

When an attorney is acting as a third-party neutral, it is imperative that the attorney inform all parties about the nature of the attorney's role. This is particularly true in the case of parties to the dispute that do not have legal representation. ABA Model Rule 2.4(b) states:

> "A lawyer serving as a third-party neutral shall inform unrepresented parties that the lawyer is not representing them. When the lawyer knows or reasonably should know

that a party does not understand the lawyer's role in the matter, the lawyer shall explain the difference between the lawyer's role as a third-party neutral and a lawyer's role as one who represents a client."

There is a conflict of interest if an attorney acts as a third-party neutral in a matter involving a party that the attorney represents. Despite this conflict, the attorney may still be permitted to act as the third-party neutral if all parties give their informed, written consent. ABA Model Rule 1.12(a) states:

> "A lawyer shall not represent anyone in connection with a matter in which the lawyer participated personally and substantially as a judge or other adjudicative officer or law clerk to such a person or as an arbitrator, mediator or other third-party neutral, unless all parties to the proceeding give informed consent, confirmed in writing."

This conflict also covers all other attorneys in the disqualified lawyer's firm if the disqualified lawyer is not properly and timely screened.

Lawyers Before Legislative and Administrative Bodies

An attorney may appear before legislative and administrative bodies. These appearances can take several different forms. First, the attorney could appear on their own behalf to offer suggestions or other testimony, depending on the facts and circumstances of the proceedings. If the attorney appears before a legislative or administrative body on behalf of a client, ABA Model Rule 3.9 states: "A lawyer representing a client before a legislative body or administrative agency in a nonadjudicative proceeding shall disclose that the appearance is in a representative capacity and shall conform to the provisions of Rules 3.3(a) through (c), 3.4(a) through (c), and 3.5."

The general rule is that attorneys representing clients in legislative or administrative proceedings must follow all of the rules that apply in court with respect to candor and professional courtesy. For example, ABA Model Rule 3.9, Comment 1 states:

> "In representation before bodies such as legislatures, municipal councils, and executive and administrative agencies acting in a rule-making or policy-making capacity, lawyers present facts, formulate issues and advance argument in the matters under consideration. The decision-making body, like a court, should be able to rely on the integrity of the submissions made to it. A lawyer appearing before such a body must deal with it honestly and in conformity with applicable rules of procedure."

Prosecutors and Other Government Lawyers

ROLE

The role of a prosecuting attorney differs from that of a criminal defense attorney. In general, the prosecutor has a greater responsibility to approach the case in an unbiased manner and seek justice rather than a particular desired outcome. ABA Model Rule 3.8, Comment 1 states:

> "A prosecutor has the responsibility of a minister of justice and not simply that of an advocate. This responsibility carries with it specific obligations to see that the defendant is accorded procedural justice, that guilt is decided upon the basis of sufficient evidence, and that special precautions are taken to prevent and to rectify

the conviction of innocent persons. The extent of mandated remedial action is a matter of debate and varies in different jurisdictions."

PUBLICITY AND CRIMINAL PROSECUTORS

The ABA Model Rules contemplate that the accused may be harmed by public statements made by the prosecutor, or other person assisting the investigation, that relate to the criminal proceeding. With this in mind, ABA Model Rule 3.8(f) states:

> "[E]xcept for statements that are necessary to inform the public of the nature and extent of the prosecutor's action and that serve a legitimate law enforcement purpose, refrain from making extrajudicial comments that have a substantial likelihood of heightening public condemnation of the accused and exercise reasonable care to prevent investigators, law enforcement personnel, employees or other persons assisting or associated with the prosecutor in a criminal case from making an extrajudicial statement that the prosecutor would be prohibited from making under Rule 3.6 or this Rule."

DUAL ROLES

There are several potential problems that may arise when an attorney serves as a witness in the client's judicial proceeding, but one of the main problems is potential conflicts of interest. The attorney's testimony could contradict that of the client, or the attorney could testify in a way that otherwise damages the client's case. Comment 6 to ABA Model Rule 3.7 states:

> "Determining whether or not such a conflict exists is primarily the responsibility of the lawyer involved. If there is a conflict of interest, the lawyer must secure the client's informed consent, confirmed in writing. In some cases, the lawyer will be precluded from seeking the client's consent."

A dual role, both as witness and advocate, taken on by an attorney may confuse the trier of fact, who could be unsure of which role the attorney is playing when making a given statement. Comment 2 to ABA Model Rule 3.7 states:

> "The tribunal has proper objection when the trier of fact may be confused or misled by a lawyer serving as both advocate and witness. The opposing party has proper objection where the combination of roles may prejudice that party's rights in the litigation. A witness is required to testify on the basis of personal knowledge, while an advocate is expected to explain and comment on evidence given by others. It may not be clear whether a statement by an advocate-witness should be taken as proof or as an analysis of the proof."

Because of the inherent problems with an attorney acting as both witness and advocate, ABA Model Rule 3.7(a) states that "[a] lawyer shall not act as advocate at a trial in which the lawyer is likely to be a necessary witness" unless one of the following exceptions applies:

(1) the testimony relates to an uncontested issue;
(2) the testimony relates to the nature and value of legal services rendered in the case; or
(3) disqualification of the lawyer would work substantial hardship on the client.

PROBABLE CAUSE AND THE ACCUSED'S RIGHT TO COUNSEL

Prosecutors are expected to support the filtering process of determining who should be prosecuted and who should not. This requires prosecutors to examine the evidence and determine whether or not the accused should be prosecuted. ABA Model Rule 3.8(a) states that a prosecutor shall "refrain from prosecuting a charge that the prosecutor knows is not supported by probable cause." Prosecutors shall also "make reasonable efforts to assure that the accused has been advised of the right to and the procedure for obtaining, counsel and has been given reasonable opportunity to obtain counsel." ABA Model Rule 3.8(b)

Prosecutors are expected to provide greater assistance to the accused than other attorneys owe to the opposing side. This is all done in the interest of seeking justice for the accused. Therefore, a prosecutor shall "not seek to obtain from an unrepresented accused a waiver of important pretrial rights, such as the right to a preliminary hearing." ABA Model Rule 3.8(c). Furthermore, with respect to evidence, ABA Model Rule 3.8(d) states that a prosecutor shall

> "make timely disclosure to the defense of all evidence or information known to the prosecutor that tends to negate the guilt of the accused or mitigates the offense, and, in connection with sentencing, disclose to the defense and to the tribunal all unprivileged mitigating information known to the prosecutor, except when the prosecutor is relieved of this responsibility by a protective order of the tribunal."

SUBPOENAING ATTORNEY(S)

The Model Rules generally frown on subpoenaing a criminal defense attorney as a means of obtaining evidence. One reason for this is that it is in the public's interest that criminal defendants feel protected when dealing with counsel; there is also the desire for integrity of the attorney-client privilege. Before a prosecutor can subpoena another lawyer to present evidence about a past or present client, ABA Rule 3.8(e) requires that the prosecutor reasonably believe the following:

(1) the information sought is not protected from disclosure by any applicable privilege;
(2) the evidence sought is essential to the successful completion of an ongoing investigation or prosecution; and
(3) there is no other feasible alternative to obtain the information.

HIGH STANDARDS

The highest ethical duties are placed on criminal prosecutors. The reasoning behind this is that prosecutors participate in criminal proceedings where individuals are facing the power of the government and can lose their freedom and be jailed. The U.S. generally takes the approach that it is better for a guilty party to go free than an innocent party to be wrongly incarcerated in a criminal proceeding. The fact that many government attorneys work in non-criminal areas of the law does not preclude them from aspects of a heightened ethical standard. For example, government attorneys are expected not to pursue actions against parties that are obviously unfair. Additionally, government attorneys have a responsibility to develop complete records in litigation matters and not abuse the status of the government to compel unjust settlements or other resolutions to cases.

Safekeeping Funds and Other Property

Safekeeping Funds and Other Property of Clients

ABA Model Rule 1.15(a) states:

> "A lawyer shall hold property of clients or third persons that is in a lawyer's possession in connection with a representation separate from the lawyer's own property. Funds shall be kept in a separate account maintained in the state where the lawyer's office is situated, or elsewhere with the consent of the client or third person. Other property shall be identified as such and appropriately safeguarded. Complete records of such account funds and other property shall be kept by the lawyer and shall be preserved for a period of [five years] after termination of the representation."

In many instances, it may be appropriate for an attorney to maintain a single account for the funds of multiple clients. However, one client's funds may not be used for the representation of another client.

SAFEKEEPING FUNDS

REQUIREMENTS FOR ADVANCE FUNDING

An attorney who is advanced funds from a client in order to pay anticipated costs, expenses, and/or attorney's fees must place these funds into the lawyer's client trust fund account. ABA Model Rule 1.15(c) states: "A lawyer shall deposit into a client trust account legal fees and expenses that have been paid in advance, to be withdrawn by the lawyer only as fees are earned or expenses incurred." The attorney's ability to rightfully withdraw such funds is only justified if the withdrawals are not disputed by the client. A careful accounting of funds is mandatory, and detailed billing practices are highly advisable.

SHARED INTEREST IN FUNDS

Situations may arise where an attorney possesses funds in which both the attorney and a client share an interest. For example, this may occur if an attorney has negotiated a settlement on behalf of a client (having agreed that the attorney fees would be deducted before the client received the remainder) and the opposing side has disbursed the funds to the attorney. The attorney must divide the funds according to the fee agreement. In the case of a dispute over the money, ABA Model Rule 1.15(e) states:

> "When in the course of representation a lawyer is in possession of property in which two or more persons (one of whom may be the lawyer) claim interests, the property shall be kept separate by the lawyer until the dispute is resolved. The lawyer shall promptly distribute all portions of the property as to which the interests are not in dispute."

FUNDS INVOLVING A THIRD PARTY

Problems may arise where an attorney holds funds in which both a client and a third party claim an interest. An attorney who knew of a third person's potential lawful claim to funds yet disbursed

83

such funds to a client could be in violation of applicable law. As Comment 4 to ABA Model Rule 1.15 states:

> "A lawyer may have a duty under applicable law to protect such third-party claims against wrongful interference by the client. In such cases, when the third-party claim is not frivolous under applicable law, the lawyer must refuse to surrender the property to the client until the claims are resolved. A lawyer should not unilaterally assume to arbitrate a dispute between the client and the third party, but, when there are substantial grounds for dispute as to the person entitled to the funds, the lawyer may file an action to have a court resolve the dispute."

SAFEKEEPING NON-MONETARY PROPERTY

An attorney who comes into possession of money belonging to a client and/or a third party must take great care to isolate those funds from the attorney's own funds. Additionally, the attorney should keep the money in an account where it will earn reasonable interest and be free from risk of loss. Similar principles apply when the attorney is entrusted with non-cash property. ABA Model Rule 1.15(a) requires that the attorney segregate the property, identify it as belonging to the client, and protect it from damage or loss. Small items can be placed in safe deposit boxes, while larger items must be placed in appropriate places where they will be best preserved and protected.

ACTING AS CUSTODIAN

Attorneys must keep safe the money and property of clients. ABA Model Rule 1.15(a) and (d) list several requirements with which attorneys must comply while safeguarding client's money/property:

- Whenever money/property is placed with an attorney on behalf of the client, the attorney must notify the client promptly;
- While the attorney is safeguarding the client's property, the attorney must keep complete, accurate, and up-to-date records of all of the money/property kept by the attorney. These records must be kept by the attorney for 5 years after the representation has ended;
- The attorney must also render appropriate accountings of all of the money/property held; and
- The attorney must pay over money or deliver property promptly to the client at the appropriate time.

Establishing and Maintaining Client Trust Accounts

ENTRUSTED FUNDS IN A SEPARATE ACCOUNT

When an attorney is entrusted with safeguarding funds, it is imperative that the attorney avoids commingling those funds with their own funds. However, ABA Model Rule 1.15(b) states that "[a] lawyer may deposit the lawyer's own funds in a client trust account for the sole purpose of paying bank service charges on that account, but only in an amount necessary for that purpose." Additionally, Rule 1.15, Comment 1, dictates that "[s]eparate trust accounts may be warranted when administering estate monies or acting in similar fiduciary capacities." Attorneys in the position of safeguarding large sums of money for extended periods of time should seek safe, interest-bearing accounts to hold the money so that the client does not miss out on the interest potential of the money.

IOLTA ACCOUNTS

When an attorney is entrusted with client funds, it is the attorney's duty to set these funds aside from the attorney's own funds. The type and configuration of the account is determined by the amount of money and/or the length of time the attorney anticipates holding the funds. For large amounts of money expected to be held for a long period of time, the attorney must place the funds in an account that will bear interest. For amounts of money for which the fees charged by a bank would surpass any interest earned, the attorney should place these funds into a pooled client account. Many attorneys put these pooled accounts into Interest On Lawyer Trust Account (IOLTA) programs. These pooled accounts contain enough money to earn interest that exceeds the fees charged by the bank. Once any bank fees have been paid, the excess interest is forwarded to the state bar association or a designated legal fund for the public good.

Communication About Legal Services

Advertising and Other Public Communications About Legal Services

"ADVERTISING" AND "SOLICITATION"

In the legal context, understanding and distinguishing between the concepts of "advertising" and "solicitation" are important because different ethical rules apply to each method. In general, both advertising and solicitation are means by which attorneys procure clients. The main difference is that advertising is a method by which an attorney or law firm seeks to appeal to a large segment of society or to society as a whole. This is often accomplished through television and print advertisements. On the other hand, solicitation refers to the more direct approach of an attorney seeking an audience with a specific individual or group for the purposes of obtaining business from that individual or group.

ATTORNEY ADVERTISING

Attorney advertising has been determined to be commercial speech, protected by the 1st Amendment to the U.S. Constitution (as well as state constitutions). As such, any governmental regulation of attorney advertising is subject to intermediate scrutiny. Under *Central Hudson*, commercial speech that neither concerns unlawful activity nor is misleading may be regulated if:

- the government asserts a substantial interest in support of the regulation;
- the restriction on commercial speech directly and materially advances that interest; and
- the regulation is narrowly drawn.

ACCURACY OF COMMUNICATIONS

The constitutional protections applied to prevent certain types of government regulations on attorney advertising do *not* protect the attorney from the repercussions of making false statements. Therefore, an attorney is subject to discipline for making false statements. Specifically, under ABA Model Rule 7.1:

> "A lawyer shall not make a false or misleading communication about the lawyer or the lawyer's services. A communication is false or misleading if it contains a material misrepresentation of fact or law, or omits a fact necessary to make the statement considered as a whole not materially misleading."

This rule applies to all communications and not just advertisements.

MISLEADING STATEMENTS

Some truthful statements may also be misleading, according to Comment 2 to Rule 7.1:

> "Truthful statements that are misleading are also prohibited by this Rule. A truthful statement is misleading if it omits a fact necessary to make the lawyer's communication considered as a whole not materially misleading. A truthful statement is also misleading if there is a substantial likelihood that it will lead a reasonable person to formulate a specific conclusion about the lawyer or the lawyer's services for which there is no reasonable factual foundation."

MISLEADING ADVERTISEMENT

ABA Model Rule 7.1, Comment 3 states:

> "An advertisement that truthfully reports a lawyer's achievements on behalf of clients or former clients may be misleading if presented so as to lead a reasonable person to form an unjustified expectation that the same results could be obtained for other clients in similar matters without reference to the specific factual and legal circumstances of each client's case. Similarly, an unsubstantiated comparison of the lawyer's services or fees with the services or fees of other lawyers may be misleading if presented with such specificity as would lead a reasonable person to conclude that the comparison can be substantiated. The inclusion of an appropriate disclaimer or qualifying language may preclude a finding that a statement is likely to create unjustified expectations or otherwise mislead a prospective client."

Recall that advertisements that are false, rather than misleading, are also prohibited by Rule 7.1.

FORMS OF MEDIA RESTRICTIONS

Generally, an attorney has few limitations on advertising. The attorney is subject to the general rules against false and misleading statements contained in ABA Model Rule 7.1. As far as the types of media employed by the attorney for their advertising campaign, there are no limitations. ABA Model Rule 7.2(a) allows a lawyer to "advertise services through written, recorded or electronic communication, including public media," subject to Rule 7.1 (prohibiting false or misleading communications) and Rule 7.3 (governing direct contact with prospective clients).

NON-MISLEADING ADVERTISEMENTS

For advertising information about fields of practice and specialization, ABA Model Rule 7.4 imposes the following limitations:

(a)   A lawyer may communicate the fact that the lawyer does or does not practice in particular fields of law.

(b)   A lawyer admitted to engage in patent practice before the United States Patent and Trademark Office may use the designation "Patent Attorney" or a substantially similar designation.

(c)   A lawyer engaged in Admiralty practice may use the designation "Admiralty," "Proctor in Admiralty" or a substantially similar designation.

(d)   A lawyer shall not state or imply that a lawyer is certified as a specialist in a particular field of law, unless:
(1)   the lawyer has been certified as a specialist by an organization that has been approved by an appropriate state authority or that has been accredited by the American Bar Association; and
(2)   the name of the certifying organization is clearly identified in the communication.

NAMING PAST CLIENTS SERVED

Attorneys may employ persuasive methods in advertisements to attract clients. An attorney may, for example, deem it effective to use the names of past or regular clients to demonstrate their effectiveness in providing legal counsel. Listing recurring clients is not barred by the Rules of Professional Conduct. However, ABA Model Rule 7.2, Comment 2 requires the consent of regularly-represented clients to use that fact in advertisements.

REQUIRED CONTENT IN ADVERTISEMENTS

Attorney advertisements must contain certain information. For example, ABA Model Rule 7.2(c) requires that attorney advertisements include the name and office address of at least one lawyer or law firm responsible for its content. This requirement helps to assure that those subject to the advertisement: 1) clearly understand that an attorney or law firm is responsible for the advertisement; and 2) have a method for reaching that attorney or law firm.

PAYING FOR RECOMMENDATIONS

Under ABA Model Rule 7.2(b), "[a] lawyer shall not give anything of value to a person for recommending the lawyer's services . . . ." This Rule nevertheless permits a lawyer to do the following:

(1) pay the reasonable costs of advertisements or communications permitted by this Rule;

(2) pay the usual charges of a legal service plan or a not-for-profit or qualified lawyer referral service. A qualified lawyer referral service is a lawyer referral service that has been approved by an appropriate regulatory authority;

(3) pay for a law practice in accordance with Rule 1.17; and

(4) refer clients to another lawyer or a non-lawyer professional pursuant to an agreement not otherwise prohibited under these Rules that provides for the other person to refer clients or customers to the lawyer, if

(i) the reciprocal referral agreement is not exclusive, and

(ii) the client is informed of the existence and nature of the agreement.

RECIPROCAL REFERRAL ARRANGEMENTS

Regarding reciprocal referral agreements, ABA Model Rule 7.2, Comment 8 states:

"A lawyer also may agree to refer clients to another lawyer or a non-lawyer professional, in return for the undertaking of that person to refer clients or customers to the lawyer. Such reciprocal referral arrangements must not interfere with the lawyer's professional judgment as to making referrals or as to providing substantive legal services. Except as provided in Rule 1.5(e), a lawyer who receives referrals from a lawyer or non-lawyer professional must not pay anything solely for the referral, but the lawyer does not violate . . . this Rule by agreeing to refer clients to the other lawyer or non-lawyer [if] the reciprocal referral agreement is not exclusive and the client is informed of the referral agreement. Reciprocal referral agreements should not be of indefinite duration and should be reviewed periodically to determine whether they comply with these Rules. This Rule does not restrict referrals or divisions of revenues or net income among lawyers within firms comprised of multiple entities."

Solicitation – Direct Contact with Prospective Clients

SOLICITATION OF NEW CLIENTS

Generally, the Rules of Professional Conduct frown upon soliciting new clients. There are exceptions to this rule, but the basic premise is that it is a better public policy to let potential clients seek out attorneys. For instance, a person who has recently suffered a personal or economic loss could be improperly influenced if contacted by an attorney. With this in mind, ABA Model Rule

7.3(a) only permits the financially-motivated solicitation of professional employment "by in-person, live telephone or real-time electronic contact" when the contacted person:

(1) is a lawyer; or

(2) has a family, close personal, or prior professional relationship with the lawyer.

Even if communication with a client is not prohibited by ABA Model Rule 7.3(a), Rule 7.3(b) lists two circumstances under which an attorney may not "solicit professional employment by written, recorded or electronic communication or by in-person, telephone or real-time electronic contact":

(1) the prospective client has made known to the lawyer a desire not to be solicited by the lawyer; or

(2) The solicitation involves coercion, duress or harassment.

USING AN AGENT

ABA Model Rule 7.3(a), which addresses solicitation of prospective clients, does not specifically forbid an attorney from using an agent to solicit clients. However, there is a catch-all provision in ABA Model Rule 8.4(a) that states that it is professional misconduct for an attorney to "violate or attempt to violate the Rules of Professional Conduct, knowingly assist or induce another to do so, or do so through the acts of another." This makes the attorney susceptible to discipline for using an agent to violate Rule 7.3(a), or any other Rule to which the attorney is subject.

ROLE OF FEES

Model Rule 7.3(a) prohibits an attorney from using in-person, live telephone or real-time electronic contact to solicit professional employment from a prospective client if pecuniary gain is a significant motive for such solicitation. However, real-time solicitation is permissible if the prospective client is another lawyer or has a family, personal, or prior professional relationship with the attorney.

LABELING REQUIREMENTS

The Rules of Professional Conduct seek to protect the public from misleading advertisements. For example ABA Model Rule 7.3(c) requires:

"Every written, recorded or electronic communication from a lawyer soliciting professional employment from a prospective client known to be in need of legal services in a particular matter shall include the words 'Advertising Material' on the outside envelope, if any, and at the beginning and ending of any recorded or electronic communication, unless the recipient of the communication is a person specified in paragraphs (a)(1) or (a)(2)."

These requirements do not apply to communications from the attorney to close friends, relatives, clients, former clients, and other lawyers. ABA Model Rule 7.3, Comment 4.

CLAIMS OF SPECIALIZATION

Problems can arise when attorneys mislead potential clients with claims as to their status as certified specialists in a particular area.

Under ABA Model Rule 7.4(d), a lawyer can state or imply that they are certified as a specialist in a particular field of law if the following factors are met:

(1) the lawyer has been certified as a specialist by an organization that has been approved by an appropriate state authority or that has been accredited by the American Bar Association; and

(2) the name of the certifying organization is clearly identified in the communication.

This Rule applies to "communications," which include everything from advertisements to informal conversations.

SELECTING A LAW FIRM'S NAME

Comment 1 to ABA Model Rule 7.5 states:

> "A firm may be designated by the names of all or some of its members, by the names of deceased members where there has been a continuing succession in the firm's identity or by a trade name such as the "ABC Legal Clinic." A lawyer or law firm may also be designated by a distinctive website address or comparable professional designation. Although the United States Supreme Court has held that legislation may prohibit the use of trade names in professional practice, use of such names in law practice is acceptable so long as it is not misleading. . . . The use of such names to designate law firms has proven a useful means of identification. However, it is misleading to use the name of a lawyer not associated with the firm or a predecessor of the firm, or the name of a non-lawyer."

ENTERING PUBLIC SERVICE

Under the Rules of Professional Conduct, the name of a law firm cannot be misleading. This, in part, requires that the names of any members of the law firm included in the name be the actual names of practicing attorneys. For a named partner/member entering public service, ABA Model Rule 7.5(c) states: "The name of a lawyer holding a public office shall not be used in the name of a law firm, or in communications on its behalf, during any substantial period in which the lawyer is not actively and regularly practicing with the firm."

Group Legal Services

PREPAID LEGAL SERVICE PLANS

Group and prepaid legal service plans have gained popularity. The idea behind such plans is to provide clients with access to legal representation at affordable costs. ABA Model Rule 7.3(d) states:

> "Notwithstanding the prohibitions in paragraph (a), a lawyer may participate with a prepaid or group legal service plan operated by an organization not owned or directed by the lawyer that uses in-person or telephone contact to solicit memberships or subscriptions for the plan from persons who are not known to need legal services in a particular matter covered by the plan."

Solicitation in this fashion is unlikely to result in improper attorney influence over a client facing a stressful legal issue.

Lawyers' Duties to the Public and the Legal System

Voluntary Pro Bono Service

PRO BONO WORK APPROACH

The Rules of Professional Conduct make recommendations as to the amount of pro bono work that an attorney should complete in a year. The rules do *not* mandate these recommendations nor make attorneys subject to discipline if the guidelines are not met. ABA Model Rule 6.1 encourages lawyers "to render at least (50) hours of pro bono publico legal services per year." Non-cumulative examples of such service involves work with:

(1)   persons of limited means; or
(2)   charitable, religious, civic, community, governmental and educational organizations in matters that are designed primarily to address the needs of persons of limited means.

CONFLICTS WITH PAYING CLIENTS

With two exceptions, the ABA Model Rules allow a lawyer to "serve as a director, officer or member of a legal services organization, apart from the law firm in which the lawyer practices, notwithstanding that the organization serves persons having interests adverse to a client of the lawyer." The exceptions that prohibit such service are:

(a)   if participating in the decision or action would be incompatible with the lawyer's obligations to a client under Rule 1.7; or
(b)   where the decision or action could have a material adverse effect on the representation of a client of the organization whose interests are adverse to a client of the lawyer.

LIMITED LEGAL SERVICES PROGRAM

Pursuant to Comment 1 of ABA Model Rule 6.5, a limited legal services program is any program where an attorney offers services such as advice or the completion of legal forms that will assist persons to address their legal problems without further representation by a lawyer. In these programs, such as legal-advice hotlines, advice-only clinics, or pro se counseling programs, a client-lawyer relationship is established, but there is no expectation that the lawyer's representation of the client will continue beyond the limited consultation. Such programs are normally operated under circumstances in which it is not feasible for a lawyer to systematically screen for conflicts of interest as is generally required before undertaking a representation.

RELAXED CONFLICT OF INTEREST RULES

Because of the desire to promote pro bono service and the increased difficulty in checking for conflicts in pro bono cases, the rules pertaining to conflicts of interests are generally relaxed for pro bono work. ABA Model Rule 6.5, Comment 3 states:

> "Because a lawyer who is representing a client in the circumstances addressed by this Rule ordinarily is not able to check systematically for conflicts of interest, paragraph (a) requires compliance with Rules 1.7 or 1.9(a) only if the lawyer knows that the

91

representation presents a conflict of interest for the lawyer, and with Rule 1.10 only if the lawyer knows that another lawyer in the lawyer's firm is disqualified by Rules 1.7 or 1.9(a) in the matter."

ORGANIZATIONS SEEKING TO CHANGE THE LAW

It is common for attorneys to participate with organizations that actively seek changes in state and/or federal law. These changes may lead to ethical questions, depending on whether the attorney has clients that will be harmed or helped by the change. ABA Model Rule 6.4 states that:

> "A lawyer may serve as a director, officer or member of an organization involved in reform of the law or its administration notwithstanding that the reform may affect the interests of a client of the lawyer. When the lawyer knows that the interests of a client may be materially benefited by a decision in which the lawyer participates, the lawyer shall disclose that fact but need not identify the client."

Political Contributions to Obtain Engagements or Appointments

PROHIBITED POLITICAL CONTRIBUTIONS

While attorneys and law firms are permitted and encouraged to participate in the political process, making certain types of political contributions is prohibited. Specifically, ABA Model Rule 7.6 states:

> "A lawyer or law firm shall not accept a government legal engagement or an appointment by a judge if the lawyer or law firm makes a political contribution or solicits political contributions for the purpose of obtaining or being considered for that type of legal engagement or appointment."

The rationale is stated in Comment 3 to Rule 7.6:

> "When lawyers make or solicit political contributions in order to obtain an engagement for legal work awarded by a government agency or to obtain appointment by a judge, the public may legitimately question whether the lawyers engaged to perform the work are selected on the basis of competence and merit."

POLITICAL EMPLOYMENT

Some types of political employment are less prone to potential abuses and are thus not subject to the purview of ABA Model Rule 7.6. Comment 3 to Rule 7.6 lists the following services that are not "government legal engagement":

> "(a) substantially uncompensated services; (b) engagements or appointments made on the basis of experience, expertise, professional qualifications and cost following a request for proposal or other process that is free from influence based upon political contributions; and (c) engagements or appointments made on a rotational basis from a list compiled without regard to political contributions."

The common denominator is money; Rule 7.6 ultimately seeks to avoid attorneys "purchasing" lucrative employment through political contributions.

Judicial Ethics

Maintaining the Independence and Impartiality of the Judiciary

ABA CODE OF JUDICIAL CONDUCT

The ABA Code of Judicial Conduct is a working document that sets out the model rules of ethics for the judiciary. It applies to "all full-time judges." A judge is defined as "anyone who is authorized to perform judicial functions, including an officer such as a justice of the peace, magistrate, court commissioner, special master, referee, or member of the administrative law judiciary."

BEHAVIOR EXPECTATIONS

"A judge shall act at all times in a manner that promotes public confidence in the independence, integrity, and impartiality of the judiciary, and shall avoid impropriety and the appearance of impropriety." ABA Code of Judicial Conduct Rule 1.2. This applies to a judge's "professional and personal conduct," pursuant to Comment 1 of Rule 1.2.

LIMITATIONS ON RELATIONSHIPS

Rule 2.4(B) of the ABA Code of Judicial Conduct states: "A judge shall not permit family, social, political, financial, or other interests or relationships to influence the judge's judicial conduct or judgment."

This rule is intended to avoid even the appearance of impropriety. It is imperative that judges manage their various relationships in such a way that does not undermine the integrity of the judicial system. If a judge where viewed as ruling favorably for someone with whom the judge had a prior business or social relationship, the honesty and integrity of the court would be questioned.

UNDERSTANDING OF PRESTIGE

Judges occupy a position of great respect and power. This power is not to be used as a source of improper influence. Rule 1.3 of the ABA Code of Judicial Conduct states: "A judge shall not abuse the prestige of judicial office to advance the personal or economic interests of the judge or others, or allow others to do so."

PERMISSIBLE USES OF PRESTIGE

A judge may employ the prestige of the office in writing a letter of recommendation. Comment 2 to Rule 1.3 states:

> "A judge may provide a reference or recommendation for an individual based upon the judge's personal knowledge. The judge may use official letterhead if the judge indicates that the reference is personal and if there is no likelihood that the use of the letterhead would reasonably be perceived as an attempt to exert pressure by reason of the judicial office."

DISCRIMINATION LIMITATIONS

Rule 3.6(A) of the ABA Code of Judicial Conduct states that "[a] judge shall not hold membership in any organization that practices invidious discrimination on the basis of race, sex, gender, religion, national origin, ethnicity, or sexual orientation." According to Comment 1 to this rule, the concern is that such association "creates the perception that the judge's impartiality is impaired."

93

Further, under Rule 3.6(B), "[a] judge shall not use the benefits or facilities of an organization if the judge knows or should know that the organization practices invidious discrimination on one or more of the bases identified in [Rule 3.6(A)]."

PROHIBITED ORGANIZATIONS

In addition to the various specific prohibitions condemning judicial discrimination or the association with organizations who practice invidious discrimination, Comment 1 to Rule 3.6 of the ABA Code of Judicial Conduct states:

> "A judge's public manifestation of approval of invidious discrimination on any basis gives rise to the appearance of impropriety and diminishes public confidence in the integrity and impartiality of the judiciary. A judge's membership in an organization that practices invidious discrimination creates the perception that the judge's impartiality is impaired."

"When a judge learns that an organization to which the judge belongs engages in invidious discrimination, the judge must resign immediately from the organization." ABA Code of Judicial Conduct Rule 3.6, Comment 3.

FINANCIAL PRIVACY

Like other citizens, judges should be afforded a certain level of privacy as to their financial affairs. However, these rights also must be tempered by the overriding public interest of ensuring an objective and uncompromised judiciary. Comment 1 of Rule 3.11 of the ABA Model Code of Judicial Conduct states:

> "Judges are generally permitted to engage in financial activities, including managing real estate and other investments for themselves or for members of their families. Participation in these activities, like participation in other extrajudicial activities, is subject to the requirements of this Code. For example, . . . it would be improper for a judge to use his or her official title or appear in judicial robes in business advertising, or to conduct his or her business or financial affairs in such a way that disqualification is frequently required."

"JUDICIAL CANDIDATE" DEFINED

The ABA Model Judicial Code defines "[j]udicial candidate" as "any person, including a sitting judge, who is seeking selection for or retention in judicial office by election or appointment." The Terminology section of the Code further states:

> "A person becomes a candidate for judicial office as soon as he or she makes a public announcement of candidacy, declares or files as a candidate with the election or appointment authority, authorizes or, where permitted, engages in solicitation or acceptance of contributions or support, or is nominated for election or appointment to office."

Several rules regulating judicial conduct distinguish between a judge and a judicial candidate.

LIMITATIONS ON POLITICAL INVOLVEMENT FOR JUDGES AND JUDICIAL CANDIDATES

"A judge or candidate for judicial office shall not engage in political or campaign activity that is inconsistent with the independence, integrity, or impartiality of the judiciary." ABA Model Judicial Code, Canon 4. The rationale behind this policy is that "[p]ublic confidence in the independence and impartiality of the judiciary is eroded if judges or judicial candidates are perceived to be subject to political influence." *Id*. at Rule 4.1, Comment 3.

This prohibition does not prevent judges or judicial candidates from "register[ing] to vote as members of a political party." *Id*.

PROHIBITED CONDUCT

Pursuant to Rule 4.1(A) of the ABA Model Judicial Code, neither a judge nor a judicial candidate may:

- act as a leader in, or hold an office in, a political organization;
- make speeches on behalf of a political organization;
- seek, accept, or use endorsements from a political organization;
- personally solicit or accept campaign contributions other than through a campaign committee authorized by Rule 4.4;
- use or permit the use of campaign contributions for the private benefit of the judge, the candidate, or others;
- use court staff, facilities, or other court resources in a campaign for judicial office;
- knowingly, or with reckless disregard for the truth, make any false or misleading statement;
- make any statement that would reasonably be expected to affect the outcome or impair the fairness of a matter pending or impending in any court; or
- in connection with cases, controversies, or issues that are likely to come before the court, make pledges, promises, or commitments that are inconsistent with the impartial performance of the adjudicative duties of judicial office.

REQUIRED CONDUCT FOR JUDICIAL CANDIDATES

A candidate for judicial office shall:

(1) act at all times in a manner consistent with the independence, integrity, and impartiality of the judiciary;

(2) comply with all applicable election, election campaign, and election campaign fund-raising laws and regulations of [the] jurisdiction;

(3) review and approve the content of all campaign statements and materials produced by the candidate or his or her campaign committee, as authorized by Rule 4.4, before their dissemination; and

(4) take reasonable measures to ensure that other persons do not undertake on behalf of the candidate activities, other than those described in Rule 4.4, that the candidate is prohibited from doing by Rule 4.1.

ABA Model Code of Judicial Conduct Rule 4.2(A).

CONDUCT THAT IS TEMPORALLY PERMISSIBLE FOR JUDICIAL CANDIDATES BUT NOT JUDGES

There are several forms of conduct that are generally prohibited for judges and judicial candidates, see Rule 4.1(A)(3)–(7), but are permissible for judicial candidates "not earlier than [a jurisdictionally-set time period] before the first applicable primary election, caucus, or general or retention election." Rule 4.2(B)–(C).

Under Rule 4.2(C), for a **partisan judicial election**, a judicial candidate may, outside of the jurisdictionally-set time period, perform the following:

(1) identify himself or herself as a candidate of a political organization; and

(2)   seek, accept, and use endorsements of a political organization.

Pursuant to Rule 4.2(B), for a **non-partisan judicial election**, a judicial candidate may, outside of the jurisdictionally-set time period, perform the following:

- publicly endorse or oppose candidates for the same judicial office for which he or she is running;
- attend or purchase tickets for dinners or other events sponsored by a political organization or a candidate for public office;
- seek, accept, or use endorsements from any person or organization other than a partisan political organization; and
- contribute to a political organization or candidate for public office, but not more than [a jurisdictionally-set amount] to any one organization or candidate.

Also under Rule 4.2(B), in a **non-partisan judicial election**, a judicial candidate may, outside of the jurisdictionally-set time period, "establish a campaign committee" and "speak on behalf of his or her candidacy through any medium, including but not limited to advertisements, websites, or other campaign literature."

CANDIDATES FOR APPOINTIVE JUDICIAL OFFICES

Under Rule 4.3 of the ABA Model Judicial Code, a judge who is a candidate for an **appointive** judicial office may:

(A)   communicate with the appointing or confirming authority, including any selection, screening, or nominating commission or similar agency; and

(B)   seek endorsements for the appointment from any person or organization other than a partisan political organization.

JUDGES WHO BECOME CANDIDATES FOR NONJUDICIAL OFFICES

Rule 4.5 of the ABA Model Judicial Code requires the following of judges who become candidates for nonjudicial office:

(A)   Upon becoming a candidate for a nonjudicial elective office, a judge shall resign from judicial office, unless permitted by law to continue to hold judicial office.

(B)   Upon becoming a candidate for a nonjudicial appointive office, a judge is not required to resign from judicial office, provided that the judge complies with the other provisions of this Code.

JUDICIAL CAMPAIGN COMMITTEE

A judicial candidate may set up a committee to run an election campaign. The judicial candidate "is responsible for ensuring that his or her campaign committee complies with applicable provisions of this Code and other applicable law." ABA Model Judicial Code, Rule 4.4(A). The main provisions regarding campaign committees are in Rule 4.4(B) and require that the committee:

- Receive only reasonable amounts that do not in the aggregate exceed statutorily set amounts;
- Not receive contributions outside of the statutorily set timeframe; and
- "[C]omply with all applicable statutory requirements for disclosure and divestiture of campaign contributions . . . ."

96

Performing the Duties of Judicial Office Impartially, Competently, and Diligently

PRECEDENCE TO JUDICIAL DUTIES

"The duties of judicial office, as prescribed by law, shall take precedence over all of a judge's personal and extrajudicial activities." ABA Model Judicial Code, Rule 2.1. The Model Rules encourage, but do not require, that judges "participate in activities that promote public understanding of and confidence in the justice system." *Id.*, Comment 2.

PUBLIC AND NONPUBLIC COMMENTS ON CASES

The ABA Model Judicial Code prohibits certain public and nonpublic statements by judges. Rule 2.10(A) states: "A judge shall not make any public statement that might reasonably be expected to affect the outcome or impair the fairness of a matter pending or impending in any court, or make any nonpublic statement that might substantially interfere with a fair trial or hearing."

A judge can make public statements about cases "in the course of official duties" and "comment on any proceeding in which the judge is a litigant in a personal capacity." Rule 2.10(D).

ADMINISTRATIVE DUTIES

In performing administrative duties, judges must do the following:

- Perform their duties "without bias or prejudice." Rule 2.3(A).
- Perform their duties with diligence and competence. Rules 2.5(A).
- "[C]ooperate with other judges and court officials in the administration of court business." Rule 2.5(B).
- Make administrative appointments "impartially and on the basis of merit" and "avoid nepotism, favoritism, and unnecessary appointments." Rule 2.13(A).

Generally, a judge may not appoint a lawyer to a position if the lawyer, the lawyer's spouse, or the lawyer's domestic partner donated more than a statutory amount to the judge's election campaign within a statutory time period. ABA Model Judicial Code, Rule 2.13(B). This prohibition does not apply where:

(1) the position is substantially uncompensated;
(2) the lawyer has been selected in rotation from a list of qualified and available lawyers compiled without regard to their having made political contributions; or
(3) the judge or another presiding or administrative judge affirmatively finds that no other lawyer is willing, competent, and able to accept the position.

DISCIPLINARY RESPONSIBILITIES

"Taking action to address known misconduct is a judge's obligation." ABA Model Judicial Code, Rule 2.15, Comment 1.

A judge must **"inform the appropriate authority"** when the judge has **knowledge** that another judge or lawyer has committed an ethical violation "that raises a **substantial question** regarding [that individual's] honesty, trustworthiness, or fitness." ABA Model Judicial Code, Rules 2.15(A)–(B).

A judge must **"take appropriate action"** in the following circumstances:

- The judge has "a **reasonable belief** that the performance of a lawyer or another judge is **impaired** by drugs or alcohol, or by a mental, emotional, or physical condition." Rule 2.14.
- The judge "**receives information** indicating a **substantial likelihood** that another [judge or lawyer] has committed" an ethical violation. Rules 2.15(C)–(D).

"'Appropriate action' means action intended and reasonably likely to help the judge or lawyer in question address the problem and prevent harm to the justice system." Rule 2.14, Comment 1.

Ex Parte Communications

Generally, "[a] judge shall not initiate, permit, or consider ex parte communications . . . concerning a pending or impending matter . . . ." ABA Model Judicial Code, Rule 2.9. There are five exceptions:

1. Ex parte communications for administrative or emergency purposes are allowed, provide that the judge: 1) reasonably believes will not give one side an advantage; 2) promptly notifies other parties of the substance of the communication; and 3) gives the other parties a chance to respond;
2. Written advice of a disinterested expert, if the judge gives parties notice and a chance to respond;
3. Consultations with court staff and officials;
4. For purposes of settlement; and
5. When authorized by law.

Disqualification

Rule 2.11 of the ABA Model Judicial Code requires that a judge "disqualify himself or herself in any proceeding in which the judge's impartiality might reasonably be questioned." The Code lists the following circumstances as examples warranting disqualification:

6. The judge has a bias concerning the parties or lawyers;
7. The judge has personal knowledge of facts in dispute;
8. The judge or a close relation is substantively involved in the case (even as a witness) or has an economic interest in the outcome;
9. A party, attorney, or firm in the case has donated more than a statutory set amount to the judge's election campaign; and
10. The judge has made a public statement committed to a particular result.

RULE OF NECESSITY

"The rule of necessity may override the rule of disqualification. For example, a judge might be required to participate in judicial review of a judicial salary statute, or might be the only judge available in a matter requiring immediate judicial action, such as a hearing on probable cause or a temporary restraining order. In matters that require immediate action, the judge must disclose on the record the basis for possible disqualification and make reasonable efforts to transfer the matter to another judge as soon as practicable." ABA Model Judicial Code, Rule 2.11, Comment 3.

WAIVING DISQUALIFICATION

Judicial disqualification may be waived by the parties. See ABA Model Judicial Code, Rule 2.11(C). To do so, the following steps must be followed:

11. The judge discloses on the record the basis for the disqualification;
12. The judge asks the parties to consider, outside the presence of the court and its staff, whether to waive the disqualification; and
13. The parties agree on record that the judge may participate in the proceeding.

RECEIVING GIFTS

The general rule is that "[a] judge shall not accept any gifts, loans, bequests, benefits, or other things of value, if acceptance is prohibited by law or would appear to a reasonable person to undermine the judge's independence, integrity, or impartiality." ABA Model Judicial Code, Rule 3.13(A).

Rule 3.15(A) requires a judge to publicly report the following:

(1)   compensation received for extrajudicial activities as permitted by Rule 3.12;
(2)   gifts and other things of value as permitted by Rule 3.13(C), unless the value of such items, alone or in the aggregate with other items received from the same source in the same calendar year, does not exceed $[insert amount]; and
(3)   reimbursement of expenses and waiver of fees or charges permitted by Rule 3.14(A), unless the amount of reimbursement or waiver, alone or in the aggregate with other reimbursements or waivers received from the same source in the same calendar year, does not exceed $[insert amount].

Under Rule 3.13(B), a judge is **not required** to report the following gifts:

- items with little intrinsic value (plaques, certificates, trophies, and cards);
- gifts, loans, bequests, benefits, or other things of value from individuals whose appearance or interest in a proceeding before the judge would in any event require disqualification;
- ordinary social hospitality;
- commercial or financial opportunities and benefits, if also made to similarly-situated non-judges;
- rewards and prizes given to competitors or participants in random drawings, contests, or other events that are open to non-judges;
- scholarships, fellowships, and similar benefits or awards, if also made to similarly-situated non-judges;
- printed resource materials supplied by publishers on a complimentary basis for official use; or
- gifts, awards, or benefits associated with the business, profession, or other separate activity of a spouse, a domestic partner, or other family member of a judge residing in the judge's household, but that incidentally benefit the judge.

Under Rule 3.13(C), a judge must report the following gifts:

- gifts incident to a public testimonial;
- invitations to the judge and the judge's spouse, domestic partner, or guest to attend without charge:
  o   an event associated with a bar- or law-related function; or

- an event associated with any of the judge's educational, religious, charitable, fraternal or civic activities permitted by this Code, if the same invitation is offered to nonjudges who are engaged in similar ways in the activity as is the judge; and

- gifts, loans, bequests, benefits, or other things of value, if the source is someone who has come or is likely to come before the judge, or whose interests have come or are likely to come before the judge.

JUDGE ACTING AS A FIDUCIARY

The ABA Model Judicial Code defines "fiduciary" as including "relationships such as executor, administrator, trustee, or guardian."

A judge may serve as a fiduciary for a family member "if such service will not interfere with the proper performance of judicial duties." Rule 3.8(A). Such service is "subject to the same restrictions on engaging in financial activities that apply to a judge personally." Rule 3.8(C). If a person serving as a fiduciary becomes a judge, that person must comply with Rule 3.8 as soon as practicable, in no event later than one year after becoming a judge.

A judge shall not serve as a fiduciary if:

- Such service will interfere with the proper performance of judicial duties; or
- The judge as fiduciary will likely be engaged in proceedings that would ordinarily come before the judge, or if the estate, trust, or ward becomes involved in adversary proceedings in the court on which the judge serves, or one under its appellate jurisdiction.

ACTING AS ARBITRATOR/MEDIATOR

"A judge shall not act as an arbitrator or a mediator or perform other judicial functions apart from the judge's official duties unless expressly authorized by law." ABA Model Judicial Code, Rule 3.9.

Rule 3.9 "does not prohibit a judge from participating in arbitration, mediation, or settlement conferences performed as part of assigned judicial duties. Rendering dispute resolution services apart from those duties, whether or not for economic gain, is prohibited unless it is expressly authorized by law." *Id.* at Comment 1.

Extrajudicial Activities

EXTRAJUDICIAL ACTIVITIES

The ABA Model Judicial Code encourages judges "to engage in appropriate extrajudicial activities." Rule 3.1, Comment 1. Further, "[a] judge may accept reasonable compensation for extrajudicial activities permitted by this Code or other law unless such acceptance would appear to a reasonable person to undermine the judge's independence, integrity, or impartiality." Rule 3.12.

When engaging in extrajudicial activities, a judge shall **not** do the following:

(A) participate in activities that will interfere with the proper performance of the judge's judicial duties;
(B) participate in activities that will lead to frequent disqualification of the judge;
(C) participate in activities that would appear to a reasonable person to undermine the judge's independence, integrity, or impartiality;
(D) engage in conduct that would appear to a reasonable person to be coercive; or

(E) make use of court premises, staff, stationery, equipment, or other resources, except for incidental use for activities that concern the law, the legal system, or the administration of justice, or unless such additional use is permitted by law.

GOVERNMENTAL HEARINGS OR CONSULTATIONS

"A judge shall not appear voluntarily at a public hearing before, or otherwise consult with, an executive or a legislative body or official, except:

(A) in connection with matters concerning the law, the legal system, or the administration of justice;

(B) in connection with matters about which the judge acquired knowledge or expertise in the course of the judge's judicial duties; or

(C) when the judge is acting pro se in a matter involving the judge's legal or economic interests, or when the judge is acting in a fiduciary capacity."

ABA Model Judicial Code, Rule 3.2.

GOVERNMENTAL COMMITTEES OR COMMISSIONS

There is a strong desire in the ABA Model Judicial Code to negate the influence upon and by judges when it comes to non-legal policy issues. To that end, Rule 3.4 states: "[a] judge shall not accept appointment to a governmental committee, board, commission, or other governmental position, unless it is one that concerns the law, the legal system, or the administration of justice."

OFFICER, DIRECTOR, TRUSTEE, OR ADVISOR

Under Rule 3.11(B) of the ABA Model Judicial Code, a judge may manage or participate in:

(1) a business closely held by the judge or members of the judge's family; or

(2) a business entity primarily engaged in investment of the financial resources of the judge or members of the judge's family.

Otherwise, "[a] judge shall not serve as an officer, director, manager, general partner, advisor, or employee of any business entity . . . ." *Id.*

A judge may serve as an officer, director, trustee, or non-legal advisor of an educational, religious, charitable, fraternal, or civic organization not conducted for profit, unless the organization:

(a) will be engaged in proceedings that would ordinarily come before the judge; or

(b) will frequently be engaged in adversary proceedings in the court of which the judge is a member, or in any court subject to the appellate jurisdiction of the court of which the judge is a member.

ABA Model Judicial Code, Rule 3.7(A)(6).

FUNDRAISING ACTIVITIES FOR NON-PROFIT ORGANIZATIONS

A judge may assist "an organization or entity in planning related to fund-raising, and participating in the management and investment of the organization's or entity's funds." ABA Model Judicial Code, Rule 3.7(A)(1). A judge may not directly solicit contributions for such an organization, except from members of the judge's family and fellow judges. *Id.* at Rule 3.7(A)(2).

MPRE Practice Test #1

1. Attorney Harrison, who specializes in tax law, advises one of his corporate clients about a little-known tax loophole that saves the corporation a substantial amount in tax liability. The "loophole" involves withholding certain income information that is not readily discoverable by the IRS, so has little risk for the corporation. Grateful for the tax break, the corporation sends Attorney Harrison on an all-expenses-paid weekend trip to Las Vegas. Attorney Harrison spends the weekend gambling and drinking. At one point, he is asked by management to leave the casino due to public intoxication and disturbing the peace. Is Attorney Harrison subject to discipline?

   a. No. Although the casino asked him to leave, there were no criminal charges filed against him.
   b. No, because the IRS did not audit the corporation's tax return or otherwise discover the loophole.
   c. Yes, for gambling and public intoxication.
   d. Yes, for conduct involving dishonesty and fraud.

2. Attorney Gregg, recently admitted to the bar, is hired as an associate attorney at the Law Offices of Powell, Evans, and McGinnis, P.C. The professional corporation was formed for the sole purpose of the practice of law and is composed of two shareholders and four associates. Associates are salaried employees and are not shareholders or officers in the corporation. All of the shares of the corporation are held by two partners, Powell and Evans, with the exception of 33 shares held by the widow and executor of the estate of Attorney McGinnis, who recently passed away and whose estate is awaiting probate. Attorney Powell is the president and Attorney Evans is the vice president of the corporation. Stephanie Powell, the wife of Attorney Powell and a non-lawyer, is the office manager. She is a salaried employee and serves as the secretary/treasurer for the corporation. Is it appropriate for Attorney Gregg to practice at Powell, Evans, and McGinnis under the current corporate structure?

   a. Yes, because the associates are salaried employees, not shareholders in the corporation.
   b. Yes, because Mrs. Powell is not engaging in the practice of law.
   c. No, because Mrs. Powell, a non-lawyer, is an officer of the corporation.
   d. No, because Mrs. McGinnis, a non-lawyer, is holding stock as an executor of a will.

3. Attorney Hill, a solo practitioner specializing in family law, plans on taking an extended leave of absence to care for her husband, who recently had a stroke. Attorney Bradley, also a solo practitioner, has agreed to assist Attorney Hill by reviewing her client files and taking any actions needed to protect the interests of the clients. Attorney Hill delivers all of her client files to Attorney Bradley and obtains his assurance that he will treat all information in the files confidentially. Attorney Hill then provides written notice to all of her clients, advising them that their files have been delivered to Attorney Bradley for handling, but also advising that the clients could retain another attorney should they so desire. Is Attorney Hill subject to discipline?

   a. Yes, because she failed to obtain consent from her clients before delivering their files to Attorney Bradley.
   b. Yes, because she will be on leave of absence and therefore unable to supervise the work of Attorney Bradley.
   c. No, because Attorney Bradley agreed to keep the client information confidential.
   d. No, because finding alternative representation was reasonable due to her current family situation.

4. Attorney Morgan was previously employed by Connecticut Insurance Company where he primarily investigated and defended claims for personal injury from automobile accidents. Attorney Morgan recently went into private practice, specializing in personal injury claims. Mr. Tucker comes to Attorney Morgan's office asking for representation in his personal injury claim. At the initial consultation, Attorney Morgan recognizes that he investigated Mr. Tucker's claim against Connecticut Insurance Company while still employed there. The claim remains unresolved. How should Attorney Morgan proceed?

   a. Decline representation of Mr. Tucker
   b. Disclose the conflict of interest to Mr. Tucker and agree to represent him only upon his written consent
   c. Contact Connecticut Insurance Company and offer to act as mediator because he is familiar with both the claim and the defense
   d. Refer Mr. Tucker to an associate within his firm

5. Attorney Marsh, a personal injury attorney, is taking his morning run around the perimeter of a large park near his home. Just ahead of him, he sees another runner start to cross the street using the crosswalk at an intersection. An SUV turns at the intersection and into the crosswalk, striking the runner. The runner suffers severe injuries. Attorney Marsh witnessed the entire event and clearly saw that the driver of the SUV was texting on his cell phone while he turned into the intersection. The driver claimed innocence and told police that he had both hands on the steering wheel at the time of the accident. After recovering from his injuries, the runner begins to look for legal representation. He is advised by his family that police had questioned a witness at the scene who was an attorney. The runner contacts Attorney Marsh and asks if he would be willing to represent him. Attorney Marsh agrees to the representation but requires the runner to sign a consent allowing Attorney Marsh to also testify on his behalf at trial. Attorney Marsh knows that the driver's phone records show a text being sent at the time of the accident, but recognizes that the runner's case will be much stronger if he testifies about what he witnessed at the time. Is it proper for Attorney Marsh to represent the runner?

    a. Yes, because he was the only witness who saw the driver texting.
    b. Yes, because his client consented to Attorney Marsh providing testimony.
    c. No, because Attorney Marsh witnessed the accident.
    d. No, because he was the only witness who saw the driver texting.

6. Attorney Case is defending a client against charges of tax evasion. In preparing the client for deposition, the client reveals that, before he was represented by Attorney Case, he had committed perjury while testifying before the grand jury that indicted him. Attorney Case is subject to discipline if he:

    a. Continues to represent the client.
    b. Does not inform the prosecutor of the perjury.
    c. Informs the prosecutor of the perjury.
    d. Continues to represent the client without the client admitting his perjury to the court.

7. Attorney Hart represented 12 plaintiffs in a suit for sexual harassment against a restaurant owner who previously employed them. The defendant offered to settle the suit for a lump sum of $120,000. The defendant will not settle any of the claims unless all are settled. Attorney Hart evaluates each of his client's damages and allocates the $120,000 amongst the 12 plaintiffs based on the nature and extent of their interactions with the defendant. Attorney Hart meets individually with each of his clients and advises them of the amount they will receive from the settlement. To protect the confidentiality of the clients and preserve the settlement, Attorney Hart does not disclose to any plaintiff the amount to be received by any other plaintiff. Each of the plaintiffs agrees to the settlement. Is Attorney Hart subject to discipline for structuring the settlement agreement according to these terms?

    a. No, because Attorney Hart was in the best position to evaluate the merits of each plaintiff's claim.
    b. Yes, because no individual plaintiff knew the amount to be received by any other plaintiff.
    c. No, because disclosing the individual settlement amounts might have jeopardized the whole settlement.
    d. No, because Attorney Hart reasonably believed the allocations were fair, and because each plaintiff agreed to the amount.

8. Attorney James represents the plaintiff in a claim for assault. During the investigation of the claim, Attorney James identifies an eyewitness to the altercation at issue in the case. He interviews the witness and realizes that her recollection of the event is contrary to that of his client, and if believed by the jury, could establish that his client was actually at fault for the altercation. The witness advises that she does not want to get involved in the case and is considering a vacation in order to be out of the country during the time of the trial. Attorney James advises the witness that she is under no obligation to appear and asks her to proceed with her vacation out of the country. Were Attorney James' actions improper?

   a. No, because the witness did not want to testify.
   b. No, because Attorney James did not offer the witness any inducement to discourage the witness from testifying.
   c. Yes, because Attorney James asked the witness to leave the jurisdiction of the court.
   d. Yes, because the witness had not been subpoenaed to testify at trial.

9. Attorney Lane recently joined a midsize firm as an associate attorney and is working hard to build his caseload. He recognizes that a recent downturn in the economy has led to the inability of many potential clients to pay their legal expenses. He brainstorms several options to present to the firm's shareholders in an effort to assist potential clients in paying their fees. Which of the following would be improper for the shareholders to approve?

   a. Accepting credit cards for payment of fees
   b. Accepting property for payment of fees
   c. Arranging for clients to obtain bank loans for the purpose of paying fees
   d. Accepting publication rights concerning the case as payment of fees

10. Attorney Paul is an associate in a midsize firm that represents a number of corporations that own and manage rental properties. Attorney Paul also serves on the board of directors of a local legal aid organization that provides free legal assistance to low-income clients. The legal aid services include representation in landlord-tenant disputes and, in fact, some of the legal aid client disputes are against corporations represented by Attorney Paul's firm. The legal aid organization falls on hard financial times and cannot continue providing free services to all of its clients. One of the directors proposes that the organization withdraw from representation of all landlord-tenant actions because they often require much of an attorney's time. Attorney Paul recognizes that this will leave some of the organization's clients without representation in disputes against some of his firm's corporate clients. The board of directors is prepared to vote on the proposal. Which of the following best describes Attorney Paul's obligations under the Model Rules?

   a. Attorney Paul may continue to serve on the board of directors, but may not participate in the vote.
   b. Attorney Paul may continue to serve on the board of directors as well as participate in the vote.
   c. Attorney Paul should resign from the board of directors and refrain from voting on the proposal.
   d. Attorney Paul must report his participation on the board of directors to the state bar association because his participation violates the Rules of Professional Conduct.

11. Attorney Henry is an associate at a small firm that specializes in estate planning. Attorney Henry's grandmother seeks to hire her granddaughter to draft her last will and testament. As part of her will, the grandmother instructs Attorney Henry to bequeath certain items to her family and friends. Included in her instructions is a bequest of her substantial jewelry collection to Attorney Henry. Will Attorney Henry be subject to discipline if she prepares her grandmother's will as instructed?

   a. Yes, because an attorney cannot prepare for any client an instrument giving a substantial gift to that attorney.
   b. Yes, because an attorney cannot prepare a will for this client because they are relatives.
   c. No, because an attorney can prepare for a client a will that gives the attorney a substantial gift if it is made knowingly and voluntarily.
   d. No, because an attorney can prepare for a client a will that gives the attorney a substantial gift if they are relatives.

12. A construction company enters into a contract with a purchaser to construct a new home. Judge Alexander's wife owns and operates a landscaping business. She has an existing service agreement with the construction company to provide landscaping for the new homes they build. While Judge Alexander's wife is landscaping the property, the owner files a breach of contract action against the construction company. The action is filed in the jurisdiction in which Judge Alexander presides. The construction company sends a Christmas gift to Judge Alexander that is not part of his wife's compensation under the service agreement. Is it improper for Judge Alexander to accept the gift?

   a. Yes, because the gift was made in relation to his wife's business and could reasonably be perceived as intended to influence the judge in the performance of his duties.
   b. Yes, unless the owner gave the same gift to Judge Alexander.
   c. No, because the construction company does not have a direct business relationship with Judge Alexander.
   d. No, because a judge is not prohibited from accepting gifts.

13. Attorney Ferrara is a solo practitioner. She has no partners and is not associated with any other attorneys. She has several billboards throughout town advertising her practice as "specializing in employment law, including wrongful discharge." Mrs. Connor schedules a consultation with Attorney Ferrara to discuss the facts of her recent discharge from employment with a local school district. At the end of the meeting, Attorney Ferrara advises that her current workload will not allow her to take on a case as complex as Mrs. Connor's. She offers to provide Mrs. Connor with the names of several other attorneys who specialize in employment law. She recommends Mrs. Connor timely meet with another attorney to preserve her rights. Mrs. Connor declines a referral and leaves Attorney Ferrara's office. Six months later, Mrs. Connor consults with another attorney who advises her that the statute of limitations for wrongful discharge expired several months ago. Is Attorney Ferrara subject to liability?

   a. Yes, because Attorney Ferrara failed to advise Mrs. Connor of the statute of limitations for her case.
   b. Yes, because Attorney Ferrara's billboard advertising was false and misleading.
   c. No, because Attorney Ferrara had the right to decline representation of Mrs. Connor if she cannot competently represent her interests due to workload, regardless of advertising that she specializes in employment law.
   d. No, because Attorney Ferrara complied with the rules of professional conduct and acted reasonably in declining the representation.

14. Attorney Locke has been retained by Mr. Kemp to represent him in a heavily contested divorce proceeding. Mr. Kemp's wife stands to recover a substantial amount of Mr. Kemp's fortune and he is quite irate about this potential outcome. Early on, he asks Attorney Locke a number of questions about the extent of attorney-client privilege. As the case proceeds, Mr. Kemp reveals a great deal of information regarding the couple's contentious and sometimes violent relationship. Just before trial, Mr. Kemp threatens Attorney Locke that he had better limit his wife's recovery because otherwise he "has a gun and will be forced to take care of [his] wife" to keep her from the money. Knowing Mr. Kemp's history, Attorney Locke considers this a reasonable threat to the wellbeing of Mr. Kemp's wife. Is it appropriate for Attorney Locke to disclose Mr. Kemp's comments to law enforcement?

    a. No, because the disclosure would be prejudicial to Mr. Kemp in his divorce proceedings.

    b. No, because Mr. Kemp has never attempted to kill his wife in spite of their contentious history.

    c. Yes, because the information concerns a future crime and therefore is not protected by attorney-client privilege.

    d. Yes, because the information is necessary to prevent an action reasonably certain to result in death or bodily harm.

15. Which of the following correctly states an attorney's responsibility to report alleged professional misconduct?

    a. An attorney must report a partner in his law firm when he reveals he has been withdrawing client funds and investing them for personal gain.

    b. An attorney must report opposing counsel for representing a client with whom he has been involved romantically for the past year.

    c. An attorney must report a fellow associate in his law firm who has been sued by his brother-in-law for breach of contract arising from a failed business venture.

    d. An attorney must report a local bankruptcy attorney for personally filing for her own bankruptcy.

16. Attorney Kitt is retained by Mr. Ray to file a lawsuit against a subcontractor for breach of contract. Once he files the petition, Attorney Kitt does little to pursue the case, opting instead to work on other cases with higher settlement value. Defense counsel files written discovery to the plaintiff, but Attorney Kitt does not inform his client, respond to the discovery, or file a motion for extension of time to respond. Defense counsel files a notice to depose the plaintiff. Attorney Kitt does not advise his client of the date of the deposition. He intends to call defense counsel to propose a later date for the deposition, but fails to do so. Neither the plaintiff nor Attorney Kitt appear at the deposition. Upon motion of the defendant, a default judgment is entered against the plaintiff. Attorney Kitt promises his client he will get the default judgment set aside. He prepares a motion to set aside, but does not file it with the court until after he finishes another trial. His motion is denied. Is Attorney Kitt subject to discipline?

    a. No, because the court should have granted the plaintiff's motion to set aside the default judgment.

    b. No, as long as Attorney Kitt reimburses his client for any attorney fees he has already paid.

    c. Yes, because Attorney Kitt failed to respond to discovery, appear at a scheduled deposition, or timely file a motion to set aside the default judgment.

    d. No, because defense counsel did not give Attorney Kitt notice of his intent to file a motion for default judgment or give him a chance to remedy the issues.

17. Acme Insurance Company is a large property insurance provider that serves insured businesses in New York, including many hospitals. Recently, Acme has been inundated with hospital claims for clean-up and business interruption because of a pandemic. The pandemic was a novel event and Acme has been forced to make difficult coverage decisions on these claims. The New York legislature appointed a committee to conduct hearings regarding the sufficiency and improvement of property insurance arising from pandemic claims. Acme employs a team of in-house attorneys to handle regulatory compliance work. Attorney Butler is part of the legal team. At Acme's direction, Attorney Butler testified in the property insurance hearings before the state committee. Attorney Butler's testimony supported the position of Acme. However, Attorney Butler did not disclose to the committee his relationship to Acme. Acme paid for his time and expenses to attend the hearings. Did Attorney Butler engage in improper conduct?

  a. Yes, because he did not disclose to the committee that he was appearing as Acme's in-house counsel.
  b. Yes, because Acme paid Attorney Butler for testifying before the committee.
  c. No, because Attorney Butler could not reveal his relationship to Acme due to attorney-client privilege.
  d. No, because Attorney Butler could not reveal his relationship to Acme due to attorney-client evidentiary privilege.

18. Mrs. Mann and Mrs. Hart co-own a business, Sweet and Savory Catering. The partnership dissolves and the two become involved in a contentious dispute when Mrs. Hart uses part of the business's profits to invest in stock, a violation of the partnership agreement. Mrs. Mann retains Attorney Fletcher to represent her in settlement negotiations with Mrs. Hart. The parties and their attorneys have met several times. While the negotiations are ongoing, Attorney Fletcher runs into Mrs. Hart at a Christmas party for which Mrs. Hart's new business is catering food. Mrs. Hart asks how Attorney Fletcher is doing, and the two discuss their individual holiday travel plans. Was Attorney Fletcher's conduct appropriate?

  a. Yes, because Mrs. Hart approached Attorney Fletcher.
  b. Yes, because Attorney Fletcher and Mrs. Hart discussed holiday plans.
  c. No, because any discussions between Attorney Fletcher and Mrs. Hart have an appearance of impropriety.
  d. No, because Mrs. Hart is represented by counsel in the negotiations.

19. Attorney Marsh, a personal injury attorney, is taking his morning run around the perimeter of a large park near his home. Just ahead of him, he sees another runner start to cross the street using the crosswalk at an intersection. An SUV turns at the intersection and into the crosswalk, striking the runner. The runner suffers severe injuries. Seeing an opportunity to build his client base, Attorney Marsh runs ahead to the accident scene and approaches the runner. He recognizes her as a fellow attorney from local bar functions that the two have attended. He hands her a business card and advises that he witnessed the entire event and clearly saw that the driver of the SUV was texting on his cell phone while he turned into the intersection. He offers to represent the runner in a lawsuit against the SUV driver. Before the runner can respond, she is loaded into an ambulance by paramedics and transported from the scene. Later, after she recovers from her injuries, she finds Attorney Marsh's business card amongst her items from the accident. She recalls being approached by him at the accident scene in what she believes to be complete lack of moral and professional behavior. She plans to report him to the state licensing board. Were Attorney Marsh's actions at the scene of the accident subject to discipline?

 a. No, because he witnessed the accident and believed he could help her recover damages from the driver.
 b. No, because the runner is also an attorney.
 c. Yes, because a lawyer is prohibited from soliciting business from potential clients for monetary gain.
 d. Yes, because the runner did not want him to solicit her business.

20. In a medical malpractice case against a local primary care physician, the plaintiff is represented by a seasoned attorney with a reputation for obtaining substantial verdicts for his injured clients. Defense counsel for the physician and the corporation for which he is employed seeks to place his clients in the best light to potential jurors. He encourages his clients to accelerate the release of a planned advertising campaign, including mailed brochures and local billboards focusing on the outstanding quality of care provided by the corporation's physicians. The campaign is released the week prior to jury selection, providing publicity that biases the prospective jurors in favor of the defendants. Will defense counsel be subject to discipline for making this request for advertising?

 a. Yes, because the advertising campaign resulted in false information being released in court.
 b. Yes, because the advertising campaign was an attempt to influence prospective jurors.
 c. No, because the defendants had already planned to release an advertising campaign.
 d. No, because defense counsel did not directly contact any prospective jurors.

21. Attorney Green represents Mr. Snow in the sale of his business as he prepares to retire. During negotiations, Attorney Green grows increasingly frustrated with Mr. Snow's affirmative statements to the buyer regarding the profitability of the business. Attorney Green believes the statements may go beyond mere "puffing." He advises Mr. Snow to avoid making these statements. He documents this in writing and places a copy in the legal file. The buyer subsequently files suit against both Attorney Green and Mr. Snow, alleging fraud. Attorney Green and Mr. Snow retain separate counsel. In response to discovery requests, Attorney Green advises his counsel that he would like to produce the written document, which will be favorable to this defense but potentially damaging to Mr. Snow. Is it proper for Attorney Green to release this information?

    a. Yes, because the information was disclosed in a prior business transaction before the fraud claim was filed.

    b. Yes, because Attorney Green is revealing the information to defend himself against a civil claim.

    c. No, because no criminal charges have been brought against Attorney Green.

    d. No, because the information will be prejudicial to Mr. Snow.

22. Mr. Abernathy is sued in a landlord/tenant action in a Kansas trial court. Mr. Abernathy's cousin, Vincent, is an attorney practicing just across the state line in Missouri. Vincent is licensed to practice law in Missouri only. Mr. Abernathy calls Vincent and asks if he will represent him in the landlord/tenant trial. Which of the following best states Vincent's professional responsibility?

    a. Vincent must decline his cousin's request because he is not licensed to practice law in Kansas.

    b. Vincent should advise his cousin to tell the court he is representing himself without counsel. Vincent will then be allowed to attend the trial and argue the case for Mr. Abernathy because his name does not appear on the record.

    c. Vincent may file a motion to appear pro hac vice and, if granted by the court, he may represent Mr. Abernathy in Kansas.

    d. Vincent may represent his cousin, but only so long as he does so on a pro bono basis.

23. Attorney Blue opened a client trust account at First National Bank. First National requires a $10 monthly service charge to manage the account. Attorney Blue deposits money from his firm's operating account into the client trust account each month to cover the service fee. He takes the added measure of depositing $20 monthly to ensure that the service fee never depletes the client funds held in the account. Attorney Blue keeps detailed records regarding deposits into the client account. Is Attorney Blue's management of the client trust account appropriate?

    a. No, because he deposits more into the client trust account than is needed to cover the service fee.

    b. No, because Attorney Blue is commingling the firm's money with the client trust funds.

    c. Yes, because deposits from the firm's account are protecting the client funds.

    d. Yes, because he maintains detailed records delineating his funds from the client funds.

24. Attorney Stone practices for a large firm in St. Louis, Missouri. The firm has offices in St. Louis and just across the state line in Collinsville, Illinois. Attorney Stone is licensed in Missouri only, but routinely works out of the Collinsville office, providing legal services in Illinois. An attorney at another St. Louis firm reports Attorney Stone to the Missouri Bar. Which of the following is the most accurate statement regarding disciplinary authority?

a. Missouri has disciplinary authority because this is where Attorney Stone is licensed.
b. Illinois has disciplinary authority because this is where the violation (practicing without a license) occurred.
c. Both Missouri and Illinois have jurisdiction because Attorney Stone is subject to disciplinary authority in both jurisdictions for the same conduct.
d. Illinois has no jurisdiction because Attorney Stone has no license within the state to discipline.

25. An attorney represents Metropolis General Hospital in a medical malpractice lawsuit filed against it by the plaintiff, a former patient of the hospital. The suit is filed in a jurisdiction that requires the plaintiff to file an affidavit of merit, no later than 30 days after filing the petition, attesting that the care at issue has been reviewed by a qualified healthcare provider who determined it failed to meet a reasonable standard of care. No affidavit has been filed by the plaintiff and the deadline for filing expired 10 days ago. Is it appropriate for defense counsel to proceed with a motion for default judgment for failure to file the affidavit?

a. No, because defense counsel should notify the plaintiff's counsel of his intent to file the motion before proceeding.
b. No, because doing so would constitute a failure to extend professional courtesy to another member of the bar.
c. Yes, because defense counsel is representing the best interest of the hospital.
d. Yes, because defense counsel has determined, after review by a qualified healthcare provider, that the hospital provided a reasonable standard of care.

26. Attorney Booth was employed by the US Department of Homeland Security. During his tenure, a number of investigations into suspected cyberattacks were completed. Attorney Booth was not a part of the investigation team and had no knowledge of any facts or findings of the investigations. Last year, Attorney Booth left the Department and started his own private practice. He was recently contacted by a potential client who had been charged with several causes of action, apparently disclosed in one of the Department's cybersecurity investigations. Before Attorney Booth agrees to represent the client, he contacts the Department and obtains its written consent to the representation. May Attorney Booth represent the client?

a. Yes, because he was neither a part of nor had any knowledge of the facts of the Department of Homeland Security's investigation.
b. Yes, because the Department of Homeland Security consented to the representation.
c. No, because he was employed by the Department of Homeland Security during the time of the investigation.
d. No, because the actions he is being asked to defend arose directly from the Department of Homeland Security's investigation.

27. Attorney Tillman is retained by Mr. Walton to defend him in an action for breach of contract. Mr. Walton is 82 years old, widowed, and has no family other than a niece with whom he rarely communicates. As Attorney Tillman prepares his defense, he becomes concerned about Mr. Walton's cognition and capacity to make decisions for himself. In fact, Attorney Tillman suspects the breach of contract arose from Mr. Walton's failure to understand the terms of the agreement. Attorney Tillman contacts the niece, who informs him she is in poor health and unable to assist with the care of her uncle. As there are no other known family members, Attorney Tillman files a petition to have a public administrator appointed as Mr. Walton's guardian. Mr. Walton is quite angry, accusing Attorney Tillman of taking unauthorized action and disclosing information that is protected by the attorney-client privilege. Is Mr. Walton likely to prevail in his objections to Attorney Tillman's actions?

   a. Yes, because Mr. Walton did not authorize Attorney Tillman to act on his behalf other than to defend him in the breach of contract action.
   b. Yes, because Attorney Tillman released confidential financial and health information without his consent.
   c. No, because Attorney Tillman sought the consent of Mr. Walton's only relative before proceeding with a guardianship action.
   d. No, because Attorney Tillman reasonably believed that Mr. Walton could not act in his own best interest.

28. Attorney McGinnis is a partner in a midsize law firm. She specializes in bankruptcy law. She agrees to represent Beta Inc., one of the firm's corporate clients, in bankruptcy proceedings. Shortly thereafter, another case she is handling for the firm is set for trial. The trial would be more lucrative for the firm, so she transfers Beta's case to an associate attorney in the firm. The associate disputes the new assignment based on his unfamiliarity with bankruptcy law. He argues that he lacks reasonable time to gain sufficient legal competence to handle Beta's case without assistance from Attorney McGinnis. Attorney McGinnis believes the associate can handle the assignment independently. Did Attorney McGinnis properly handle this case?

   a. Yes, because the associate is licensed to practice any type of law.
   b. Yes, Attorney McGinnis has the right to withdraw from Beta's case because handling it would cause her financial hardship.
   c. No, because Attorney McGinnis did not seek Beta's consent to transfer the case to the associate.
   d. No, because Attorney McGinnis was aware of the associate's lack of competence to handle the case, but failed to provide oversight to protect Beta's interests.

29. An attorney and client enter into an agreement as follows:

- The client pays a retainer fee of $2,500 in advance of services being provided
- The attorney agrees to return any portion of the retainer remaining after completion of services
- The attorney provides the client with monthly statements outlining fees for the work performed

The $2,500 retainer fee is deposited in the attorney's client trust account. The attorney sends monthly statements to the client, outlining her total fees of $2,000, but does not withdraw any of the $2,500 retainer fees until the case is concluded. At that time, she writes two checks on the client trust account: one to herself for $2,000 and one to the client for $500. Was the attorney's conduct proper?

a. Yes, because the attorney deposited the retainer fee in her client trust account.
b. Yes, because the attorney provided the client with accurate monthly billing statements.
c. No, because the attorney's failure to withdraw her fees as they were billed resulted in improper commingling of her funds with the client's funds.
d. No, because the attorney requested an advanced payment against her fees.

30. Attorney Salvador represents five family members who filed a claim against Chicago General Hospital for the alleged wrongful death of their family member who was treated at the hospital. The case is settled at mediation. On late Friday afternoon prior to a long holiday weekend, defense counsel had five settlement checks delivered to Attorney Salvador, one for each of the attorney's clients. Attorney Salvador deposits the checks into a client trust account. On Tuesday morning after the holiday weekend, he contacts the client spokesperson for the family and advises that the checks were deposited the week prior and were ready for the clients. The clients pick up the checks the following day. Was Attorney Salvador's conduct proper?

a. No, because he should have notified his clients on Friday when he received the checks.
b. No, because the funds should have been kept separate from the client trust account.
c. Yes, because the clients did not object to the delayed delivery.
d. Yes, because the clients could not have done anything with the funds over the holiday weekend due to bank closures.

31. Attorney Michaels represents an elected county official who is suing a local television station for slander. After one of the pretrial hearings, as Attorney Michaels leaves the courthouse, a number of news reporters are waiting with questions. In response to one of the reporter's questions, Attorney Michaels reveals the identity of the news reporter who broke the story that is the subject of the slander claim. Are Attorney Michaels' actions improper?

a. No, because a trial of the matter had not yet commenced.
b. No, because the statement related to a matter of public record.
c. Yes, because prospective jurors might hear Attorney Michaels' statement.
d. Yes, because Attorney Michaels identified a prospective witness in the case.

32. Attorney Byrne is a solo practitioner who handles a variety of cases, but has most recently spent a large amount of time handling motor vehicle cases. At her husband's annual office Christmas party, she is approached by one of his co-workers who recently had abdominal surgery. The co-worker explained that complications from the surgery resulted in a prolonged stay, additional surgery, and a permanent colostomy. She believes the complications arose from negligent care by the surgeon and she would like to sue him to recover her medical bills and for pain and suffering. Attorney Byrne told the co-worker that she would be happy to represent her because one of her specialties is personal injury. She adds that she has recovered full damages for her clients in the last two cases she tried. The last two cases Attorney Byrne handled were related to motor vehicle accidents, not personal injury, but her statements regarding awarding of damages were accurate. She provides a business card to the co-worker who subsequently schedules a consultation with Attorney Byrne. Is Attorney Byrne subject to discipline?

   a. No, because the co-worker approached Attorney Byrne for advice; Attorney Byrne did not initiate the conversation.
   b. No, because the statements regarding damage awards were truthful.
   c. Yes, because Attorney Byrne's statements regarding her specialties were false and misleading.
   d. Yes, because the discussion was a direct solicitation for business by Attorney Byrne.

33. A local store owner hires an attorney to provide legal counsel on business matters that occasionally arise. The state in which the store is located recently instituted a mandate requiring all patrons to wear a mask while inside any business as a measure to reduce the spread of a pandemic. The store owner contacts his attorney to ask whether any businesses have been prosecuted for refusing to abide by the mandate. He also asks whether the $500 fine established by the mandate could be imposed for each patron found within the store or as a one-time fine at the time the infraction is discovered. The attorney correctly advises that the fine could only be imposed once per infraction, not per patron; and that, to date, no businesses within the county have been prosecuted. Several days later, the attorney is advised that the store owner has posted a "no masks allowed" sign on their door, in direct violation of the mandate. Is the attorney subject to discipline?

   a. Yes, because he had reason to believe the information would encourage the store owner to violate the mandate.
   b. Yes, because the attorney aided the store owner in violating the mandate.
   c. No, but only if the attorney did not bill the store owner for the legal advice.
   d. No, because the attorney provided only factual information regarding the mandate.

34. Attorney Smith, recently admitted to the bar and struggling to pay off his student loan debt, advises the partners in his firm that he does not intend to complete any CLE courses. He reminds his partners that their state does not require CLEs and argues that he cannot afford them. The partners are concerned because Attorney Smith does not carry malpractice insurance. They are also concerned that he won't be motivated to study on his own. Is Attorney Smith's action proper?

   a. No, because Attorney Smith cannot maintain competence without attending CLE courses.
   b. Yes, because Attorney Smith may independently pursue continuing study and education to maintain competence.
   c. No, because Attorney Smith does not have malpractice insurance.
   d. Yes, because the state in which Attorney Smith practices does not offer free CLE courses.

35. Attorney Curry is employed as corporate counsel for Future Tech, a large technology company. Future Tech routinely provides exceptional summer interns with scholarships up to $5,000 for their final year of college expenses if those interns agree to work for Future Tech for at least one year after graduation. If the intern chooses not to work for Future Tech or does not remain employed for a full year, they must repay the scholarship on a prorated basis. Ms. Blake is a top intern who receives $2,000 in scholarship funds. She returns to work at Future Tech after graduation, but leaves for another position after six months of employment. At year's end, Future Tech's accounting department discovers that Ms. Blake did not fulfill her one-year commitment. Accounting contacts Attorney Curry and advises that Ms. Blake owes the company $1,000 (her prorated amount for six months). Attorney Curry contacts Ms. Blake, who responds that she has no intent to repay the $1,000. Attorney Curry consults with the President of Future Tech and advises that the company has a valid claim against Ms. Blake that is enforceable in small claims court. However, the time and effort to pursue the claim, including Attorney Curry's appearance in court, might be more than it is worth to recover the $1,000. He recommends that Future Tech forego enforcement of the repayment. The president agrees. Was Attorney Curry's conduct proper?

   a. No, because he gave legal advice based on economic factors.
   b. No, because his advice not to pursue the small claim violated his duty to diligently pursue the company's cause of action.
   c. Yes, because the president accepted Attorney Curry's advice and decided against enforcing the claim.
   d. Yes, because his advice could include both legal and economic factors.

36. Mr. Kohls schedules a consultation with Attorney Evans. He says that he and Mrs. Kohls have decided to divorce. The couple resides in a state that recognizes accelerated proceedings for "no-fault" dissolution cases. They desire to dissolve the marriage amicably with an equal division of assets, and plan to file and pursue their own divorce case. Mr. Kohls asks Attorney Evans to work with them in preparing the settlement agreement. The couple has an established relationship with Attorney Evans, as several years ago he prepared their wills and trusts and helped them purchase a new home. Attorney Evans believes he can represent both Mr. Kohls and Mrs. Kohls fairly without a conflict of interest, but he clearly outlines the following to both parties: (1) he advises them to consider separate counsel for the divorce, but will assist with a settlement agreement as long as both parties remain in complete agreement; (2) if a conflict develops, he will withdraw his representation for both parties; and (3) separate communications between Attorney Evans and either party will not be kept confidential from the other party. Both Mr. Kohls and Mrs. Kohls agree to the terms and sign an agreement to jointly retain Attorney Evans. Was it appropriate for Attorney Evans to represent both parties?

   a. No, because Attorney Evans cannot condition representation upon waiver of client confidentiality.
   b. No, because Attorney Evans did not advise the couple in writing that they should seek independent counsel before entering into an agreement with him.
   c. Yes, because there is minimal risk that either party's interest will be materially prejudiced.
   d. Yes, because Attorney Evans has previously represented both parties jointly.

37. Attorney Connor agrees to represent a client, Mr. Bean, in a personal injury action on a contingency fee basis. An agreement is signed by the client, agreeing to pay the attorney 30 percent of any amount recovered in the action. Six months later, Attorney Connor has acquired a significant number of cases. Mr. Bean's case is moving slowly and Attorney Connor recognizes that he could likely take on more lucrative cases if he wasn't representing Mr. Bean. He approaches Mr. Bean with an amended agreement and advises that the fee has been increased to 40 percent. He tells Mr. Bean that the fee increase is non-negotiable, but if he refuses to sign the agreement, Attorney Connor will find another attorney to take his case for the original fee. Mr. Bean feels he has no real choice in the matter and signs the agreement. The case proceeds to trial and Mr. Bean receives a modest damages award. He offers Attorney Connor the original 30 percent contingency fee, but refuses to pay 40 percent. Attorney Connor files suit against Mr. Bean for breach of contract. Is Attorney Connor likely to prevail in his claim against Mr. Bean?

   a. No, because the increase in fees could not be accomplished without an adverse effect on Mr. Bean.
   b. No, because no good cause existed for Attorney Connor to increase the contingency fee.
   c. Yes, because Attorney Connor offered to find another attorney to assume representation of Mr. Bean for the original fee.
   d. Yes, because a 40 percent contingency fee is still reasonable for a personal injury action.

38. In a trial without a jury, the judge overrules the defendant's motion to suppress certain evidence. Plaintiff's counsel, who tried a case before the same judge in a similar case the week prior, recognizes that the judge's ruling on the same motion is in direct contradiction to his ruling in the prior trial. The prior case is currently under advisement, awaiting a decision by the judge. After the court adjourns for the day, plaintiff's counsel asks to talk to the judge in chambers and explains his concern that the judge's ruling on the motion to suppress in the prior case was in error and may impact the outcome of the case. He asks if the judge would like to reopen the case for a briefing by both parties and further consideration of the motion. The judge reopens the case, requesting supplementary briefs from both parties for further consideration. Was it proper for the judge to communicate with plaintiff's attorney on this issue?

   a. Yes, because both parties were given an opportunity to present their arguments in regard to the motion during the trial.
   b. Yes, because plaintiff's counsel did not argue that the judge should change his ruling.
   c. No, because the judge allowed and considered communication on this matter before advising defense counsel.
   d. No, because plaintiff's counsel's communication caused the judge to reopen a case that had been taken under advisement.

39. Attorney Jefferson represents Mr. Hanks in a breach of contract action against an electrician. Mr. Hanks also has a personal injury claim against his neighbor, Mr. Thomas, but is represented by another attorney for this claim. Mr. Thomas asks Attorney Jefferson to defend him in the suit filed against him by Mr. Hanks.

Is it proper for Attorney Jefferson to represent Mr. Thomas in his defense against the claim of Mr. Hanks?

   a. No, because Attorney Jefferson is already representing Mr. Hanks in the breach of contract suit.
   b. Yes, because Mr. Thomas knows that Attorney Jefferson is already representing Mr. Hanks, but has no issue with the dual representation.
   c. Yes, because the representation is for two different causes of action.
   d. No, because both matters could eventually be appealed in the same court, requiring Attorney Jefferson to argue two conflicting causes of action.

40. Mrs. Rudolph sustains an injury at Metropolis General Hospital that she believes was the result of negligent care. She wants to file a lawsuit against the hospital but does not have money to pay attorney fees. She files a pro se medical malpractice action against Metropolis General Hospital. Attorney Dixon, defense counsel for Metropolis General, advises that he believes Mrs. Rudolph has a valid claim and recommends the hospital try to settle the case before either side incurs any additional costs. Mrs. Rudolph agrees to mediation. She presents to the office of the mediator, Attorney Dixon, as instructed for the mediation. Through the course of the day, it becomes evident to the mediator that Mrs. Rudolph does not have a good understanding of the mediation process. She confides in Attorney Dixon some key details that he believes are pertinent to the settlement value of the case and should be communicated to Metropolis General. However, Mrs. Rudolph makes several statements to Attorney Dixon, such as, "I know I can share this with you as counsel," and "I know this is protected by attorney-client privilege." Attorney Dixon disregards the statements and proceeds with providing the information to Metropolis General. Were Attorney Dixon's actions proper?

   a. No, because he is acting as a neutral party but showing bias toward the hospital.
   b. No, because he should have advised Mrs. Rudolph that he is a neutral party and does not represent her.
   c. Yes, because a mediator's role is to reach a resolution of the case by disclosing all pertinent information.
   d. Yes, because Mrs. Rudolph did not explicitly advise Attorney Dixon that the information she disclosed was confidential.

41. Judge Bailey is Chief Justice of the Alabama Supreme Court. As part of his duties, he has the power to appoint bailiffs for the Supreme Court as well as the state's appellate courts. It is unusual for two different panels of appellate judges to be in session simultaneously, but Judge Bailey appoints a full-time bailiff for each courtroom and each panel, resulting in several bailiffs who are only able to work part-time hours. Were Judge Bailey's appointments appropriate?

    a. Yes, because the appointments were within the powers granted to Judge Bailey as Chief Justice.

    b. Yes, because the appointments assured adequate staffing of bailiffs for all appellate courts.

    c. No, because the appointments were unnecessary given the typical sessions of the appellate judges.

    d. No, because appointing a bailiff for each court displayed favoritism for the appellate courts over other state courts.

42. Attorney Miller is hired by his client to file a lawsuit against a hospital for medical complications he sustained as a patient. Attorney Miller files the suit based on three separate counts, one of which is negligent credentialing. After the defendant files an answer to the petition, Attorney Miller discovers recent binding case law that refused to recognize a cause of action for negligent credentialing in his jurisdiction. Attorney Miller filed a motion to withdraw the negligent credentialing count and continued with litigation of the remaining two counts. Is Attorney Miller subject to sanction?

    a. Yes, because he should have given his client the opportunity to seek reversal of the existing law.

    b. Yes, because he should have known of the recent decision when the petition was filed.

    c. No, because he timely withdrew the count once he discovered it was no longer supported by existing law.

    d. No, because he did not know about the recent decision when he filed the petition.

43. An attorney specializing in family law enters into a partnership with a financial planner. The partnership provides legal assistance for dissolution of marriage, along with financial advice on division of assets and creation of a comprehensive long-term financial plan. The financial planner only performs the work he is authorized to perform as a certified financial planner (CFP). The attorney is careful to separate his practice to ensure that the financial planner doesn't affect his compliance with his professional obligations. Is the attorney subject to discipline under the Rules of Professional Conduct?

    a. Yes, because partnerships are prohibited between attorneys and non-attorneys.

    b. Yes, because some of the activities of the partnership constitute the practice of law.

    c. No, because the attorney has ensured that the financial planner is not affecting his professional obligations as an attorney.

    d. No, because the financial planner performs only the work he is authorized to perform as a certified financial planner (CFP).

44. Attorney Sharp became reacquainted with a college friend who is now a licensed psychiatrist. The two played golf together and, after discussing their specialties, determined that they might be able to assist their respective clients with a referral arrangement. The psychiatrist, Dr. Lee, specializes in the treatment of post-traumatic stress disorder, often arising from traumatic family situations; Attorney Sharp, specializing in family law, often represents clients who need psychiatric support after family dissolution. The psychiatrist advises that he keeps business cards of local attorneys, but would be willing to refer clients exclusively to Attorney Sharp in the future. Attorney Sharp, in turn, offers to provide Dr. Lee's name to his clients that need psychiatric counseling. The two enter into a formal agreement, but place a disclaimer on all referral sheets to inform clients of the arrangement. Is Attorney Sharp subject to discipline?

   a. Yes, because Dr. Lee agreed to refer his clients exclusively to Attorney Sharp.
   b. Yes, because Attorney Sharp offered something of value to Dr. Lee.
   c. No, because Dr. Lee is a non-attorney professional.
   d. No, because the referral sheets provide clients with an appropriate disclaimer.

45. Attorney Scott specializes in family law and has gained a reputation for aggressively advocating for her female clients to recover large settlements in divorce proceedings. This has proven to be lucrative for her financially, as she typically receives a substantial percentage of the settlement in fees. When retained by a client, Attorney Scott enters into an agreement whereby she receives 25 percent of her client's divorce settlement before trial, or 33 percent if an award is received at trial. Is Attorney Scott subject to discipline?

   a. Yes, because contingent fees are prohibited in a domestic relations matter.
   b. Yes, because the fee is unreasonable based on the skill required to negotiate a divorce settlement.
   c. No, because the clients consent to the arrangement by signing an agreement when they retain Attorney Scott.
   d. No, because this fee arrangement allows clients to obtain representation that they might not otherwise be able to afford.

46. Mrs. Tucker, a research pharmacist, moves from the Midwest to California to accept a position with a pharmaceutical company. She searches for a home and is interested in purchasing a property for sale by the owner without assistance from a realtor or an attorney. A friend recommends Art Levy, an attorney, to help Mrs. Tucker negotiate the sale and assist with closing. Attorney Levy contacts the seller and advises that he is facilitating price negotiations as a disinterested intermediary. Upon obtaining the seller's asking price, Attorney Levy advises Mrs. Tucker that the asking price is fair, but that she could likely negotiate for a lesser amount. Mrs. Tucker makes an offer to the seller for the full asking price. The parties complete the sale, both satisfied with the outcome. Is Attorney Levy subject to discipline?

   a. Yes, because he told the seller he was a disinterested intermediary.
   b. Yes, because Mrs. Tucker agreed to pay the full asking price when she could have negotiated for a lower price.
   c. No, because the house sold for the seller's asking price.
   d. No, because Attorney Levy advised Mrs. Tucker truthfully that the asking price was fair.

47. A defendant is on trial for rape. During closing arguments, the prosecutor accurately reviews the testimony for the jury. He concludes by stating, "The defendant's whole case is based on the testimony of his brother, who claims that the defendant was with him at the time of the rape. I believe the defendant's brother is lying to protect him, and I think you know he's lying, too." The prosecutor reasonably believes the defendant's brother is lying. Is the prosecutor subject to discipline?

    a.   Yes, because the prosecutor asserted his personal opinion about the witness's credibility.
    b.   Yes, because the prosecutor asserted his personal opinion about the beliefs of the jurors.
    c.   No, because the prosecutor accurately summarized the testimony in this case.
    d.   No, because the prosecutor reasonably believed that the witness lied.

48. Attorney Ray practices in a small firm with one partner. His partner represents a plaintiff in a personal injury case that is scheduled for a two-week trial beginning in 20 days. The partner unexpectedly dies in a motor vehicle accident. Attorney Ray obtains consent from the plaintiff to assume representation in the pending lawsuit. Attorney Ray files a motion for continuance of the trial, stating that he has doubled his caseload by assuming his partner's cases, and does not believe he will have adequate time to become familiar enough with the case to try it in 20 days. Defense counsel objects to the motion, but the court grants the continuance. Is Attorney Ray subject to discipline?

    a.   Yes, because the continuance could prejudice the defendant.
    b.   Yes, because Attorney Ray evoked sympathy over the death of his partner and used this to influence the court's decision.
    c.   No, because Attorney Ray's request was accurate and reasonable.
    d.   No, because the continuance will give Attorney Ray's client an advantage in this case.

49. A moderate-sized firm specializing in small business law is seeking to expand its practice by representing larger corporations. The firm is retained by Acme Inc. to handle all of its corporate work. At its monthly meetings, the firm's attorneys are asked to give detailed reports on the legal work they are completing for Acme. The purpose is to educate the attorneys on the breadth of services the firm has to offer Acme. When Acme's COO incidentally becomes aware of this, he sends an email to the firm's managing partner, advising that he believes Acme's confidentiality is being violated in these monthly discussions. Is it proper for the firm's attorneys to give detailed reports of their work for Acme?

    a.   Yes, because absent Acme's instructions otherwise, the attorneys may discuss client information with other attorneys in the firm.
    b.   Yes, the attorneys in the firm may discuss Acme's information, regardless of Acme's instructions otherwise, so long as the information is not to the detriment of Acme.
    c.   No, because discussing Acme's information increases the risk of improper disclosure to persons outside the firm.
    d.   No, because the attorneys may not disclose confidential information, even within the firm, unless it is necessary to provide adequate representation to Acme.

50. Several college students are charged as minors in possession of alcohol at a college fraternity party. Wayne, one of the students at the party, seeks representation from Attorney Walters against the charges. The charges were brought in Texas, where a minor is defined as a person less than 21 years of age. Wayne discloses to Attorney Walters that his state-issued driver's license indicates he is 22 years old, but admits that this is a fake ID. Wayne asks Attorney Walters not to reveal his true date of birth at the trial on the minor in possession charge. Attorney Walters advises Wayne that he will be questioned as a witness at the trial, to which Wayne responds that he will not reveal his true age. At trial, Attorney Walters asks Wayne his date of birth and Wayne gives the false date listed on his fake ID. Attorney Walters does nothing in response to Wayne's answer. Is Attorney Walters subject to discipline?

    a. Yes, because he used Wayne's date of birth in defense of the charges with knowledge that it was false.

    b. Yes, because Wayne violated the law by obtaining a fake ID.

    c. No, because the information disclosed by Wayne was protected by attorney-client privilege.

    d. No, because Wayne's real date of birth was not at issue in the trial.

51. Attorney Thorpe, a plaintiff's attorney, is campaigning for election as a local circuit court judge. Attorney Hope previously practiced in a firm with Attorney Thorpe, but the partnership dissolved primarily because Attorney Hope found Attorney Thorpe very difficult to work with. According to Attorney Hope, his former partner was ill-tempered, impatient, and quick to anger, which resulted in the firm losing a number of loyal clients. At a local bar association function at which candidates were allowed to introduce themselves, a news reporter polled the attendees for their opinions and comments. Attorney Hope was approached by the reporter. He commented on camera that he believed Attorney Thorpe would be a very poor choice for a judge based on his temperament and demeanor. Were Attorney Hope's comments improper?

    a. Yes, because the comments were derogatory to the judiciary.

    b. Yes, because attorneys are prohibited from making public statements about judicial candidates.

    c. No, because Attorney Hope was not campaigning against Attorney Thorpe.

    d. No, because Attorney Hope reasonably believed his comments about Attorney Thorpe.

52. Attorney Rose is representing Mrs. Ride in a personal injury case resulting from a motor vehicle accident. He agrees to represent Mrs. Ride on a contingency fee basis, but requires her to pay expenses such as deposition and expert witness fees as they are billed on a monthly basis. Early in the investigation of the case, Mrs. Ride advises that she cannot afford to pay the expenses and asks Attorney Rose to pay for them, deducting them later from the anticipated settlement or damages award. Attorney Rose declines Mrs. Ride's request, and suggests she consider taking out a loan to pay the expenses. Believing she has a good case, Attorney Rose goes a step further and offers to co-sign as a guarantor on Mrs. Ride's loan. Is it appropriate for Attorney Rose to assist Mrs. Ride with her loan?

    a. Yes, because Attorney Rose accepted the case on a contingency fee basis.

    b. Yes, because the loan is being used to pay for expenses incurred in the investigation of the claim, which Attorney Rose agreed to pursue.

    c. No, because Attorney Rose is financing Mrs. Ride's claim.

    d. No, because Attorney Rose is providing his credit to Mrs. Ride.

53. Mrs. White hires Attorney Boone to draft her will. As Attorney Boone prepares the will, he realizes that Mrs. White is in need of expendable income to pay off certain debt. He notes that Mrs. White owns several hundred shares of Microsoft. Recognizing this as a means to help both Mrs. White and himself financially, Attorney Boone offers to purchase the shares from Mrs. White for 95 percent of their current market value. In a written agreement, Attorney Boone clarifies that this is a private purchase, and advises Mrs. White to consider seeking legal advice from another attorney. He gives Mrs. White 24 hours to accept or decline the offer. The following day, Mrs. White returns a signed copy of the agreement to Attorney Boone accepting the offer. Is Attorney Boone subject to discipline?

   a. No, because he advised Mrs. White to seek the advice of another attorney.
   b. No, because the offer was reasonable.
   c. No, because Mrs. White gave informed consent.
   d. Yes, because 24 hours was not sufficient time to consider the offer.

54. Attorney Patrick was retained by Mrs. Dennis to bring a medical malpractice suit against a local surgeon. In preparing the case for trial, Attorney Patrick finds correspondence to another attorney within Mrs. Dennis's documents. He questions Mrs. Dennis to ensure that any attorney-client relationship between Mrs. Dennis and the other attorney has been terminated. Mrs. Dennis confirms, explaining that she paid the other attorney $1,000 as a retainer, but despite her frequent inquiries, the attorney did no work on the file for six months. The week prior, Mrs. Dennis called and advised him that she was looking for another attorney. He reluctantly returned her retainer. Mrs. Dennis tells Attorney Patrick that she "just wants to forget it," explaining that the other attorney is a family friend. Attorney Patrick believes the other attorney was negligent in failing to work on Mrs. Dennis's case for six months. Is Attorney Patrick subject to discipline if he does not report the other attorney's conduct?

   a. Yes, because Attorney Patrick has knowledge that the other attorney was guilty of professional misconduct.
   b. Yes, because Mrs. Dennis received no legal services from her retainer fee.
   c. No, because Mrs. Dennis was satisfied with the return of her retainer fee.
   d. No, because Mrs. Dennis did not agree to Attorney Patrick reporting the information.

55. An attorney represents the seller in negotiations regarding the sale of a well-established bakery in a historic downtown suburban area. The seller advises the attorney in confidence that, due to the current pandemic, the once very profitable bakery has shown only modest profits this year. It appears the buyer may be losing interest and when he asks specific questions regarding the bakery's recent financial performance, the attorney responds, "This bakery is a local treasure… where else can you make so many people happy with steady profits from the sale of wholesome products?" The buyer purchases the bakery but is quickly discouraged by the marginal profits. Is the attorney subject to discipline?

   a. Yes, because he knowingly inflated the profitability of the bakery to the buyer.
   b. Yes, because he made a false statement of material fact to the buyer.
   c. No, because the attorney was representing the best interest of the seller.
   d. No, because embellishment or exaggeration ("puffing") does not rise to the level of a false statement of material fact.

56. A class action lawsuit is filed against a pharmacist for allegations of diluting chemotherapy medications in order to increase profits. The class is made up of patients and family members injured by receiving the non-therapeutic medications. The pharmacist's liability insurance carrier denies coverage because the allegations constitute willful actions by the pharmacist. Without insurance, the pharmacist cannot find a defense attorney to represent him. The court appoints Attorney Lincoln, a seasoned personal injury trial attorney who practices with a large law firm that supports pro bono work. The case garners a great deal of publicity and is generally viewed as morally reprehensible by the public. Attorney Lincoln is particularly offended by the case because his wife recently died of cancer.

Which of the following most accurately describes Attorney Lincoln's professional responsibility?

    a. He must proceed with representing the pharmacist because he was appointed by the tribunal.

    b. He may seek approval to decline representation by advising the court that his wife recently died of cancer, which he believes will impair his relationship with the client.

    c. He may avoid appointment by arguing that it will create an unreasonable financial burden on him.

    d. He may avoid appointment by arguing that, as a personal injury attorney, he is unqualified to effectively represent the pharmacist's interests.

57. Mr. Horn retains Attorney Short to defend him when his ex-wife files for modification of alimony. Mr. Horn's sister knows that he has been struggling financially and believes the ex-wife's claim is unjustified. She contacts Attorney Short and advises that she has mailed him $1,500 to assist with her brother's legal fees. She requests that Attorney Short not disclose the payment to Mr. Horn because she believes he would be embarrassed by the assistance. Is it proper for Attorney Short to accept the sister's payment?

    a. No, because Attorney Short is neither informing Mr. Horn nor obtaining his consent to accept the payment.

    b. No, because the sister is paying fees for legal services that were not provided to her.

    c. Yes, because the sister's payment is not being made to influence the attorney's defense of the case.

    d. Yes, because Mr. Horn's bill will be reduced in proportion to the amount received from his sister.

58. District Attorney Coble is the lead prosecutor in the trial of a defendant accused of armed robbery of a convenience store. The defendant claims he was at his brother's house at the time of the robbery. An employee of the convenience store testifies at trial, stating she identified the defendant from a notebook of photos shown to her by the police. A recording of the 911 call reporting the robbery and describing the accused is also offered into evidence. The defendant is convicted and sentenced for the robbery. Sometime after the trial, defense counsel uncovers additional evidence that the convenience store employee initially chose a photograph of a different person, not the defendant, from those shown to her by police. Defense counsel further learns that District Attorney Coble knew of this evidence but did not disclose it to the defense. District Attorney Coble argues that defense counsel did not request this evidence through pretrial discovery. Is District Attorney Coble subject to discipline?

    a. No, because defense counsel failed to make a pretrial discovery request for the evidence.
    b. No, because District Attorney Coble did not have to initially disclose evidence that was discovered later.
    c. Yes, because the defendant was convicted solely on the photo identification by the employee.
    d. Yes, because the subsequently discovered evidence tends to negate the defendant's culpability for the offense.

59. An attorney practices in a small firm specializing in estate planning. At the church she attends, she discovers there is a Sunday morning Bible study group for seniors aged 60 and older. She attends the Bible study one Sunday morning and brings coffee mugs as free gifts, along with business cards. She describes her services to the seniors and encourages them to schedule an appointment with her to discuss their estate planning needs. Her sales gimmick is, "Bring in your coffee mug for a refill and a 10 percent discount on the drafting for your will." Is the attorney subject to discipline?

    a. No, because the attorney is a member of the church and therefore has an established relationship with the other church members.
    b. No, because the attorney is responding to a potential need in the church community and, by offering a discount, would not be performing the services with the motive of financial gain.
    c. Yes, because the attorney has reason to believe some of these seniors are already represented by other attorneys in the church.
    d. Yes, because the attorney is soliciting legal business from persons who are not current clients.

60. A solo practitioner specializes in personal injury cases. He agrees to represent a plaintiff on a contingency fee basis in a lawsuit against a driver who collided with him in a motor vehicle accident. Through discovery, the attorney learns that the defendant is claiming the accident occurred as a result of a rare medical condition that may have led to him "blacking out" while driving. The attorney recognizes that deposing the defendant's expert medical witness will require a thorough understanding of a medical condition with which he is unfamiliar. He wants to continue representing the plaintiff, so he makes the decision to contact a fellow attorney who specializes in medical malpractice and has tried cases involving this particular medical condition. The second attorney agrees to participate in trial for the purpose of presenting evidence regarding the medical condition. They agree to split the contingency fee in proportion to the services performed. The plaintiff's attorney will provide the plaintiff with a written statement explaining the division of fees at the conclusion of the case. Is the arrangement between the two attorneys appropriate?

a. Yes, because the fees will be divided in proportion to the services performed.
b. Yes, because the fee paid by the plaintiff will not increase in spite of the additional attorney.
c. No, because the plaintiff was not advised of the agreement between the two attorneys.
d. No, because the plaintiff's attorney will not provide the plaintiff with an explanation of the fee division until the end of the case.

Answer Key and Explanations for Test #1

1. D: Model Rule 8.4(c) states that professional misconduct includes engaging in conduct involving dishonesty, fraud, deceit, and misrepresentation. By assisting his client in tax evasion, Attorney Harrison is subject to discipline for dishonest conduct, regardless of whether his client is audited.

Although gambling, intoxication, and disturbing the peace may not have been the best behavioral choices, they do not fall within the intent of Model Rule 8.4, which is the interference with the administration of justice.

2. C: Model Rule 5.4(d) states that a lawyer must not practice with or in the form of a professional corporation or association authorized to practice law for a profit if a non-lawyer owns an interest in or is a corporate director or officer of the corporation. Mrs. Powell, a non-lawyer, is serving as an officer of the corporation, so it is not appropriate for Attorney Gregg to practice with the corporation. One exception to this rule is that a fiduciary representative of the estate of a lawyer may hold the interest of the lawyer for a reasonable time during administration. Under this condition, it is appropriate for Mrs. McGinnis to hold her deceased husband's stock awaiting probate.

The restrictions imposed by Rule 5.4(d) are not negated by the fact that the associates do not hold shares, nor by the fact that Mrs. Powell is not practicing law. The intent of the rule is to prohibit the formation of a professional corporation between lawyers and non-lawyers.

3. A: With limited exceptions, Model Rule 1.6(a) prohibits an attorney from revealing information relating to the representation of a client unless the client gives informed consent. It was improper for Attorney Hill to turn over her client files containing confidential information without obtaining informed consent from her clients. The issue is not supervision of Attorney Bradley nor his assurances to maintain confidentiality. While finding alternative representation may have been necessary, Attorney Hill should not have proceeded with doing so until she had obtained consent from her clients.

4. A: Model Rule 1.9 provides that a lawyer who has formerly represented a client in a matter shall not thereafter represent another person in the same matter unless the former client gives informed consent. Attorney Morgan should decline representation of Mr. Tucker because he previously represented Connecticut in the same matter. Further, Model Rule 1.10(a) prohibits lawyers associated in a firm from representing a client when any one of them practicing alone would be prohibited from doing so pursuant to Rule 1.9. As such, referring Mr. Tucker to another associate in the firm would be prohibited.

While informed consent is an exception to the prohibition against representation, the consent from the former client (in this case, Connecticut Insurance Company) is required, not the consent from Mr. Tucker.

5. C: Model Rule 3.7(a) prohibits a lawyer from representing a client at a trial in which the lawyer is likely to be a necessary witness unless: (1) the testimony relates to an uncontested issue, (2) the testimony relates to the nature and value of legal services rendered in the case, or (3) disqualification of the lawyer would work substantial hardship on the client. Because Attorney Marsh is the only one who saw the driver texting, he is likely a necessary witness. The case is contested by the driver, but does not relate to legal services, so exceptions (1) and (2) do not apply. Because there are cell phone records available to establish the runner's case against the driver,

Attorney Marsh's disqualification will not be a substantial hardship to the case, so exception (3) does not apply. Therefore, Rule 3.7(a) prohibits Attorney Marsh from representing the runner. The rule applies regardless of the client's consent.

6. C: With limited exception, Model Rule 1.6 prohibits a lawyer from revealing information relating to the representation of a client unless the client gives informed consent. Exceptions include situations such as disclosure to prevent the commission of a crime, protect another from death or bodily harm, or to defend the attorney from charges against him. The information revealed by this client does not qualify as one of these exceptions. Because the client acted before Attorney Case represented him, it would be a violation of the rules for Attorney Case to reveal the client's confidential information. Attorney Case is not required to withdraw as counsel, nor would it be appropriate for him to condition his continued representation upon the client's disclosure to the court.

7. B: When an attorney represents two or more clients, Model Rule 1.8(g) prohibits the attorney from participating in making an aggregate settlement of his clients' claims unless each client gives his/her written consent. The attorney disclosure must include the existence and nature of all the claims, and of the participation of each person in the settlement. Attorney Hart obtained consent from each of his clients, but without disclosure of the amounts received by the other plaintiffs. Although Attorney Hart believes he is in the best position to evaluate his clients' damages, it is not his place to decide the best outcome for each. This holds true regardless of whether the settlement might be jeopardized by disclosure, and regardless of whether the plaintiffs agreed to their allocated amount.

8. C: Model Rule 3.4(f) prohibits a lawyer from requesting a person other than a client to refrain from voluntarily giving relevant information to another party unless: (1) the person is a relative or an employee or other agent of a client, and (2) the lawyer reasonably believes that the person's interests will not be adversely affected by refraining from giving such information. Here, the eyewitness does not appear to fall within any of these exceptions, and therefore Attorney James should not have asked her to refrain from testifying. The rule requires only that the attorney ask the witness to refrain from testimony. It does not require inducement. The rule is binding even though the witness did not want to be involved at the trial and regardless of whether she had been subpoenaed.

9. D: Model Rule 1.8(d) states that a lawyer cannot make or negotiate an agreement giving the lawyer literary or media rights to a portrayal or account based in substantial part on information relating to the representation. There are no prohibitions in the rules against assisting a client in obtaining a bank loan or accepting a credit card as a form of payment. Further, Model Rule 1.8(i) allows an attorney to accept property in payment for services, such as an ownership interest in a business, provided that it does not involve acquiring a proprietary interest in a cause of action.

10. A: Model Rule 6.3 states that a lawyer may serve as a director, officer, or member of a legal services organization apart from the law firm in which the lawyer practices, notwithstanding that the organization serves persons having interests adverse to a client of the lawyer. The lawyer shall not knowingly participate in a decision or action of the organization where the decision or action could have a material adverse effect on the representation of a client of the organization whose interests are adverse to a client of the lawyer.

Attorney Paul may remain on the board of directors even though the legal aid organization represents clients with interests adverse to those of the clients represented by his firm. However, Attorney Paul should not vote on this proposal because it could have a material adverse effect on the representation of legal aid clients with interests adverse to the firm's clients. The rule does not prohibit Attorney Paul from serving on the board of directors, so he does not have to resign. Further, he is not required to report to the state bar association because he has not violated any rules.

11. D: Model Rule 1.8(c) states that a lawyer must not solicit any substantial gift from a client, including a testamentary gift; or prepare on behalf of a client an instrument giving the lawyer or a person related to the lawyer any substantial gift, unless the lawyer or other recipient of the gift is related to the client. Attorney Henry is allowed to prepare the will, including a gift to herself, because the client is her grandmother. Here, the key element is not the appropriateness of the representation or the knowledge/voluntary nature, but rather that the attorney and client are related.

12. A: Model Rule of Judicial Conduct 3.13(a) prohibits a judge from accepting any gifts, loans, bequests, benefits, or other things of value if acceptance would appear to a reasonable person to undermine the judge's independence, integrity, or impartiality. The gift to Judge Alexander could reasonably be perceived as intended to influence the judge's decision in favor of the construction company. This would not be mitigated by an equal gift from the owner. A direct business relationship is not required by the rule. Finally, a judge is prohibited from accepting gifts under certain circumstances, including those imposed by Rule 3.13(a).

13. D: Model Rule 1.1 states that a lawyer must provide competent representation to a client, which requires the thoroughness and preparation reasonably necessary for the representation. Attorney Ferrara knew that she would not have the time to properly prepare for Mrs. Connor's case. Therefore, she acted reasonably by declining the representation and recommending she meet with another attorney. The facts do not indicate that Attorney Ferrara's advertising was false or misleading. She declined representation due to workload, not because she doesn't practice employment law. Finally, she had no duty to give notice of the statute of limitations because she recommended Mrs. Connor consult with another attorney to preserve her rights.

14. D: Model Rule 1.6(b)(1) allows an attorney to reveal information relating to the representation of a client to the extent the lawyer reasonably believes necessary to prevent reasonably certain death or substantial bodily harm. If Attorney Locke does not reveal the information, it will likely result in the harm or death of his client's wife. The attorney-client privilege does provide protection of confidential information; however, despite being protected, there is an exemption to the rule for information related to death and bodily harm. The analysis does not change in relation to the likelihood based on a history of similar crimes, nor does it change based on its prejudicial effect.

15. A: Model Rule 8.3(a) requires an attorney to report another attorney for conduct that raises a substantial question as to that lawyer's honesty, trustworthiness, or fitness as a lawyer. The attorney would be required to report his partner because misappropriating client funds raises a substantial question as to the partner's honesty.

Questionable moral judgment (as in opposing counsel's relationship with his client), family disputes, and mismanagement of personal finances are not necessarily a reflection on an attorney's fitness to practice law.

16. C: Model Rule 1.3 requires an attorney to act with reasonable diligence and promptness in representing a client. Attorney Kitt's failure to file discovery responses, appear at the deposition, or timely file a motion to set aside the default judgment shows a lack of diligence and promptness in pursuing the plaintiff's case against the defendant. Nothing within the rules requires one party to give notice to the other party of an intent to seek a default judgment. The issue here is lack of diligence, so return of attorney fees will not affect Attorney Kitt's liability.

17. A: Model Rule 3.9 requires an attorney representing a client before a non-adjudicative proceeding to disclose that the appearance is in a representative capacity. Attorney Butler's failure to disclose to the committee that he was appearing as a representative of his employer, Acme, was a violation of Rule 3.9. The rule, however, does not preclude Acme from paying Attorney Butler for his services, nor is it negated by attorney-client privilege.

18. B: Model Rule 4.2 states that, in the course of representing a client, a lawyer shall not communicate about the subject of the representation with a person the lawyer knows to be represented by another lawyer in the matter, unless the lawyer has the consent of the other lawyer or is authorized to do so by law or a court order. Although Mrs. Hart was represented by another attorney and Attorney Fletcher communicated with her, the communication was not about the partnership dispute or ongoing negotiations, but rather about holiday plans. Rule 4.2 applies even if the represented party initiates the communication. Because the two did not discuss the subject of the representation, Attorney Fletcher's conduct was not inappropriate, regardless of any appearance of impropriety.

19. B: Model Rule 7.3(b) prohibits an attorney from soliciting professional employment from a prospective client with the significant motive of pecuniary gain. However, the rule outlines certain exceptions, including when the prospective client is another attorney, unless the other attorney makes known a desire not to be solicited or if the solicitation involves coercion, duress, or harassment. The runner was also an attorney, but she did not ask Attorney Marsh to refrain from the solicitation. Further, the solicitation did not involve coercion, duress, or harassment. As such, Attorney Marsh was not prohibited from soliciting business from the runner. This exception is neither negated nor supported by Attorney Marsh's witnessing of the accident or his motives to help the runner.

20. B: Model Rule 3.5(a) prohibits an attorney from communicating or attempting to influence a prospective juror or other official by means prohibited by law. Defense counsel instructed the defendants to release advertising at a time that would likely influence the opinions of prospective jurors in their favor. There is no indication that the information was false, and although the campaign was already planned, it was released early in order to directly impact the jury selection. The rule does not require direct contact, only an attempt to influence.

21. B: Model Rule 1.6(b)(5) allows an attorney to reveal confidential information to establish a defense on behalf of the lawyer in a controversy between the lawyer and the client. Because the buyer is suing both Mr. Snow and Attorney Green over the same real estate transaction, Attorney Green may reveal the information to defend himself. Model Rule 1.6 applies to both civil and criminal actions. Although the disclosure may be prejudicial to Mr. Snow, the rule still allows Attorney Green to defend himself against a legal action.

22. C: Model Rule 5.5(a) states that a lawyer may not practice law in a jurisdiction in violation of that jurisdiction's regulation of the legal profession. As a rule, Vincent could not practice in Kansas without a license (as required by Kansas regulations). Under limited circumstances, however, an attorney admitted to the bar in one state may seek to temporarily provide legal services in another state, through "admission pro hac vice" [Rule 5.5(c)].

In option B, Vincent could assist Mr. Abernathy in representing himself, but he cannot appear and represent him without being licensed in Kansas. Further, in option D, the unauthorized practice of law is not negated by waiver of legal fees.

23. A: Although Model Rule 1.15(a) prohibits the commingling of attorney and client funds, Model Rule 1.15(b) provides that a lawyer may deposit the lawyer's own funds in a client trust account for the sole purpose of paying bank service charges on that account, but only in an amount necessary for that purpose. Attorney Blue acted inappropriately by depositing more of the firm's funds in the client trust account than were necessary to pay the service fee. While deposits from the firm's account may ultimately protect the client's funds, these deposits exceed that which is necessary to pay the service fee. The fact that Attorney Blue keeps detailed records is irrelevant if there is impermissible commingling of funds.

24. C: Model Rule 8.5(a) states that a lawyer admitted to practice in a jurisdiction is subject to the disciplinary authority of that jurisdiction, regardless of where the lawyer's conduct occurred. While option A is technically correct and option B is incorrect, the rule goes on to state, "A lawyer not admitted to practice in this jurisdiction is also subject to the disciplinary authority of this jurisdiction if the lawyer provides or offers to provide any legal services in this jurisdiction." This would mean that both Missouri and Illinois have jurisdiction. This is supported by the rule that concludes with the statement, "A lawyer may be subject to the disciplinary authority of both this jurisdiction and another jurisdiction for the same conduct." Therefore, option C is the most accurate response.

25. C: In filing the motion for default judgment, defense counsel is acting in the best interest of his client: the hospital. This includes expediting litigation (Model Rule 3.2) and diligent and prompt representation (Model Rule 1.3).

While Model Rule 3.4 generally covers fairness to opposing counsel, nothing within the rule requires defense counsel, procedurally or as a professional courtesy, to warn opposing counsel of a default judgment. While an independent review by a qualified healthcare provider is appropriate, the reviewer's opinion would not form the basis for the motion for default judgment, so option D is not the best answer.

26. A: Model Rule 1.11(a)(2) states that a lawyer who has formerly served as a public officer or employee of the government shall not otherwise represent a client in connection with a matter in which the lawyer participated personally and substantially as a public officer or employee unless the appropriate government agency gives its informed consent, confirmed in writing, to the representation. The purpose of Rule 1.11 is to prevent former government employees from unfairly exploiting knowledge they obtained by virtue of their employment. Attorney Booth had nothing to do with the Department of Homeland Security's investigation and thus had no knowledge to exploit. Although the Department consented, it was unnecessary. Even though Attorney Booth was employed by the department during the time of the investigation, and even though the facts from the investigation gave rise to the current causes of action, he did not participate "personally or substantially" in the investigation and had no knowledge of the facts from the investigation.

27. D: Model Rule 1.14(b) provides that when a lawyer reasonably believes that a client has diminished capacity or is at risk of substantial physical, financial, or other harm unless action is taken and cannot adequately act in the client's own interest, the lawyer may take reasonably necessary protective action, including consulting with individuals or entities that have the ability to take action to protect the client and, in appropriate cases, seeking the appointment of a guardian ad litem, conservator, or guardian. Further, when taking this action, the lawyer is impliedly authorized under Rule 1.6(a) to reveal information about the client, but only to the extent reasonably necessary to protect the client's interests.

28. D: Model Rule 1.1 requires an attorney to provide competent representation to a client. Competent representation requires the legal knowledge, skill, thoroughness, and preparation reasonably necessary for the representation. Further, Model Rule 1.16(d) states that, upon termination of representation, a lawyer shall take steps to the extent reasonably practicable to protect a client's interests. Attorney McGinnis failed to oversee the associate's work as would have been reasonably practicable to protect Beta's interests. Licensure does not necessarily equate to competence in all areas of the law. The facts do not indicate a financial hardship in retaining the case, and even if this were the case, financial hardship is not by itself a justifiable reason to withdraw representation. Finally, Beta's consent may have been required by the firm, but the issue here is competence to handle the case.

29. C: Model Rule 1.15 requires an attorney to hold property of clients separate from the attorney's own property. Once the funds were identified as belonging to the attorney (in the form of fees earned), they should have been removed from the client account.

It is permissible to require an advanced payment, so long as those fees are kept in the client trust account. Here, although the billing statements were accurate, the funds remained impermissibly commingled in the client account.

30. A: Model Rule 1.15(d) states that a lawyer must promptly deliver to the client or third person any funds or other property that the client or third person is entitled to receive and, upon request by the client or third person, shall promptly render a full accounting regarding such property. Attorney Salvador received the funds on Friday and had an obligation under the rule to promptly notify his clients that the checks were available and to deliver them if the clients so requested. Waiting over the weekend without notifying the clients is not "prompt" delivery. The fact that banks may be closed or that the clients did not object does not relieve Attorney Salvador of his responsibility to notify them. Depositing the checks in the client trust account is appropriate (as opposed to keeping them separate), but not until the clients have been notified and agree to the deposit.

31. B: Model Rule 3.6(a) prohibits an attorney from making an extrajudicial statement that the lawyer knows or reasonably should know will be disseminated by means of public communication and will have a substantial likelihood of materially prejudicing an adjudicative proceeding in the matter. However, there is an exception for information contained in a public record. Because the county official has sued the television station for slander, the identity of the reporter is a matter of public record. The rule addresses "prejudicing an adjudicative proceeding which can occur before a trial commences." While prospective jurors may learn of the statement, and while the reporter may be a potential witness, the important point from this rule is that attorneys are allowed to make statements of public record.

32. C: Model Rule 7.1 prohibits a lawyer from making a false or misleading communication about the lawyer or the lawyer's services. A communication is false or misleading if it contains a material misrepresentation of fact or law, or omits a fact necessary to make the statement considered as a whole not materially misleading. Attorney Byrne made statements to her husband's co-worker about her specialties that were misleading. "Personal injury" does not equate to medical malpractice. The statement could lead to an expectation by the co-worker that Attorney Byrne specializes in medical malpractice. While the statement about awards was truthful, it could be misleading if not accompanied by a disclaimer regarding motor vehicle accidents. Regardless of whether the conversation was a solicitation by Attorney Byrne or was initiated by the co-worker, the rule does not provide an exception for statements that are false or misleading.

33. D: Model Rule 1.2(d) states that a lawyer cannot counsel a client to engage or assist a client in conduct that the lawyer knows is criminal or fraudulent. However, the lawyer may discuss the legal consequences of any proposed course of conduct with a client and may counsel or assist the client in making a good faith effort to determine the application of a law.

Providing factual information regarding the mask mandate, regardless of whether he billed for the services, did not rise to the level of "assisting" the store owner to violate the mandate. Further, the attorney was not required to make a determination as to how the store owner used the information.

34. B: According to Model Rule 1.1, in order to maintain the requisite knowledge and skill, a lawyer should keep abreast of changes in the law. The rule, however, does not specify that the knowledge be obtained through CLE. Independent study can be just as effective. Neither malpractice insurance nor the availability of free education courses impacts the competence requirements of Rule 1.1.

35. D: Model Rule 2.1 allows an attorney rendering advice to refer not only to law but to other considerations such as moral, economic, social, and political factors that may be relevant to the client's situation. Attorney Curry properly gave advice that included both legal and economic factors. The determination of whether Attorney Curry's conduct was proper depends on the rule, not upon whether the president of Future Tech accepted his advice or not. Further, Attorney Curry's duty to diligently pursue any cause of action is still subject to other controlling rules, including Rule 2.1.

36. C: Model Rule 1.7 prohibits an attorney from representing a client if the representation creates a concurrent conflict of interest. However, a lawyer may represent a client if: (1) the lawyer reasonably believes that they will be able to provide competent and diligent representation to each affected client; (2) the representation is not prohibited by law; (3) the representation does not involve the assertion of a claim by one client against another client represented by the lawyer in the same litigation or other proceeding before a tribunal; and (4) each affected client gives informed consent, confirmed in writing.

Here, there is little risk that either Mr. Kohls or Mrs. Kohls' interests will be compromised by Attorney Evans's representation, and they both consented in writing to the representation. While Attorney Evans previously represented both parties in previous matters, this would not automatically make joint representation appropriate in the divorce proceedings. With regard to attorney-client privilege, the prevailing rule is that the privilege does not attach between commonly represented clients. Finally, the rules do not require an attorney to recommend independent counsel before clients agree to joint representation.

37. B: Model Rule 1.16(b) allows an attorney to withdraw from representing a client for a number of delineated reasons, including perpetration of a crime or fraud, unreasonable financial burden, and when "other good cause for withdrawal exists." Attorney Connor's fee increase does not meet any valid reason for withdrawal and is essentially being made so he can earn more money. While the fee increase will clearly reduce the amount of Mr. Bean's recovery, it would be speculative to comment on how adverse the effect would be on him. While Attorney Connor offered to find another attorney, and regardless of whether the fee is reasonable, he had no valid reason to withdraw from representation.

38. C: Model Rule of Judicial Conduct 2.9 prohibits a judge from considering ex parte communications concerning a pending or impending matter. Even though defense counsel was allowed to present evidence on the motion during trial, this ex parte communication with plaintiff's counsel could influence the judge's original opinion regarding the evidence, regardless of whether plaintiff's counsel asked for a change in the ruling.

39. A: According to Model Rule 1.7, a lawyer must receive informed consent from one client before representing another client in the event that representing the second client would have a directly adverse effect on the first client. This is true even though the representation involves two unrelated causes of action. While Mr. Thomas knows of the conflict, Mr. Hanks has no knowledge and has not given his consent to the representation. The important professional conduct issue here is the conflict between two clients, not how it might impact the attorney's arguments on appeal.

40. B: Model Rule 2.4(b) states that a lawyer serving as a third-party neutral shall inform unrepresented parties that the lawyer is not representing them. When the lawyer knows or reasonably should know that a party does not understand the lawyer's role in the matter, the lawyer shall explain the difference between the lawyer's role as a third-party neutral and a lawyer's role as one who represents a client.

Mrs. Rudolph is unrepresented and has made statements indicating she does not understand Attorney Dixon's role. Attorney Dixon should explain the difference between the role of a retained attorney and a mediator. While the disclosure of certain statements by Mrs. Rudolph may be favorable to the hospital, the issue is not bias by the mediator, but rather the failure to clarify his role. The rule is not trumped by the goal of resolution. Further, Attorney Dixon had reason to know that Mrs. Rudolph was confused based on her implicit statements. An explicit statement that the information was confidential is not required.

41. C: Model Rule of Judicial Conduct 2.13 states that, in making administrative appointments, a judge shall (1) exercise the power of appointment impartially and on the basis of merit; and (2) avoid nepotism, favoritism, and unnecessary appointments.

Judge Bailey appointed more bailiffs than necessary for the caseload of the courts, resulting in several bailiffs having insufficient work. Judge Bailey's actions did not amount to favoritism, even though the decision was unwarranted given the current caseload. Finally, while Judge Bailey had the power of appointment, he was still required to exercise that power within the rules.

42. C: Model Rule 3.1 states that a lawyer shall neither bring or defend a proceeding, nor assert or controvert an issue therein, unless there is a basis in law and fact for doing so that is not frivolous. Attorney Miller made a good faith argument and withdrew it when it became clear it was no longer valid. The comments to Rule 3.1 recognize that the law is never static. Therefore, Attorney Miller should not be held to a standard of "should have known" about recent changes in the law. However, the fact that it was unknown at the time of filing does not imply that Attorney Miller can keep arguing an invalid point or agree to continue with a frivolous claim at the request of his client.

43. B: Model Rule 5.5(a) prohibits a lawyer from assisting another person in the unauthorized practice of law. Partnerships are allowed between attorneys and non-attorneys, so long as the non-attorney is not practicing law.

While the attorney and financial planner in this scenario are careful to separate their work by discipline, the key point is that the "partnership" is providing legal services and not just the licensed attorney.

44. A: Model Rule 7.2(b)(4) prohibits a lawyer from compensating, giving, or promising anything of value to a person for recommending the lawyer's services, except that a lawyer may refer clients to another lawyer or a non-lawyer professional pursuant to an agreement if the reciprocal referral agreement is not exclusive. Attorney Sharp may not refer clients to Dr. Lee because the referral agreement is exclusive. The fact that Dr. Lee is a non-attorney and that he is being given something of value does not prohibit the arrangement. On the contrary, the disclaimer does not exempt the arrangement. The issue is the exclusivity of the arrangement.

45. A: Model Rule 1.5(d) prohibits a lawyer from entering into an arrangement for any fee in a domestic relations matter, the payment or amount of which is contingent upon the securing of a divorce or upon the amount of alimony or support or property settlement. Attorney Scott is prohibited from entering into this contingency fee arrangement with her divorce clients, regardless of whether they consent to the arrangement. The reasonableness of the amount does not impact this rule, nor does the fact that it might ease the burden of a client who might otherwise have difficulty paying attorney fees.

46. A: Model Rule 4.3 states that, in dealing on behalf of a client with a person who is not represented by counsel, a lawyer shall not state or imply that the lawyer is disinterested. Mrs. Tucker hired Attorney Levy, who acted on her behalf to negotiate the sale. Attorney Levy falsely told the seller, who was unrepresented, that he was acting as a disinterested intermediary. Neither the fact that Attorney Levy was truthful with Mrs. Tucker about the value of the property nor the fact that the seller received his asking price negate Attorney Levy's liability for the misrepresentation. Finally, Attorney Levy did not have an obligation to require Mrs. Tucker to negotiate for a lower amount.

47. A: Model Rule 3.4(e) prohibits an attorney in trial from stating a personal opinion about the credibility of a witness. The prosecutor is subject to discipline for stating his personal opinion that the defendant's brother is lying. Rule 3.4 applies regardless of whether the testimony is accurate and the attorney reasonably believes it. The issue is that the prosecutor stated his own beliefs, not that he alluded to the beliefs of the jurors.

48. C: Although Model Rule 3.2 requires a lawyer to make reasonable efforts to expedite litigation consistent with the interests of the client, it also notes that there will be occasions when a lawyer may properly seek a postponement for personal reasons. Attorney Ray requested a continuance to prepare for the trial of a case with which he was unfamiliar in order to continue competently representing a client of this firm. There is no factual basis in this question to assume that the court's decision was influenced by sympathy. If Attorney Ray had been granted a continuance for an improper reason, the defendant would have cause to argue that the continuance was prejudicial to his case and gave a favorable advantage to the plaintiff. Here, the court determined that Attorney Ray had a valid reason for seeking the continuance.

49. A: Lawyers in a firm may, in the course of the firm's practice, disclose to each other information relating to a client of the firm unless the client has instructed that particular information be confined to specific lawyers (Model Rule 1.6, Comment 5). These discussions would be prohibited if Acme instructed the firm that the information be withheld. Although the discussions may increase the risk of disclosure by virtue of the fact that more people know the information, Rule 1.6 still allows information sharing within the firm.

50. A: Model Rule 3.3(b) states that a lawyer who represents a client in an adjudicative proceeding and who knows that a person intends to engage, is engaging, or has engaged in criminal or fraudulent conduct related to the proceeding shall take reasonable remedial measures, including, if necessary, disclosure to the tribunal. Attorney Walters knew of Wayne's intent to give false testimony at trial regarding his date of birth. Attorney Walters failed to take reasonable remedial measures, such as disclosing the perjury to the court. The obligations outlined in the rule are not negated by attorney-client privilege. Further, the issue in this case is not that Wayne obtained a fake ID, but rather that he lied about his real date of birth, which effectively disposed of a charge based on age.

51. D: Model Rule 8.2 prohibits a lawyer from making a statement that the lawyer knows to be false or with reckless disregard as to its truth or falsity concerning the qualifications or integrity of a judge, adjudicatory officer, public legal officer, or of a candidate for election or appointment to judicial or legal office. Here, Attorney Hope made comments about Attorney Thorpe's temperament and demeanor in regard to his qualifications to serve as a judge based on Attorney Hope's reasonable belief after practicing with him as a partner. Attorney Hope's comments were not directed at the integrity of the judiciary. His comments were not prohibited in general, but must be based on reasonable belief. The rule applies to any comments regarding a candidate, not just those made by an opponent.

52. B: Model Rule 1.8(e) prohibits an attorney from providing financial assistance to a client in connection with litigation except when advancing costs and expenses of litigation, the payment of which may be contingent upon the outcome of the matter. Because Attorney Rose's financial assistance (by co-signing Mrs. Ride's loan) will be used for expenses of litigation, it is proper under the rules. A contingency fee arrangement does not make advancement of any and all funds appropriate. They must be used for the expenses of litigation. Attorney Rose is not financing Mrs. Ride's litigation, and while he is using his credit to assist her financially, this is allowable for the payment of litigation expenses.

53. D: Model Rule 1.8(a) prohibits an attorney from entering into a business transaction with a client or knowingly acquiring an ownership, possessory, security, or other pecuniary interest adverse to a client unless: (1) the transaction and terms on which the lawyer acquires the interest are fair and reasonable to the client and are fully disclosed and transmitted in writing in a manner that can be reasonably understood by the client; (2) the client is advised in writing of the desirability of seeking and is given a reasonable opportunity to seek the advice of independent legal counsel on the transaction; and (3) the client gives informed consent, in a writing signed by the client, to the essential terms of the transaction and the lawyer's role in the transaction, including whether the lawyer is representing the client in the transaction. Although Attorney Boone complied with the requirements of a written agreement, outside legal advice, and informed consent, he did not give Mrs. White a reasonable opportunity to confer with another attorney when he imposed the 24-hour deadline. Even though the offer may have been reasonable, the key missing element was the time to seek legal advice.

54. D: Ordinarily, an attorney has the duty to report another attorney's violation of the Model Rules if the violation raises a substantial question as to honesty, trustworthiness, or fitness to practice. However, because the information about the violation is protected by the attorney-client privilege, Attorney Patrick is not subject to discipline if he chooses not to report the other attorney without Mrs. Dennis's consent.

55. D: Model Rule 4.1 prohibits an attorney from knowingly making a false statement of material fact, or failing to disclose a material fact, to a third person. However, under generally accepted standards of negotiation, certain types of statements, such as estimated price or value, are considered "puffing" and do not rise to the level of a false statement of material fact.

56. B: Model Rule 6.2 states that a lawyer shall not seek to avoid appointment by a tribunal to represent a person except for good cause, such as: (a) representing the client is likely to result in violation of the Rules of Professional Conduct or other law; (b) representing the client is likely to result in an unreasonable financial burden on the lawyer; or (c) the client or the cause is so repugnant to the lawyer as to be likely to impair the client-lawyer relationship or the lawyer's ability to represent the client. Here, the actions of the pharmacist are likely repugnant to the public in general, but also specifically to Attorney Lincoln, who lost his wife to cancer. This is arguably "good cause" for seeking release from the court's appointment.

As the attorney works for a large firm that supports pro bono work, it is unlikely that an argument of unreasonable financial hardship will prevail as good cause. Further, because this is an attorney with both litigation and personal injury experience, the argument that he is unqualified will probably not prevail either.

57. A: Model Rule 1.8(f) prohibits an attorney from accepting compensation for representing a client from anyone other than the client, unless the client gives informed consent. Attorney Short cannot accept payment from Mr. Horn's sister without his consent. As long as Mr. Horn consents, there is no prohibition against his sister from paying, even though the services were not provided to her personally. While it would be improper for the sister to attempt to influence Attorney Short's defense, or for Attorney Short to receive double payment for services, the primary issue here is Mr. Horn's consent.

58. D: Model Rule 3.8 requires a prosecutor to promptly disclose to the appropriate court any new, credible, and material evidence creating a reasonable likelihood that a convicted defendant did not commit an offense for which the defendant was convicted. District Attorney Coble failed to provide the exculpatory evidence regarding photo identification, a violation of the rule. The rule applies even if the evidence is initially unknown but discovered later. This is not contingent upon defense counsel requesting the information. Finally, the facts of the question indicate there was other evidence used to convict the defendant, such as the 911 recording, so the photo may not have been the sole basis of the conviction. Regardless, District Attorney Coble had a duty under the rule to disclose this evidence.

59. D: Model Rule 7.3 prohibits an attorney from soliciting business from prospective clients. Here, the attorney knows or should reasonably know that this population needs legal services for estate planning. She is making personal contact with them, offering to provide those services with a significant motive to early attorney fees (regardless of the discount).

60. C: Although Model Rule 1.1 states that an attorney may retain or contract with another attorney to assist in providing legal services to a client, the comments to the rule further state that the lawyer should "ordinarily obtain informed consent from the client to do so." Here, the attorney entered into an agreement with another attorney without informing his client. This is not remedied by the fact that the fees are divided without an increase in the amount, or that an explanation is provided at the end of the case.

MPRE Practice Test #2

1. Attorney Kidd is a partner in a large firm. He specializes in transactional law, but the firm has a number of divisions with attorneys specializing in many areas of the law. When working on a particularly complex business transaction for a client, Kidd encounters a taxation question that could affect the outcome of the case. He is unfamiliar with the most recent tax laws, so he consults with a partner in the firm's tax division. He does not identify the client to the partner, nor does he advise the client that he is consulting with another attorney. Kidd asks the partner to keep track of his hours so that they may be included in the monthly invoice to the client. Was it proper for Kidd to consult with his partner?

    a. Yes, because they are partners in the same firm.
    b. Yes, because he did not reveal the client's identity to his partner.
    c. No, because the total attorney fees will be increased for the client.
    d. No, because he did not obtain the client's consent to the consultation.

2. Attorney Pfeiffer has been practicing transactional law for over 20 years and has gained a favorable reputation within his community. Ready for a change, he considers running for judicial office against Judge Abernathy, the current judge who is up for reelection. Pfeiffer knows little of Abernathy's professional background and queries the state judicial commission regarding any grievances or discipline on record for the judge. The commission responds in writing that Abernathy was disciplined as a result of two grievances filed against him. Based on this information, Pfeiffer makes the decision to run for office against Abernathy. During his campaign, he uses the information released by the commission in his campaign ads against the judge. Of note is that the commission's rulings are a matter of public record. It is subsequently brought to Pfeiffer's attention that the judge only received one grievance and that the commission's written response mistakenly reported two. Is Pfeiffer subject to discipline?

    a. Yes, because the error in the commission's letter does not excuse his false statement of material fact.
    b. Yes, because Judge Abernathy was the subject of only one grievance, not two.
    c. No, because he did not knowingly misrepresent any fact concerning Judge Abernathy.
    d. No, because this is a contested election in which either party may make a statement regarding the other party.

3. Attorney Evans is a seasoned defense attorney at a small firm specializing in construction law. The firm hires a new associate, attorney Franklin, to assist with Evans's caseload. Evans represents a construction company that has been sued by a homeowner for negligent construction. He instructs Franklin to review the documents provided by his client and identify any that are potentially responsive to the plaintiff's discovery requests. Franklin completes the review and provides copies of the responsive documents to Evans, who then instructs Franklin to destroy both the originals and copies of certain construction documents that may be incriminating to the defendant's case. Franklin complies with the instructions and destroys the documents. Is Franklin subject to discipline for complying with Evans's instructions?

   a. Yes, because attorney Evans violated a rule of professional conduct.
   b. Yes, because attorney Franklin cannot avoid discipline for violating a rule of professional conduct even though it was at the direction of a supervising attorney.
   c. No, because attorney Franklin had a duty to follow the direction of her supervising attorney.
   d. No, because neither attorney Evans nor attorney Franklin violated a rule of professional conduct.

4. Attorney Williams advertises his services in representing patients injured by placement of a certain brand of mesh during abdominal surgery. Mrs. Wright sees the advertisement and schedules a consultation with him. The two discuss her medical history for 30 minutes, at which time Williams advises that he cannot represent her. He explains that due to her complicated and extensive medical history, he does not feel qualified to handle her claim for injury. Williams provides her with the names of several qualified medical malpractice attorneys and advises her to seek counsel within one year to preserve any applicable statute of limitation. Is Williams subject to discipline for declining representation after consulting with Mrs. Wright?

   a. No, because Mrs. Wright did not have a reasonable expectation of establishing an attorney-client relationship.
   b. No, because he performed duties beyond those owed to Mrs. Wright.
   c. Yes, because he now possesses confidential information regarding Mrs. Wright's medical history.
   d. Yes, because his advertisement obligated him to represent any potential client who responded to the ad.

5. Jimmy King is brought in for questioning in connection with his involvement in the kidnapping of a city councilman. The kidnappers have demanded ransom from the city for the release of the victim, but the city has refused to give in to the kidnappers' demand. At Jimmy's request, attorney Reid is appointed by the court to represent him. Reid previously defended Jimmy against a burglary charge several years ago. When interrogated by the police, Jimmy refuses to make any statements regarding the kidnapping. Afterwards, in private consultation, Jimmy reveals in confidence to Reid the location of the councilman. He tells Reid that the kidnappers plan to kill the councilman if the city does not pay the ransom by midnight. Based on his experience representing him in another criminal action, Reid has reason to believe Jimmy is telling the truth. Is it proper for Reid to disclose Jimmy's statement to the police?

    a. Yes, because Jimmy 's statement is an admission of guilt, which is not protected by attorney-client confidentiality.

    b. Yes, because Jimmy's statement is not protected by attorney-client confidentiality due to the nature of the information discussed.

    c. No, because he does not know with certainty that the councilman's life is in danger.

    d. No, because Jimmy's statement is protected by attorney-client confidentiality.

6. Dr. Bradshaw is a physician and attorney. He is licensed to practice medicine in Washington, but he lives in Idaho and is licensed to practice law there. The application for his medical license renewal in Washington asks if there are any pending criminal charges against him. Dr. Bradshaw answers "no," which is a false statement because he was recently charged with a DUI in Boise. Will Dr. Bradshaw be subjected to any discipline regarding his license to practice law in Idaho?

    a. No, because the DUI occurred in Idaho, and his medical license is in Washington.

    b. No, because the misrepresentation was made on his Washington medical license renewal, and his bar license is in Idaho.

    c. Yes, because the misrepresentation on his medical license renewal constituted dishonest conduct.

    d. Yes, if he is convicted of the DUI charges.

7. Mrs. Williams, a middle school English teacher, consults with attorney Cassidy when she believes she was denied a promotion to chair of the English department because she is nearing retirement age. Cassidy agrees to represent Mrs. Williams by filing an age discrimination complaint in federal district court. Prior to trial, the federal statute upon which Mrs. Williams's complaint is based is repealed. The defendant school district files a motion to dismiss for failure to state a valid claim under federal law. Cassidy promptly files a motion to amend the current complaint. The court grants the motion and Cassidy files an amended complaint, substituting other valid federal law for the repealed statute. Is Cassidy subject to discipline?

    a. Yes, because he filed a complaint based on a law that was no longer valid.

    b. Yes, because he should have based the complaint on other valid federal law.

    c. No, because he did not know or have reason to know that the statute had been repealed at the time the complaint was filed.

    d. No, because he appropriately amended the complaint once he became aware that the statute had been repealed.

8. Judge Powell lost his reelection bid and returned to private practice at a midsize firm specializing in family law. During his tenure as a judge, he presided over the O'Connells' divorce case in which the husband was ordered to pay alimony and child support to the wife. At that time, Mr. O'Connell was employed full-time as an engineer, while Mrs. O'Connell was still completing her law degree. Upon Powell's return to private practice, Mr. O'Connell advises him that his ex-wife has completed law school, passed the bar, and is being paid a comfortable salary at a large law firm. Mr. O'Connell wants to modify the amount he is paying in alimony and child support. Since Powell is familiar with the divorce case, Mr. O'Connell requests that the former judge represent him in his petition to modify the order. Powell discloses to both Mr. O'Connell and his ex-wife the potential conflicts in representing Mr. O'Connell. Both parties agree to the representation and sign written informed consent agreements. Powell proceeds with his representation for Mr. O'Connell. Is the former judge subject to discipline?

   a. Yes, because he presided over the initial divorce hearing.
   b. Yes, because Mr. O'Connell was ordered to pay alimony and child support based on the former judge's expertise and knowledge of the law.
   c. No, because both spouses consented to the representation.
   d. No, because the change in Mrs. O'Connell's circumstances was a valid reason to seek modification of the original order.

9. Defendant Pepper is charged with burglary of a liquor store. He retains attorney Bernard to defend him against the charges. He has no criminal record, and Bernard is successful in obtaining his release on bond. Pepper denies even being at the liquor store at the time of the burglary, and the more Bernard investigates the case, the more convinced he becomes that his client is telling the truth. Pepper is terrified that a jury will not believe him and that he will be convicted and sentenced for the crime. He asks Bernard for advice on how to avoid the criminal trial. Specifically, he asks where to go to avoid being found and arrested by the police. Bernard does not answer these questions and advises his client to participate voluntarily in the criminal proceedings rather than attempt to escape. Shortly after the meeting, Pepper flees the country without advising anyone of his whereabouts. When Pepper fails to appear at trial, Bernard explains to the court what was discussed in his last meeting with the defendant. Is Bernard subject to discipline?

   a. Yes, because defendant Pepper failed to appear at the scheduled trial.
   b. Yes, because defendant Pepper refused to follow attorney Bernard's legal advice.
   c. No, because an attorney cannot be disciplined for the willful acts of his client.
   d. No, because attorney Bernard advised his client against avoiding trial and escaping from being apprehended.

10. Mr. Fender hires attorney Dodge to bring a property damage claim against his neighbor. Mr. Fender and his neighbor have a long-standing feud over various issues and Mr. Fender's sole initiative in bringing the claim is getting back at his neighbor. Mr. Fender misrepresents several facts upon which Dodge bases his petition for damages. Dodge is unaware of his client's misrepresentations. When the case goes to trial, Mr. Fender testifies as to the same mistruths included in his petition. A judgment is entered in his favor. Later, feeling remorse for his actions, Mr. Fender sends Dodge a confidential email in which he confesses to making false statements and giving false testimony at trial. He apologizes to his neighbor for suing him, which prompts defense counsel to question the legitimacy of the claim. Defense counsel submits a complaint to the disciplinary committee of the state bar, alleging that Dodge filed a frivolous action in court based on facts he knew or should have known were false. Is it proper for Dodge to produce Mr. Fender's email to the disciplinary committee?

a. Yes, because the email was received after the trial and not during attorney Dodge's representation of Mr. Fender.
b. Yes, because disclosure of the email is necessary for his defense in the disciplinary proceedings.
c. No, because Mr. Fender specified that the email was confidential.
d. No, because Mr. Fender could be prosecuted for perjury if the email is disclosed.

11. Attorney Todd represents Oceans of Happiness, a popular waterpark. The Joseph family brings a claim against the waterpark for the death of their child following a fall from a water ride. Oceans of Happiness has a valid defense to the family's claim; however, Todd advises the park to settle the claim and pay damages to the family to avoid the negative publicity a lawsuit could bring. Relying on Todd's advice, the park pays the claim. Is Todd subject to discipline?

a. No, because the park accepted his advice.
b. No, because paying the claim avoided negative publicity.
c. Yes, because he did not zealously advocate for the interests of his client.
d. Yes, because the park paid the claim even though it had a valid defense.

12. Mr. and Mrs. Preston hire attorney Hannah to represent them in a breach of contract action involving a real estate purchase. The Prestons complete much of the data gathering and fact-finding in pursuit of the claim without requiring Hannah's involvement. They assume that he is simultaneously taking actions to pursue the claim, but at a follow-up meeting they discover that he has not completed any work on the claim for over a month. Hannah explains to the Prestons that he has been busy with competing priorities. The Prestons advise they would like to hire different counsel, and Hannah agrees to return the Prestons' retainer fee. The Prestons consult with attorney Davis. They advise her of Hannah's handling of the case but tell her that they would like to forget the past and move on since they got their retainer back. Davis agrees to represent the Prestons and in compliance with their wishes, she does not report Hannah's inaction. Is Davis subject to discipline?

a. Yes, because attorney Hannah committed professional misconduct.
b. Yes, because attorney Davis agreed to represent the Prestons without confirming their termination of the attorney-client relationship with attorney Hannah.
c. No, because the Prestons requested that attorney Davis not disclose the information they shared with her about attorney Hannah.
d. No, because attorney Hannah's conduct did not rise to the level of professional misconduct.

13. Attorney Starns is one of the founding partners of the law offices of Starns and Whitley P.C. He is elected to the state legislature but has been able to successfully balance both positions. He has remained involved in most of his caseload with occasional assistance from associate attorneys in the firm, and he has been diligent in avoiding any conflict of interest between his legal duties and his legislative duties. As such, the firm has not taken any action to remove Starns's name from the firm's name. Which of the following best describes the obligations of the law offices of Starns and Whitley?

　a. Attorney Starns may continue to practice with the firm while he is in the legislature, but his name must be removed from the firm name.

　b. Attorney Starns may not practice with the firm while he is in the legislature, but his name may remain part of the firm name.

　c. Attorney Starns may not serve as both a practicing attorney and a public official, and his name should be removed from the firm name as long as he is part of the legislature.

　d. Attorney Starns may continue to practice with the firm while he is in the legislature, and his name may remain part of the firm name.

14. Several minority shareholders of the publicly traded Acme Corporation retain counsel to bring a derivative action lawsuit against the majority shareholders for mismanagement of the corporation. The action is assigned to Judge Powell's docket. Powell owns a mutual fund managed by an investment firm. Powell contacts his investment adviser and is informed that his mutual fund includes a substantial number of shares of Acme stock, but they make up a minority percentage of his total stock ownership. Since only he and his financial advisor have knowledge of the stock ownership, Powell decides to proceed with oversight of the derivative action. Is Powell subject to discipline?

　a. No, because his shares of Acme stock make up only a minority percentage of his total stock ownership.

　b. No, because only he and his financial adviser know about the shares.

　c. Yes, because he did not disclose ownership of the stock to the parties in the lawsuit.

　d. Yes, because he did not disqualify himself from the case.

15. Attorney Morgan represented Mr. Beasley in a medical malpractice claim against a local hospital. The case settled at mediation for $50,000. The hospital sent a check for this amount payable to the order of Morgan, which he deposited in a client trust account (CTA). Morgan notified Mr. Beasley of receipt of the funds and billed him $10,000 for his legal fees. Mr. Beasley disputed the amount billed by Morgan and advised that he would pay $5,000 as a reasonable fee for his work on the case. What is the proper action for Morgan to take?

　a. Retain $45,000 in the CTA and transfer $5,000 to his office account.

　b. Send $40,000 to Mr. Beasley and transfer $10,000 to his office account.

　c. Send $40,000 to Mr. Beasley, transfer $5,000 to his office account, and retain $5,000 in the CTA until the fee dispute is settled.

　d. Retain the entire $50,000 in the CTA until the fee dispute is settled.

16. Attorney Anderson represents Mrs. Parker in a breach of contract action against her former business associate. The case settled at mediation before trial. The settlement proceeds were paid to Mrs. Parker, who then paid Anderson for his legal fees and expenses. Anderson does not provide any further legal services for Mrs. Parker. Some weeks later, Anderson is contacted by the IRS, advising that Mrs. Parker is being audited. The auditor asks Anderson for detailed information regarding the settlement. Based on the questions being asked, Anderson believes any disclosures regarding the settlement would be detrimental to Mrs. Parker. He calls Mrs. Parker to advise her of the IRS request. She tells him not to provide the information to the IRS. Is it proper for Anderson to provide the information to the IRS?

    a. No, because Mrs. Parker told him not to provide the information.
    b. No, because he believes the information would be detrimental to Mrs. Parker.
    c. Yes, because the information does not involve attorney work product.
    d. Yes, because he no longer has an attorney-client relationship with Mrs. Parker.

17. Attorney Carter, a prosecutor in Los Angeles, is prosecuting defendant Bonner for charges arising from his gang affiliation. Bonner is afraid of gang retaliation if he cooperates with the prosecutor in exchange for a lesser charge. In plea negotiations, he offers to confess to a much more serious crime that took place in New York 10 years ago, if the prosecutor will drop the current gang-related charges against him. The New York case involved the armed robbery of a bank in which a security guard was shot. Another man, apparently wrongfully convicted, has been serving a sentence in federal prison for the crime for the past nine years. Bonner describes details about the New York crime that were known only to investigators, and Carter is convinced the defendant is telling the truth about his involvement in the crime. Does Carter have an ethical duty under the Model Rules to disclose this information?

    a. No, he is not required to take any further action unless there is clear and convincing evidence that a wrongfully accused person is serving a sentence for the crime.
    b. No, because the confession is protected by attorney-client privilege.
    c. Yes, he must disclose the confession to defense counsel for the wrongfully accused man.
    d. Yes, he must promptly disclose the information to an appropriate court or authority.

18. James Walton, a prominent businessman, retained attorney Bash to represent his son, James Walton Jr, referred to as "Junior" in his divorce proceedings. Junior has given written informed consent to the arrangement. Junior is known for his generous nature and Mr. Walton is concerned that this will lead to his son giving away valuable heirlooms in order to secure a speedy divorce. Junior advises Bash that his only initiative is a peaceful divorce. Mr. Walton instructs Bash to terminate any settlement negotiations if it appears that Junior is likely to give any heirlooms to his wife. Can Bash honor his agreement with Mr. Walton?

    a. No, because he agreed to an improper contingency fee arrangement.
    b. No, because the agreement limits his ability to exercise his own legal judgment.
    c. Yes, because Mr. Walton is paying his attorney fees.
    d. Yes, because Mr. Walton's request is reasonably intended to benefit his son.

19. The law firm of Bond and Clay dissolves after the partners have a major disagreement on how to manage the partnership. Attorney Bond opens his own firm, hiring several associate attorneys to assist him. He practices in direct competition with attorney Clay, who now practices as a sole practitioner. Clay hopes to build his caseload by offering a job to a corporate attorney who will bring clients with him to the practice. Clay, still embittered over the dissolution of the partnership with Bond, includes a provision in the corporate attorney's employment contract prohibiting him from working for Bond in the future should he ever terminate employment with Clay. Is this contract provision permissible?

  a. No, because the contract provision was proposed by attorney Clay, not the corporate attorney.
  b. No, because it restricts the rights of the corporate attorney to practice law.
  c. Yes, because there are no restrictions on attorney Clay to limit the professional conduct of his employee.
  d. Yes, because the corporate attorney agreed to the contract provision.

20. Attorney Fellows represents Mr. Sutherland in an action against a mechanic for negligent repair of his vehicle. Fellows sends a demand letter to the mechanic, offering to settle the matter out of court, but the mechanic does not respond. Fellows then miscalculates the date of the negligence action and misses the statute of limitations for filing suit. He discloses the mistake to Mr. Sutherland and tells him that he wants to rectify the situation. He offers to pay Mr. Sutherland an amount that will cover the expenses incurred for the additional work required to fix the negligent repairs. Fellows assures Mr. Sutherland that this is a fair offer but does not advise him to seek a separate legal opinion regarding the agreement. Although Mr. Sutherland could have obtained a greater amount of compensation had he sued Fellows for legal malpractice, he decides to accept the offer and get his car repaired. Fellows prepares a settlement agreement that same day and both parties sign it. Mr. Sutherland is not represented by separate counsel when he discusses and signs the settlement agreement. Did Fellows engage in proper conduct?

  a. Yes, because Mr. Sutherland voluntarily entered into the agreement in order to get his car repaired.
  b. Yes, because he represented Mr. Sutherland in the original action by drafting the demand letter to the mechanic.
  c. No, because Mr. Sutherland could have obtained a greater amount in damages if he had not settled with attorney Fellows.
  d. No, because of his conduct in settlement of a potential malpractice claim with Mr. Sutherland.

21. Attorney Fritz represents Golden Valley Nursing Home. The facility was recently sued by the family of Mrs. Damon, a resident that died after suffering injuries from a fall. Mrs. Damon was confused and at high-risk for falls. She required an alarm on her bed to alert staff if she attempted to ambulate without assistance. One night, Mrs. Damon got out of bed unassisted, but the bed alarm did not sound. She fell, suffering a head injury that resulted in her death. The bed was evaluated, and it was determined that the alarm was not functioning. Fritz interviewed Golden Valley's nursing director and learned that the sister of Mrs. Damon's roommate had witnessed staff having difficulty with Mrs. Damon's bed alarm the day prior to the fall. The sister mentioned to the nursing director that a staff nurse told Mrs. Damon that something was wrong with the alarm, instructing her not to get out of bed until someone from plant operations was available to fix it. Fritz asks the nursing director to approach the roommate's sister and request that she not disclose this information to the Damon family or their attorney. Is Fritz subject to discipline?

    a. No, because he did not personally approach the roommate's sister.
    b. No, because the roommate's sister was not a party to the lawsuit.
    c. Yes, because he was prohibited from requesting the sister to withhold information from another attorney.
    d. Yes, because the witness was not an employee of the nursing home.

22. While passing by a neighbor's yard when walking home from school, a young girl is bitten and injured by a terrier that has become aggressive. Attorney Hughley sees a news story on a local television station regarding several recent attacks by terriers, all with different owners. Hughley locates and approaches the parents of the most recent victim and offers to represent them in a claim for personal injury against the dog's owner. Hughley has experience with a state statute that classifies several large dog breeds as dangerous, requiring their owners to take extra precautions to ensure public safety around the dogs. Hughley knows that terriers are not included in the list of dangerous breeds, prohibiting the young girl's claim under the statute, but he believes in good faith that the terrier is dangerous and should be added to the list of breeds included in the statute. Is Hughley subject to discipline for pursuing the claim?

    a. Yes, because terriers are not classified as a dangerous breed under the statute.
    b. Yes, because it is unlikely the girl will prevail in a claim against the dog owner.
    c. No, because the girl suffered injuries from the terrier and has a right to pursue compensation from the dog owner.
    d. No, because he has a good faith belief that the dangerous breed statute should be extended to include terriers.

23. A state administrative hearing commission issues a subpoena to nurse Cannon to testify at a disciplinary hearing involving a physician. Cannon retains attorney Brown to represent her at the hearing. She believes the physician has quality of care issues but feels uncomfortable testifying as to the issues since she routinely works with him. Brown advises Cannon that she has the constitutional right, based on a Supreme Court decision, not to respond to questions that would be against her best interest to answer. At the administrative hearing, Cannon hesitates to respond to questions regarding the physician's care, but she is instructed by the judge that failure to answer constitutes a criminal offense. The judge informs Brown that the Supreme Court decision has been overruled by a subsequent decision. Nonetheless, Brown persists in advising Cannon to withhold testimony. She remains silent. As a result, she is convicted of refusing to testify. Is Brown subject to discipline?

   a. Yes, because his repeated incorrect legal advice showed a lack of competence.
   b. Yes, because nurse Cannon followed his advice and violated the law.
   c. No, because nurse Cannon made an informed decision to disobey the judge's instruction.
   d. No, because he reasonably believed that nurse Cannon was legally entitled to withhold testimony.

24. Attorney Pena represents Mr. Clemson, a prominent businessman with ties oversees. Pena establishes a client trust account (CTA) in which he deposits the payments made by Mr. Clemson to cover his business taxes as they become due. Mr. Clemson leaves for a quarterly business trip abroad, and shortly thereafter, Pena finds himself in need of a temporary loan. He tries unsuccessfully to contact Mr. Clemson for permission to access money from the CTA, but he reasonably believes that Mr. Clemson would approve a loan. He proceeds with borrowing money from the CTA and replacing it at the end of the month. After Mr. Clemson returns from his business trip, Pena discloses the loan. Mr. Clemson does not object to his conduct. Was it proper for Pena to take the loan?

   a. No, because he used the client's funds for his personal use.
   b. No, because he could not reach Mr. Clemson before taking the funds.
   c. Yes, because he was reasonably certain Mr. Clemson would not object to the loan.
   d. Yes, because upon disclosure, Mr. Clemson did not object to his conduct.

25. Attorney Adams has worked as in-house counsel for Yamasaki Corporation for 10 years when she decides to venture out and set up her own practice, specializing in transactional law. Several months into her new practice, she is approached by Mr. Good, a local businessman who asks her to negotiate a contract whereby his business would supply certain computer components to Yamasaki. Adams discloses her prior employment as counsel for Yamasaki, and both Mr. Good and the CEO of Yamasaki consent in writing to her representation of Mr. Good in the contract negotiations. She does not use any confidential information from Yamasaki in her representation of Mr. Good. The final agreement, signed by both Mr. Good and Yamasaki, contains a statement affirming that Adams is solely representing the interests of Mr. Good and that Yamasaki is waiving any potential conflict of interest from the representation. As an added measure, Adams also signs the agreement, attesting that it was a complete, true, and correct statement of the parties' agreement. However, Adams had, without the consent of Mr. Good, provided information and counsel to Yamasaki during the contract negotiations. Yamasaki had relied heavily on her advice in the terms to which it agreed. Is Adams subject to discipline?

   a. No, because she received informed written consent from Yamasaki to represent Mr. Good.
   b. No, because she did not use any of Yamasaki's confidential information in her representation of Mr. Good.
   c. Yes, because the agreement contained a false statement.
   d. Yes, because she cannot represent a new client with interests adverse to a former client.

26. Billy Bennett is arrested late one night for possession of marijuana and driving under the influence. With his one allowable phone call from the county jail, he calls and awakens his cousin Vincent. Vincent recently passed the bar and began work as an associate in a large firm, practicing personal injury law. Vincent advises his cousin that he does not handle criminal cases. Billy tells Vincent he is the only attorney he knows and begs him to try to get him released on bail. He reminds Vincent that he can make no other phone calls. Vincent goes to the county jail, but despite his best efforts he is unable to get Billy released. It is the middle of the night, so Vincent returns home. First thing the next morning, Vincent consults with an experienced criminal lawyer in this firm. The attorney is able to secure Billy's release that same morning. Was Vincent's conduct proper?

   a. No, because he had no experience in criminal law and therefore did not have the competence to represent Billy.
   b. No, because a conflict of interest existed in representing a close family member in a criminal proceeding.
   c. Yes, because neither a referral nor a consultation was a practical option under the circumstances.
   d. Yes, because he revealed that he did not handle criminal cases, but Billy still consented to his representation.

27. Attorney Stone is a solo practitioner focusing primarily on transactional and real estate law; however, his caseload is dwindling, and he is struggling financially. His brother is a chiropractor and managing partner of a large chiropractic practice in another city within the state. The two have been estranged for a number of years, but Stone decides to reach out to him for a favor. He calls and asks his brother to retain him to defend any medical malpractice cases filed against him or his partners. His brother is somewhat offended by the request considering their current relationship, but he agrees to consider the request. Was it improper for Stone to make this request of this brother?

    a. No, because the recipient of the solicitation (his brother) has a familial relationship with him.

    b. No, because he only asked for his brother to use his services without offering to represent him in a specific matter.

    c. Yes, because the brother found the request offensive.

    d. Yes, because he is prohibited from soliciting professional employment with the motive of pecuniary gain.

28. Attorney Ray enters into a written retainer agreement to provide legal services to Mr. Hart, a local real estate broker. The retainer agreement required Mr. Hart to make a $5,000 advance payment, which Ray deposited into a client trust account (CTA). The terms of the agreement also required Ray to withdraw funds from the CTA on a monthly basis to pay for legal services and to provide Mr. Hart with an accounting of the funds. Ray performed legal services but did not withdraw any funds from the CTA until the current legal matter was completed some six months later. At that time, Ray had billed $2,700 in attorney fees. He wrote two checks on the CTA: one to himself for $2,700 and one to Mr. Hart for $2,300. Is Ray subject to discipline?

    a. No, because his fee was reasonable.

    b. No, because Mr. Hart's payment was secured in a client trust account.

    c. Yes, because he required Mr. Hart to pay in advance.

    d. Yes, because he failed to withdraw his fees as they were billed on a monthly basis.

29. Attorney Brandon works for a state attorney general's consumer protection division. She is lead counsel assigned to a major data breach case against Acme Inc., a payment processing company, that is impacting thousands of consumers. At trial, judgment is entered in favor of the state with heavy penalties imposed on the defendant company. Shortly after the trial, Brandon leaves her employment with the attorney general's office and opens her own law practice. State law allows individual consumers to bring their own private cause of action against a corporation for damages arising from a data breach. State law also makes certain documents gathered by government agencies in its course of business available to the public. Five individual consumers file suit against Acme for the data breach. Acme contacts Brandon seeking representation in its defense against these consumer actions. Will Brandon be subject to discipline if she agrees to defend Acme in the private actions?

    a. Yes, because she had substantial involvement in the state's case against Acme.

    b. Yes, because the final judgment in the state's case is completely dispositive of Acme's liability.

    c. No, because she has extensive knowledge of data breach cases and, therefore, is competent to represent Acme.

    d. No, because a verdict and sentencing occurred, and thus the state is no longer involved and does not have to consent to the representation.

30. Attorney Cooper is retained by a local contractor to file a complex product liability suit against a building material manufacturer. Cooper is a sole practitioner with only a paralegal to assist him. The attorney representing the defendant manufacturer is part of a large litigation firm with many resources. The defense counsel files extensive discovery requests and numerous pleadings and motions, resulting in the suit being more time-consuming and costly than anticipated. Cooper's client wants the pretrial process to end with a trial date established sooner rather than later. Cooper advises that shortening the pretrial process will significantly decrease the odds of winning at trial. Despite Cooper's advice, his client demands the case be expedited to trial. These differences in opinion are making the case increasingly difficult to manage. Would it be appropriate for Cooper to seek court approval to withdraw from representing the plaintiff?

  a. Yes, because an attorney has the right to withdraw from representation at any time before trial begins.
  b. Yes, because the client's demands are making it unreasonably difficult for attorney Cooper to effectively represent the client.
  c. No, because an attorney is legally bound to follow the directions of the client in regard to management of a lawsuit.
  d. No, because the plaintiff did not consent to attorney Cooper withdrawing from representation.

31. Attorney Jacobs is retained by Luke Walters to bring a medical malpractice claim against a physician. While Jacobs is preparing the case, Luke tells him in confidence that he was previously involved in a hit-and-run accident in which he struck and killed a pedestrian but left the scene. The hit-and-run accident is completely unrelated to the current medical malpractice case. Luke is not a suspect in the crime, which remains unsolved. Is it proper for Jacobs to disclose to the police Luke's involvement in the hit and run accident?

  a. No, because the information was obtained in the course of the legal representation of his client.
  b. No, because he did not represent or provide legal advice to Luke regarding the hit-and-run accident.
  c. Yes, because he is an officer of the court with a duty to disclose the information.
  d. Yes, because the case remains unsolved.

32. In February, Susan Smith hires attorney Harmon to bring an employment discrimination action against her previous employer, Delta Inc. In May, a local judge appoints Harmon to defend an accused against felony drug charges. The prosecutor in the criminal case advises Harmon that he will be ready for trial in July. Meanwhile, Susan advises Harmon that she could clear her calendar to participate in her employment trial any time during the summer. Harmon advises Susan of his court appointment and the possibility that the criminal trial date may be set in the summer as well. He assures her the criminal trial will not negatively impact her civil case. At a pretrial conference, the employment trial date is set for August. Susan did not attend the pretrial conference, but Harmon called and informed her of the trial date as soon as the conference was finished. At the criminal pretrial conference the following week, the criminal case is set for trial in July. Did Harmon act properly by setting the civil trial date in August?

    a. No, because he had a duty to consult with Susan before agreeing to the trial date.
    b. No, because he had a duty to expedite the trial date to earlier in the summer.
    c. Yes, because prior to the pretrial conference, Susan consented to a summer trial date setting.
    d. Yes, because criminal trial scheduling typically takes precedence over civil trial scheduling.

33. Attorney Scarborough recently graduated law school and passed the bar. He begins work as an associate for a large multispecialty firm. In addition to billing a minimum number of professional hours, associates are expected to provide a minimum of 50 hours of pro bono legal services per year. Scarborough nears the end of the year having provided only five hours of pro bono work for a local charity. Scarborough's sister, Dr. Fair, is a successful dentist who practices in the same city. Dr. Fair pays a substantial amount in attorney fees each year for collection of outstanding patient accounts. Scarborough makes a win-win proposal to Dr. Fair. He will provide 50 hours of legal collection services to Dr. Fair's practice at a substantially reduced amount (10 percent of his normal billable rate) and submit them to the firm as pro bono hours to meet the yearly requirement. Is Scarborough's proposal improper?

    a. Yes, because the Model Rules require more than 50 hours of pro bono work per year.
    b. Yes, because Dr. Fair is a successful professional with the means to pay for legal representation.
    c. No, because he billed Dr. Fair at a substantially reduced hourly rate.
    d. No, because he also provided pro bono work to a charitable organization.

34. Attorney Sawyer represents Mr. Myers in his defective product lawsuit against a car manufacturer. The manufacturer's main defense is that it warned the plaintiff of the existing issue via US mail, advising him to take the car to an authorized dealership for replacement of a defective part. When called as witnesses, both Mr. Myers and his wife testify that they never received a notice from the manufacturer. While the trial was still proceeding, the sister of Mrs. Myers confides in Sawyer that the couple did receive a notice from the manufacturer, but they destroyed it. Sawyer confronts them, at which time Mrs. Myers admits to receipt and destruction of the notice, but she states that she did so without the knowledge of Mr. Myers. Sawyer proceeds with the trial but makes no mention of the notice in his closing argument to the jury. Is Sawyer subject to discipline?

   a. No, because he did not reference the notice in his closing argument.
   b. No, because he did not rely on Mrs. Myers's testimony once he discovered the perjury.
   c. Yes, because he failed to take reasonable remedial measures after he realized that Mrs. Myers perjured herself.
   d. Yes, because Mrs. Myers committed perjury.

35. Attorney Morris practices in a midsize firm specializing in criminal defense. She volunteers as a director on the board of a local nonprofit organization whose mission is to combat teen drug and alcohol use through education, counseling, and treatment. Morris is occasionally appointed by local courts to represent criminal defendants. Some of the criminal cases are lengthy and the fees paid by the court do not even come close to the fees she would earn defending a client who retains the services of her firm. A court notifies Morris of an appointment to represent a defendant against criminal charges for selling meth to a high school student that resulted in the student's death. Morris objects to the appointment on the basis of her personal beliefs and her position on the board of the nonprofit organization. She argues that, based on the nature of the charges against the defendant, she cannot represent him. Is Morris subject to discipline for seeking release from the appointment to represent the defendant?

   a. No, because representing the defendant will violate professional rules regarding conflict of interest.
   b. No, because representing the defendant would be so repugnant to attorney Morris as to potentially impact her relationship with the defendant.
   c. Yes, because the appointment was made as a court order.
   d. Yes, because financial burden is not a valid reason for seeking release from the appointment.

36. Attorney Moon represents Mr. Kim in his medical malpractice suit against several health care providers. The retainer agreement provides that Moon will advance legal costs and expenses provided that Mr. Kim, on demand, reimburses him for the amounts advanced. Moon retains an expert witness to review Mr. Kim's medical claims and advances the payment of the expert's billed professional fees. When Moon bills him for reimbursement, Mr. Kim refuses to pay. Moon advises Mr. Kim that he will not perform any further work on the case until he is reimbursed. Shortly thereafter, one of the defendant providers files a counterclaim against Mr. Kim for collection on his account. Having not been reimbursed, Moon does not file a responsive pleading by the 30-day deadline. A default judgment is entered on the counterclaim in favor of the provider. Mr. Kim subsequently reimburses Moon, who is then successful in setting aside the default judgment. The medical malpractice case proceeds to trial where judgment is entered in favor of Mr. Kim. Is Moon subject to discipline?

   a. No, because Mr. Kim breached the terms of the retainer agreement by failing to reimburse costs.
   b. No, because Mr. Kim did not sustain any prejudice as a result of attorney Moon's actions.
   c. Yes, because he neglected Mr. Kim's lawsuit.
   d. Yes, because he did not seek leave of court to withdraw as counsel.

37. Hometown Bank retains attorney Walker to assist in commercial real estate transactions. Duncan Development Company seeks a business loan from Hometown Bank in order to purchase a plot of land and build an office complex. The loan will be secured by a mortgage on the land and the office building. Hometown Bank will process the loan if Walker drafts the loan and mortgage documents and if Duncan Development pays Walker's fees. This type of business arrangement is common in commercial real estate deals in Ohio, the state in which Walker practices. He feels confident he can provide both Hometown Bank and Duncan Development competent and fair representation in this transaction. Both parties provide written consent to the representation after having been given sufficient opportunity to consult with independent counsel. Is it proper for Walker to prepare the loan and mortgage documents?

   a. Yes, because both Hometown Bank and Duncan Development provided informed consent to the representation.
   b. Yes, because this approach is a common practice in Ohio.
   c. No, because Duncan Development, not Hometown Bank, will pay the attorney fees.
   d. No, because the interests of Duncan Development and Hometown Bank are conflicting.

38. Attorney Richardson represents a defendant in a criminal action for possession and distribution of marijuana. Several days before the trial is scheduled to begin, the court provides the parties with a list of potential jurors. Richardson gives the list to a private investigator he frequently hires to gather evidence in his criminal cases. He asks the investigator to locate and interview the potential jurors regarding their past experiences with recreational drug use. The investigator does not disclose to the potential jurors that he is working on behalf of Richardson, and Richardson does not disclose to opposing counsel the investigator's report from the interviews. Is Richardson subject to discipline?

a. No, because the interviews were voluntary.
b. No, because the list of potential jurors was provided by the court as part of the pretrial process.
c. Yes, because he did not provide the investigator's report to opposing counsel.
d. Yes, because the investigator, at the direction of attorney Richardson, communicated with potential jurors prior to trial.

39. Attorney Meadows is a well-known expert in health law who represents the large health care corporation UHI. Meadows is called to testify before the US Senate regarding a new bill addressing medical surrogate decision-making. She testifies as to both her personal and expert professional opinion regarding the new legislation. Her opinions are also representative of UHI's position and believed to be in the best interest of the public. UHI agreed to pay Meadows her regular hourly billable rate to attend the hearing. Since Meadows is offering her own opinions, she does not disclose in her testimony that she is being paid by UHI. Is Meadows subject to discipline?

a. No, because the Senate seeks to know the content of her expert opinion, not who is paying her to testify.
b. No, because she believes that her position was in the best interest of the public.
c. Yes, because she is prohibited from accepting a fee for attempting to influence the Senate's opinion on the bill.
d. Yes, because a lawyer who appears in a legislative hearing should identify the capacity in which she appears.

40. Attorney Fox has provided estate planning services to Mr. Fender for many years. He prepared Mr. Fender's will and acted as one of the two witnesses to the execution of it. Mr. Fender's son and daughter are his sole heirs, but due to an estranged relationship with his son, Mr. Fender bequeathed his entire estate to his daughter. The executor named in the will retains Fox to assist in the probate of the will. He is subsequently advised that Mr. Fender's son concedes that the will was properly executed but plans to contest the will on the basis that his sister committed fraud in influencing their father's distribution of the estate. The second witness to the will's execution is now deceased, leaving Fox as the only witness to the execution. As such, he will likely be called as a witness in court to testify as to Mr. Fender's instructions regarding the distribution of his estate. Is it proper for Fox to continue representing the executor in probate of the will?

a. No, because he will be called as a witness in the will contest.
b. No, because it will be an undue hardship on the executor at this point in the probate process to retain different counsel.
c. Yes, because there is no contested issue of fact as to the execution of the will.
d. Yes, because the executor does not have any beneficial interest under the terms of the will.

41. Attorney Whitten practices with Brown and Associates, a large multispecialty firm, but he is hoping to downsize his practice. He has been offered an associate position with Martin and Davis, a much smaller firm. To check for conflicts of interest, Whitten is asked to provide Martin and Davis with a list of clients he represented at Brown and Associates. He complies, providing a list of names of his own clients with a description of the matters handled, as well as the same information for clients represented by other attorneys in the firm for which he performed work. Whitten did not ask any of the clients for authorization to disclose the representation or issues involved. Was it proper for Whitten to disclose this confidential information to Martin and Davis?

    a. No, because he did not obtain consent or authorization from the clients before disclosing the information.

    b. No, because he disclosed not only the names of clients he represented, but also the names of clients represented by other attorneys in the firm.

    c. Yes, if he discloses to the attorneys at Brown and Associates that he provided this information to the other firm.

    d. Yes, because he disclosed the information solely to detect and resolve conflicts of interest arising from his transition between firms.

42. The Alliance for Justice, a nonprofit civil rights organization, maintains a database of licensed attorneys in each state who are qualified and willing to represent clients in their civil rights claims. The attorneys agree to pay Alliance for Justice one-third of any attorney fees awarded by the court at the conclusion of the case. Attorney Jacobs practices in a small firm in Nebraska and agrees to be placed in the organization's database. Shortly thereafter, he is assigned a case that is eventually appealed to the Nebraska Supreme Court. At the conclusion of the case, Jacobs is awarded $150,000 in attorney fees. He sends a check to the Alliance for $50,000. Is Jacobs subject to discipline?

    a. Yes, because he shared attorney fees with a non-lawyer organization.

    b. Yes, because the amount of fees shared was not commensurate with Alliance for Justice's contribution to the case.

    c. No, because once the court awarded the fees to attorney Jacobs, he was free to share them however he chose.

    d. No, because Alliance for Justice hired attorney Jacobs to handle the case.

43. Attorney Simpson is quite pleased to sign a retainer agreement with Beta Industries to provide legal services for the corporation. The agreement establishes a rate of $300 per hour for attorney work and $150 per hour for paralegal work. These amounts are slightly higher than, but still within the range of, fees billed by other attorneys in the jurisdiction. After year two of the relationship, Simpson increases the fees to $350 per hour and $175 per hour, respectively. He does not explicitly communicate the rate change to Beta, but the company continues to pay the attorney's bills at the new rate. Is Simpson subject to discipline?

    a. Yes, because the retainer agreement was in writing.

    b. Yes, because attorney Simpson failed to obtain Beta's consent to the rate change.

    c. No, because the rate change was less than 20 percent, which is a reasonable increase.

    d. No, because Beta has the legal obligation to pay attorney Simpson for work completed, pursuant to the retainer agreement.

44. Attorney James, a solo practitioner, successfully represented Summit Development Company in an action to change the zoning of a residential neighborhood in order to accommodate the construction of Summit's planned condominiums. The rezoning is the only matter that James has handled for Summit Development. Two years after the condominiums are constructed, several of the residents approach James seeking his representation in a lawsuit against Summit Development for defective construction. Is it proper for James to represent the condominium residents?

   a. Yes, because the residents' interests are not materially adverse to those of Summit Development.
   b. Yes, because the residents' claims are unrelated to attorney James's work on the zoning matter.
   c. No, because he has not obtained written informed consent from Summit Development.
   d. No, because the residents' interests are materially adverse to those of Summit Development.

45. Attorney Cook is a sole practitioner specializing in personal injury law. Late on a Friday night, she receives a text from her uncle advising that her step-aunt has been taken to the hospital for a massive heart attack. She has suffered significant injury to her cardiac system and is not expected to survive. Her uncle advises that his wife has never drafted a will, and he asks Cook to meet him at the hospital as soon as possible in order to draft a will before she dies. Cook advises her uncle that her practice does not include real estate planning and that she lacks the knowledge and experience to prepare a will. However, she does agree to contact some attorney peers to see if they can assist. At the hospital on Saturday, the uncle begs Cook to draft the will, advising that his wife may only have a few days to live. Cook has been unsuccessful at securing any assistance from other attorneys over the weekend. She takes detailed notes of the step-aunt's wishes regarding her estate. She uses a standard form off the internet and promptly drafts the will. She delivers it to the step-aunt and has it executed. Did Cook engage in improper conduct?

   a. No, because in an emergency situation it was impractical to refer or consult with an estate planning attorney.
   b. No, because she was related to the uncle and step-aunt.
   c. Yes, because she lacked knowledge and experience in estate planning.
   d. Yes, because she lacked the legal competence to draft the step-aunt's will.

46. Mr. Nichols is a real estate developer in Texas. He has retained the services of a local attorney, Jack Hope, on a number of occasions to assist him in closing on real estate transactions. He recently developed a retirement community across the state line in Oklahoma. He asks Hope to assist with closing the deal. Hope is licensed to practice law in both Texas and Oklahoma but is not as familiar with Oklahoma law since he rarely practices there. Mr. Nichols offers Hope a fee of $25,000 for his services. Hope agrees to represent Mr. Nichols, but he advises that he is not comfortable preparing the attorney's opinion document requested by the lender without the review of a local attorney in Oklahoma. Mr. Nichols understands that he will have to hire separate counsel to review the opinion. He signs an agreement to these terms with Hope. Is Hope subject to discipline?

    a. Yes, because an attorney cannot agree to limit the amount of fees to which he is entitled in a complex transaction.

    b. Yes, because requiring the developer to pay for separate counsel when attorney Hope is already licensed in Oklahoma is unethical.

    c. No, because $25,000 was insufficient to cover the cost of the entire transaction.

    d. No, because the limitation was reasonable, and Mr. Nichols consented to the entire transaction.

47. Attorney McLaughlin practices family law as a solo practitioner in the small town of Macon. Mary Lou Jackson owns a coffee shop and bookstore just around the block from McLaughlin's law office. Mary Lou agrees to prominently display an ad for McLaughlin's practice on the paper placemats used on the coffee shop tables and in the window of the bookstore. In return, McLaughlin agrees to prominently display an ad for Mary Lou's store at his law office and to recommend her business to any of his customers new to the area. The referral agreement was not exclusive, and clients and customers are advised of the agreement in the fine print of the ads. Is McLaughlin subject to discipline?

    a. No, because he did not pay Mary Lou for the referrals.

    b. No, because the agreement was not exclusive, and clients and customers are informed of the agreement.

    c. Yes, because the agreement provided something of value to Mary Lou in return for recommending his legal services.

    d. Yes, because he asked Mary Lou to place ads for the firm at her business.

48. Mary and Margaret are arrested on charges of prostitution. They hire the same counsel, attorney Fredrickson, to represent them against the charges. Fredrickson meets with the prosecutor, who suggests that the defendants consider pleading guilty in exchange for two years' probation. The prosecutor advises that both defendants must agree to the plea agreement or it will be withdrawn. Fredrickson advises the defendants of the plea offer, but he purposefully withholds the condition that both accept the offer. Mary is willing to enter a guilty plea but Margaret refuses. The prosecutor withdraws the offer. Is Fredrickson subject to discipline?

    a. Yes, because he was willing to accept a plea that required both of his clients to consent.

    b. Yes, because he did not tell both defendants the full conditions of the plea offer.

    c. No, because he conveyed the plea offer to both of his clients.

    d. No, because the defendants had the ultimate right to accept or decline the plea offer.

49. Attorney Harrison practices at a small boutique firm specializing in tax law. Mr. Hicks retains Harrison to represent him in a dispute with the IRS. Harrison explains to Mr. Hicks that because the firm is small, he and his fellow attorneys routinely discuss cases among themselves to share expertise and experience. Mr. Hicks was previously represented by another attorney in the firm regarding a separate matter that did not have a favorable result. He advises Harrison that he has no objection to discussion of his current tax issue within the firm, apart from his former counsel. As Harrison prepares the case, he frequently discusses the facts with other attorneys in the office, including the former counsel, who assists Harrison in reaching a favorable outcome for Mr. Hicks. Is Harrison subject to discipline?

a. Yes, because Mr. Hicks expressly told attorney Harrison not to disclose information to the former counsel.
b. Yes, because a client cannot consent to the disclosure of information relevant to the representation.
c. No, because consulting with the former counsel was necessary to obtain a favorable outcome in the case.
d. No, because the former counsel was a member of attorney Harrison's firm.

50. The mayor of Reedsburg, who is also a prominent businesswoman, is being investigated for ties to the mafia and providing governmental favors in exchange for money paid to her personally. Federal prosecutor Finley contacts an informant within the mafia and asks him to secretly record conversations between himself and the mayor related to the transfer of funds from the organization to the mayor's personal accounts. The most incriminating recorded conversation occurs after the mayor retains a local transactional attorney to help her business negotiate a contract with another out of state corporation. Once Finley receives the recorded conversation, he proceeds to have the mayor arrested and indicted. Is Finley subject to discipline?

a. Yes, because the mayor had an attorney on retainer and the conversation related to the subject matter of the investigation.
b. Yes, because he did not request a court order for the informant to communicate with the mayor.
c. No, because the informant, not prosecutor Finley, recorded the conversation.
d. No, because the law permitted him to have the informant record the conversation.

51. Eric Graves was recently defeated in his bid for reelection as attorney general for the state of Utah. He decides to return to private practice in his hometown. He prints fliers announcing his return to private practice and mails them to previous clients, members of the bar, and friends and business associates he has never represented. The announcement states that he has reopened his law office, states his office address, contact information, and adds that he recently served a term as the state attorney general. Are Graves's actions proper?

a. No, because his announcement implies ability to improperly influence the state courts.
b. No, because he mailed the announcement to people who had never been his clients.
c. Yes, because all of the information in the announcement is truthful.
d. Yes, because all of the information in the announcement is public information.

52. Attorney Raymond represents Mr. Sebastian in a personal injury action arising from a motor vehicle accident. The police report lists an eyewitness to the accident. Raymond interviews the eyewitness and determines that her testimony would be favorable for Mr. Sebastian's case. Unfortunately, the eyewitness lives several hundred miles from the court where the trial will be held. To secure her testimony, Raymond offers to pay the eyewitness reimbursement for travel expenses, lost wages for the time spent at trial, and 5 percent of any damages recovered by Mr. Sebastian at trial. Are Raymond's actions proper?

    a. Yes, because all of these expenses and damages are allowable under the Model Rules.
    b. Yes, because the reimbursement is necessary to secure testimony that is imperative to his client's case.
    c. No, because he is offering an inducement to the witness.
    d. No, because none of these expenses or damages are allowable under the Model Rules.

53. Ronald Tripp, a prominent businessman, purposefully refused to file federal tax returns for five consecutive years. He receives a certified letter from the IRS notifying him of the delinquency and advising him of the penalties for tax evasion, which include imprisonment. Mr. Tripp calls his former tax attorney, Ms. Joyner, who advises him to immediately prepare the delinquent tax returns. She agrees to represent Mr. Tripp if he is required to appear at an IRS hearing. For now, she files the delinquent tax returns on Mr. Tripp's behalf, but she does so without disclosing that she is Mr. Tripp's attorney. Is Ms. Joyner subject to discipline?

    a. Yes, because she did not disclose to the IRS that she was serving as Mr. Tripp's attorney.
    b. Yes, because she assisted Mr. Tripp in criminal activity.
    c. No, because she was not aware of the criminal activity at the time Mr. Tripp decided not to file tax returns.
    d. No, because filing a tax return does not involve an official hearing or meeting with the IRS.

54. Edgerton Brothers Construction Company was formed by brothers Marty and Rick. The brothers hire attorney Sutton to help them prepare and file the required documents to establish and register the company with the state. Six months later, a subcontractor sues the partnership for breach of contract. Sutton agrees to represent the brothers in the action. The plaintiff prevails at trial and damages are assessed against the partnership. Shortly after the case is resolved, Rick discloses to Marty that he failed to provide certain documents during trial preparation that would have supported their defense of the claim. Marty consults with Sutton and requests that he file a tort action against Rick for negligence in failing to provide the missing information. He believes the breach of contract action would have had a different result had the information been available at trial. Is it proper for Sutton to represent Marty in a lawsuit against his brother?

    a. Yes, if Marty reasonably believes his brother's failure to provide the information resulted in a judgment against the partnership.
    b. Yes, because he did not know of the withheld information during his representation of the partnership at trial.
    c. No, because he represented both brothers in the breach of contract action.
    d. No, because separate counsel will represent Rick in the lawsuit brought by Marty.

55. Mr. Hall, the superintendent of the local school district, well-known within the community, is charged with the attempted murder of his estranged wife. Attorney Nixon represents the superintendent in his defense against the charges. He advises his client that he has little concern of a conviction as he believes the prosecution's case is based solely on circumstantial evidence. Nixon is shocked when the jury returns a guilty verdict for the prosecution. Mr. Hall is then sentenced to 15 years in prison. A week after the sentencing, Nixon attempts to contact the jury foreman to question him about the jury's reasoning behind the verdict. The foreman tells Nixon that he does not want to speak to him. Nixon subsequently asks his paralegal to contact the foreman and pretend to be a newspaper reporter interested in writing a story on the trial. This time, the foreman is willing to discuss the verdict. Neither Nixon nor his paralegal has any further contact with the foreman after that conversation. Is Nixon subject to discipline?

   a. Yes, because the jury foreman refused to speak with him.
   b. Yes, because he contacted a member of the jury after the jury was dismissed.
   c. No, because the paralegal, not attorney Nixon, contacted the foreman the second time.
   d. No, because neither the paralegal nor attorney Nixon contacted the jury foreman again after they obtained the information they requested.

56. Attorney Moulder recently passed the bar and opened his own law practice. He takes a variety of cases, mainly civil, in order to gain experience and pay the bills. He registers with the local courts to be appointed as defense counsel for unrepresented defendants. Shortly thereafter, he is appointed by the court to represent Tommy Williams in his defense against several criminal felony and misdemeanor counts. Moulder meets with Tommy and gathers all the relevant information regarding the charges. After several days of completing legal research and reviewing his bar study materials, Moulder realizes he lacks the knowledge and experience to provide effective representation to his client. He meets again with Tommy and advises him of his concerns, but Tommy gives his informed consent for Moulder to continue his representation. Is Moulder subject to discipline?

   a. Yes, because he lacks appropriate legal skill and understanding to represent his client.
   b. Yes, because he is not a certified specialist in criminal defense.
   c. No, because the court appointed him as defense counsel.
   d. No, because Tommy knowingly and voluntarily gave consent for his continued representation.

57. Mrs. Miner brings a claim for personal injury against Springfield City Hospital and Dr. Jameson. Mrs. Miner was seen in the emergency department and claims she was misdiagnosed by Dr. Jameson, resulting in her injuries. Attorney Mead, general counsel for the hospital, has met with the administration, nursing staff, and Dr. Jameson on a number of occasions in his investigation and management of the claim. Dr. Jameson is not employed by the hospital but rather by a contracted emergency medicine group. However, he has participated in the investigation with the good faith belief that Mead was representing his interests as well as the hospital's interests in defending the claim. Based on the context of the discussions and the questions Dr. Jameson has asked, Mead reasonably should have known that Dr. Jameson had this belief, but he did not advise Dr. Jameson to notify his insurer or seek separate legal counsel. Is Mead subject to discipline?

   a. Yes, because he did not get Dr. Jameson's written informed consent to participate in the discussions.
   b. Yes, because he did not explain to Dr. Jameson that he was only representing the hospital.
   c. No, because Dr. Jameson provided care to a patient of the hospital, he was entitled to advice from the hospital's attorney.
   d. No, because discussing the facts of a case with all involved providers is acceptable when managing a claim against the hospital.

58. The Missouri Court of Appeals, on which John Sealy is a judge, recently decided a controversial action on appeal from the trial court. The court was divided on the decision, and Sealy authored the opinion. Missouri recently legalized the use of marijuana for medical purposes. The Court of Appeals opinion interpreted the legislation as it applies to a "qualified patient" for marijuana use. Several months after the court's decision, Sealy is selected as a potential candidate for appointment to the Missouri Supreme Court. In hearings before the state judicial commission, Sealy is questioned about the controversial marijuana opinion. Sealy responds, "I correctly decided the case and would decide the same way if I hear the case as a Supreme Court justice." Is Sealy subject to discipline?

   a. Yes, because the statement indicates he will not decide the case fairly as a Supreme Court justice.
   b. Yes, because he is prohibited from discussing any court decision currently eligible for appeal.
   c. No, because he is exercising his constitutional right to free speech.
   d. No, because as a Court of Appeals judge, he is afforded immunity.

59. Mac Dyson, a former heavyweight boxing champion, is charged with rape. He hires attorney Cochran, a well-known criminal defense attorney, to represent him. Cochran advises Mac that his representation through trial will be quite costly. Mac has not been active in sports since suffering a significant head injury several years ago. He has not managed his finances well, and consequently, his expendable income is limited. He advises Cochran that he can manage a retainer fee but can't pay any additional fees at this time. Mac proposes that, in exchange for Cochran's legal services, he will transfer to him any future media rights that develop from the trial or the allegations surrounding it. Cochran advises that he will consider the proposal but recommends that Mac consult with separate counsel regarding his rights in relationship to the offer. Mac does not consult with another attorney. Will Cochran be subject to discipline if he accepts the proposal?

    a. Yes, because he is not permitted to enter into an agreement giving him the literary or media rights of his client.

    b. Yes, because he has not completed his representation of Mac.

    c. No, because Mac failed to consult with another attorney.

    d. No, because the rape case is a criminal proceeding rather than a civil action.

60. Attorney Jack Osborn recently graduated from law school and passed the bar exam. He opens his own law practice as a sole practitioner but quickly finds it difficult to retain new clients. His brother-in-law is an amateur videographer who agrees to film a short media piece to advertise Osborn's services. The resulting video shows the attorney arguing a case before what appears to be the US Supreme Court. The court justices appear to rule unanimously in favor of the attorney's client. The voice-over states that results may vary depending upon the case but concludes by stating, "Jack will fight for your rights." In actuality, Osborn has never appeared in court. The advertisement results in the attorney retaining several new clients with significant cases. Were Osborn's actions proper?

    a. No, because the advertisement implied that he had successfully appeared in court.

    b. No, because the advertisement created an unjustified expectation about the results he could achieve in court.

    c. Yes, because the advertisement was simply a dramatization.

    d. Yes, because the advertisement contained an express disclaimer.

Answer Key and Explanations for Test #2

1. A: Model Rule 1.1 requires an attorney to "provide competent representation to a client. Competent representation requires the legal knowledge, skill, thoroughness and preparation reasonably necessary for the representation." In order for Kidd to competently represent his client, it was appropriate for him to consult with his partner in order to obtain the knowledge of tax law reasonably necessary for the representation. Model Rule 1.5(e) places limitations on the division of fees between attorneys (including consent from the client), but only when they are not practicing in the same firm. The rules apply regardless of whether the identity of the client is revealed. An increase in fees for the client is allowable if the consultation is for the purpose of obtaining competence.

2. C: Model Rule 8.2(a) prohibits an attorney from making "a statement that the lawyer knows to be false or with reckless disregard as to its truth or falsity concerning the qualifications or integrity of a judge, adjudicatory officer or public legal officer, or of a candidate for election or appointment to judicial or legal office." Pfeiffer did not knowingly misrepresent any fact regarding Abernathy. The false statement is excused under the rule because Pfeiffer reasonably relied upon the accuracy of the commission's response. Just because an election is contested does not mean that the parties may make any statement regarding their opponent that they know is a misrepresentation of fact.

3. B: Model Rule 5.2(a) states that "a lawyer is bound by the Rules of Professional Conduct notwithstanding that the lawyer acted at the direction of another person." Destroying or concealing a document with potential evidentiary value is a violation of Model Rule 3.4. Franklin cannot escape liability for destroying evidence simply as a result of following Evans's instructions. While Evans's instructions violated ethical rules, Franklin is not liable simply because of Evans's conduct; she is also liable for the act of destroying the documents. A duty to obey a supervising attorney does not negate liability for an unethical act.

4. B: Pursuant to Model Rule 1.18(a), "a person who consults with a lawyer about the possibility of forming a client-lawyer relationship with respect to a matter is a prospective client." If no attorney-client relationship forms, the lawyer is prohibited from revealing any information learned from the consultation. When Williams declined representation, the only duty he owed to Mrs. Wright was that of confidentiality of the information he obtained during the consultation. By advising her to seek alternative counsel and providing her with referrals, Williams performed duties beyond those required by the rules. Mrs. Wright did have a reasonable expectation of establishing a relationship and was therefore entitled to confidentiality. This did not equate to her having an entitlement to representation.

5. B: In general, Model Rule 1.6(a) prohibits an attorney from revealing "information relating to the representation of a client unless the client gives informed consent." Rule 1.6(b), however, permits disclosure of this information in certain situations, including, as stated in Rule 1.6(b)(1), to the extent the lawyer reasonably believes necessary "to prevent reasonably certain death or substantial bodily harm." Disclosing the location to the police could prevent the councilman's death. Based on his experience, Reid can reasonably rely on Jimmy's truthfulness even though he does not know with certainty that the kidnappers will kill the councilman. Answer A is incorrect because an admission of guilt is protected by attorney-client confidentiality.

6. C: Model Rule 8.4(c) states that "it is professional misconduct for a lawyer to engage in conduct involving dishonesty, fraud, deceit or misrepresentation." Further, Model Rule 8.5(a) provides that "a lawyer admitted to practice in this jurisdiction is subject to the disciplinary authority of this jurisdiction, regardless of where the lawyer's conduct occurs." Therefore, it does not matter that the medical license renewal misrepresentation occurred in Washington, not Idaho. In fact, Dr. Bradshaw is subject to discipline in both states. Finally, the rules are addressing the misrepresentation surrounding the DUI charges, not the charges themselves; therefore, it is irrelevant whether there was a conviction on the charges.

7. D: Model Rule 3.1 prohibits an attorney from bringing or defending "a proceeding ... unless there is a basis in law and fact for doing so that is not frivolous, which includes a good faith argument for an extension, modification or reversal of existing law." Cassidy filed a complaint based on a federal statute that was valid at the time the complaint was filed. It was only after the filing that the law was repealed. Cassidy timely filed an amended complaint, curing the violation. Answers A, B, and C are incorrect because the federal statute was still valid at the time the complaint was filed.

8. C: Model Rule 1.12(a) prohibits an attorney from representing anyone "in connection with a matter in which the lawyer participated personally and substantially as a judge or other adjudicative officer or law clerk to such a person or as an arbitrator, mediator or other third-party neutral, unless all parties to the proceeding give informed consent, confirmed in writing." Here, the former judge participated personally and substantially in the divorce proceedings which would, in general, prohibit him from later representing one of the parties. However, he obtained written informed consent from both parties. Therefore, he is not subject to discipline for representing Mr. O'Connell. The fact that the former judge made a reasoned decision on child support and alimony in the divorce proceeding, or that a change in circumstances necessitates a modification, are not applicable to the conflict-of-interest issues in this question.

9. D: Model Rule 1.2(d) prohibits an attorney from helping a client "in conduct that the lawyer knows is criminal or fraudulent, but a lawyer may discuss the legal consequences of any proposed course of conduct with a client." Here, Bernard's advice attempted to prevent his client from violating the law, so it was not subject to discipline under Rule 1.2. Further, he cannot be disciplined for his client's willful conduct when he advised the client to appear in court as required, and the client chose not to follow the advice.

10. B: In general, Model Rule 1.6(a) prohibits an attorney from revealing "information relating to the representation of a client unless the client gives informed consent." Rule 1.6(b), however, permits disclosure of this information in certain situations, including, as stated in Rule 1.6(b)(5), a response "to allegations in any proceeding concerning the lawyer's representation of the client." Here, Dodge is permitted to disclose the email in order to defend himself in the disciplinary proceedings. The rule applies even after the attorney-client relationship has terminated and regardless of whether it may result in action against a client, such as the unlikely imposition of perjury charges.

11. B: Model Rule 2.1 states that, "in representing a client, a lawyer shall exercise independent professional judgment and render candid advice. In rendering advice, a lawyer may refer not only to law but to other considerations such as moral, economic, social and political factors that may be relevant to the client's situation." It was proper for Todd to consider potential negative publicity in the legal advice given to his client, and he, therefore, is not subject to discipline. While an attorney is required to pursue his client's claim "with reasonable diligence and promptness" (Model Rule 1.3), he is still entitled to refer to the considerations outlined in Rule 2.1 in deciding whether to pursue the claim. Although the park had a valid defense, this did not prohibit Todd from considering these other factors in the advice given to his client.

12. D: Generally, Model Rule 8.3(a) requires "a lawyer who knows that another lawyer has committed a violation of the Rules of Professional Conduct that raises a substantial question as to that lawyer's honesty, trustworthiness, or fitness as a lawyer in other respects, shall inform the appropriate professional authority." Here, Hannah returned the retainer and the Prestons accepted his explanation for the delay in working on their case. This does not necessarily raise a substantial question as to the attorney's honesty, trustworthiness, or fitness. Had Hannah committed professional misconduct, Davis would have the duty to report regardless of the Prestons' request otherwise. Further, there is no particular duty for Davis to confirm termination of the attorney-client relationship, but rather, she is allowed to rely on the Prestons' representations.

13. D: Model Rule 1.11 allows an attorney serving as a public official to continue practicing law provided that it does not violate any rules governing conflict of interest. Under Comment 8 of Model Rule 7.1, the name of a lawyer holding a public office shall not be used in the name of a law firm, or in communications on its behalf, during any substantial period in which the lawyer is not actively and regularly practicing with the firm. Here, Starns has avoided any conflict of interest between his role as legislator and his role as a practicing attorney. Because he continues to actively practice, the firm may continue to use his name. Answers A through C are incorrect because they either prohibit Starns from practicing law or prohibit the firm from using his name.

14. D: Model Rule of Judicial Conduct 2.11(A) requires a judge to "disqualify himself or herself in any proceeding in which the judge's impartiality might reasonably be questioned." This includes a proceeding in which the judge knows that he "has an economic interest in the subject matter in controversy" (Model Rule 2.11(3)), or in which he "has more than a de minimus interest that could be substantially affected by the proceeding" (Model Rule 2.11(2)(c)). Powell should recognize that the parties would reasonably question his impartiality if they knew he owned a substantial number of shares of Acme stock. Disclosure to the parties is insufficient to meet the requirements of the rule. Finally, the rule applies regardless of who has actual knowledge of the judge's ownership.

15. C: Model Rule 1.15(a) requires an attorney to keep a client's funds separate from his own. Comment 3 to the rule provides that a "lawyer is not required to remit to the client funds that the lawyer reasonably believes represent fees owed. However, a lawyer may not hold funds to coerce a client into accepting the lawyer's contention. The disputed portion of the funds must be kept in a trust account." In this case, $5,000 was disputed and therefore should remain in the CTA. The remaining $45,000 should be distributed ($40,000 to Mr. Beasley and $5,000 to Morgan). All of the remaining options are incorrect as they involve retaining within the CTA amounts that are undisputed.

16. A: Model Rule 1.6(a) prohibits an attorney from revealing "information relating to the representation of a client unless the client gives informed consent." The IRS is requesting information related to Anderson's representation of Mrs. Parker in the breach of contract action, but Mrs. Parker did not give consent to the disclosure. As such, it would be improper for him to release the information. The rule applies regardless of whether the information is beneficial or detrimental to the client. The rule also states that the duty of confidentiality continues after the attorney-client relationship has terminated. Finally, the rule applies beyond attorney work product to all information related to the representation.

17. D: Model Rule 3.8(g)(1) provides that "when a prosecutor knows of new, credible and material evidence creating a reasonable likelihood that a convicted defendant did not commit an offense of which the defendant was convicted, the prosecutor shall promptly disclose that evidence to an appropriate court or authority." Carter had the duty to disclose to the police or the court the information obtained through Bonner's confession. The determination of clear and convincing evidence is not one to be made by Carter, but rather by the court. Further, it is the court's duty to determine any further disclosure to the prisoner's counsel. The confession is not protected by attorney-client privilege as Carter does not represent Bonner as a client.

18. B: Model Rule 5.4(c) prohibits an attorney from allowing a non-client "to direct or regulate the lawyer's professional judgment in rendering legal services." Here, Bash agreed to proceed in a manner at odds with Junior's stated interest. Mr. Walton is not prohibited from paying Bash's fees, but not if the arrangement is meant to influence the attorney's judgment. The rule applies regardless of whether the influence or intent is in the best interest of the represented party.

19. B: Model Rule 5.6(b) prohibits an attorney from "offering or making an agreement in which a restriction on the lawyer's right to practice is part of the settlement of a client controversy." The provision in the employment contract prevents the corporate attorney from working for Clay's former partner upon termination of his employment with Clay. The prohibition set forth in Rule 5.6 trumps an employer's rights to limit an employee's conduct and negates the employee's agreement to the limitation. Since the rule prohibits both "offering or making" the agreement, the restriction is impermissible regardless of whether it was proposed by the employer or the employee.

20. D: Model Rule 1.8(h)(2) prohibits an attorney from settling a "potential claim for such liability with an unrepresented client or former client unless that person is advised in writing of the desirability of seeking and is given a reasonable opportunity to seek the advice of independent legal counsel in connection therewith." Fellows settled a potential legal malpractice claim with Mr. Sutherland without advising him in writing to seek the advice of separate legal counsel or giving him reasonable time to do so. Representing Mr. Sutherland in the original demand against the mechanic does not extend to representation in the settlement agreement in the potential legal malpractice claim. It doesn't matter that Mr. Sutherland voluntarily agreed to the terms if he did so without legal advice. The prevailing issue in this question is the conduct of Fellows, not the amount in damages from the settlement versus a legal malpractice suit.

"**21. D:** Model Rule 3.4(f) prohibits an attorney from requesting "a person other than a client to refrain from voluntarily giving relevant information to another party unless:

(1) the person is a relative or an employee or other agent of a client; and (2) the lawyer reasonably believes that the person's interests will not be adversely affected by refraining from giving such information." Further, Model Rule 8.4(a) provides that "it is professional misconduct for a lawyer to violate or attempt to violate the Rules of Professional Conduct ... through the acts of another." The roommate's sister was not an employee of the nursing home, so the exception outlined in Rule 3.4(f) does not apply. Further, Fritz used the nursing director to approach the sister, violating Rule 8.4(a)."

22. D: Model Rule 3.1 states that an attorney "shall not bring or defend a proceeding, or assert or controvert an issue therein, unless there is a basis in law and fact for doing so that is not frivolous, which includes a good faith argument for an extension, modification or reversal of existing law." The current dangerous breed statute does not include terriers; however, Hughley believes in good faith that the statute should be extended to include the breed. This good faith belief for extension of the law protects him from violation of the rule. Hughley would not be subject to discipline for bringing a frivolous claim simply because the claim is unlikely to be successful. The fact that the girl may be entitled to compensation for injuries does not overcome the requirement that the claim be based in valid law or fall within an exception such as the good faith argument for extension of the law.

23. A: Model Rule 1.1 imposes on an attorney the duty to "provide competent representation to a client. Competent representation requires the legal knowledge, skill, thoroughness and preparation reasonably necessary for the representation." Brown was not prepared and did not know that the Supreme Court decision had been overruled. Further, he failed to advise Cannon to follow the instructions of the judge after the judge advised of the change in law. This shows a lack of competence that is subject to discipline under the rules. A "reasonable belief" is not a sufficient basis upon which to give legal advice. The fact that Cannon followed Brown's advice and disobeyed the judge does not preclude the attorney's liability or application of discipline.

24. A: Model Rule 1.15(a) requires an attorney to keep a client's funds separate from his own. Pena was not allowed to use the funds in the CTA for a loan since those funds belonged to his client. The rule applies regardless of whether the attorney is able to reach the client for consent before accessing the funds or whether the client ultimately approves of the action of the attorney after the funds are accessed.

25. C: Model Rule 4.1 prohibits an attorney, in the course of representing a client, from "knowingly making a false statement of material fact or law to a third person." An attorney can violate this rule by affirming a statement by another person that the attorney knows is false. The agreement contained a statement that Adams was solely representing Mr. Good when in fact she was also providing representation to Yamasaki. Both parties signed the agreement, thereby affirming the statement, and Adams, knowing the statement was false, also signed the agreement, affirming the truth of the statement. In so doing, she violated Rule 4.1. An attorney may represent a new client with interests adverse to a former client with written informed consent of the former client. Although she obtained informed consent, and although she did not use information she obtained from prior representation, she is still subject to discipline for affirming a false statement.

26. C: Comment 3 to Model Rule 1.1 recognizes that, "in an emergency a lawyer may give advice or assistance in a matter in which the lawyer does not have the skill ordinarily required where referral to or consultation or association with another lawyer would be impractical." Although Vincent had no experience in criminal law and was without the requisite knowledge and skill to competently represent Billy, an exception existed for the emergency situation. When Billy called Vincent in the middle of the night with his one allowable phone call, it was impractical to refer to or consult with another attorney. The relationship between the cousins did not create a conflict of interest such that Vincent could not represent Billy if requested. The issue here is competence, and incompetence cannot be negated simply because a client consents.

27. A: Model Rule 7.3(b) prohibits an attorney from soliciting "professional employment by live person-to-person contact when a significant motive for the lawyer's doing so is the lawyer's or law firm's pecuniary gain, unless the contact is with a: (1) lawyer; (2) person who has a family, close personal, or prior business or professional relationship with the lawyer or law firm; or 3) person who routinely uses for business purposes the type of legal services offered by the lawyer." Since the chiropractor and Stone have a familial relationship, the attorney is not prohibited from the solicitation. Even though Stone did not offer representation for a specific matter, his request could be reasonably understood as an offer to provide legal services for pecuniary gain. The family relationship exception to the solicitation applies even though the request is looked upon unfavorably by the recipient.

28. D: Model Rule 1.15(a) requires an attorney to keep a client's funds separate from his own. Once the funds were identified as belonging to Ray (i.e., as they were earned on a monthly basis), the funds should have been removed from the client trust account. It is allowable to accept fees in advance so long as the fees are kept separately in a client trust account. The rule applies regardless of whether the fees were reasonable or not.

29. A: Model Rule 1.11(a)(2) provides that "a lawyer who has formerly served as a public officer or employee of the government shall not otherwise represent a client in connection with a matter in which the lawyer participated personally and substantially as a public officer or employee, unless the appropriate government agency gives its informed consent, confirmed in writing, to the representation." Brandon is prohibited from representing Acme in the civil data breach action because she personally and substantially participated in the criminal action as a lawyer for a state government agency. The rule applies regardless of her competence to represent Acme. Nothing in the facts indicate she sought consent to the representation from the attorney general's office. The final judgment in the criminal action was not dispositive because state law allows individual civil actions based on the same facts.

30. B: Model Rule 1.16(b)(6) permits an attorney to withdraw, among other reasons, if the representation "has been rendered unreasonably difficult by the client." Although his client has discretion in determining the objectives of litigation, Cooper is not obligated to follow the client's directions regarding how he will represent the client. Cooper is permitted to withdraw because the client's directives are making representation unreasonably difficult. Answer A is incorrect because there are limits on when an attorney may withdraw before trial. The withdrawal does not require consent from the client, but Cooper may need approval from the court.

31. A: In general, Model Rule 1.6(a) prohibits an attorney from revealing "information relating to the representation of a client unless the client gives informed consent." The information regarding the hit-and-run accident was obtained during the course of Jacobs's representation of Luke and consequently relates to that representation. As such, Jacobs should not disclose the information without Luke's consent. Luke provided the information pursuant to an attorney-client relationship regardless of the fact that the relationship was formed subsequent to the hit-and-run accident. Although Jacobs is an officer of the court, nothing within the rules requires an attorney to disclose a client's past crimes. Even though the crime remains unsolved, Jacobs is not relieved of the duty of confidentiality.

32. C: Mode Rule 1.4 requires an attorney to "explain a matter to the extent reasonably necessary to permit the client to make informed decisions regarding the representation." Prior to the civil pretrial conference, Harmon obtained Susan's informed consent to go to trial during the summer. After the pretrial conference, he timely informed her of the trial date. He also counseled her that the dual summer trial settings would not negatively impact her interests. While Harmon had an ethical duty to make "reasonable efforts to expedite litigation consistent" with Susan's interests (Rule 3.2), he did not delay the trial setting beyond the summer. Even if Answer D were factual, it is not relevant to this question regarding an attorney's duty to keep a client informed.

33. B: Model Rule 6.1 states that "every lawyer has a professional responsibility to provide legal services to those unable to pay. A lawyer should aspire to render at least (50) hours of pro bono publico legal services per year. In fulfilling this responsibility, the lawyer should: (a) provide a substantial majority of the (50) hours of legal services without fee or expectation of fee to: (1) persons of limited means or (2) charitable, religious, civic, community, governmental and educational organizations in matters that are designed primarily to address the needs of persons of limited means." Here, Dr. Fair has a successful practice with the ability to pay for attorney fees. The rule applies in spite of the substantially reduced hourly rate that Scarborough offered Dr. Fair. The five hours of service provided to a charitable organization do not amount to a "substantial majority" of the attorney's yearly pro bono requirement. The rule does not mandate 50 hours of service but rather suggests that an attorney should "aspire" to this goal.

34. C: Pursuant to Model Rule 3.3, "if a lawyer, the lawyer's client, or a witness called by the lawyer, has offered material evidence and the lawyer comes to know of its falsity, the lawyer shall take reasonable remedial measures, including, if necessary, disclosure to the tribunal." Simply not referring to the destruction of the manufacturer's notice in closing arguments is not a valid remedial measure. While Sawyer may not have relied on Mrs. Myers's testimony, he still knew of its falsity and did nothing to remediate it.

35. B: Model Rule 6.2(c) prohibits a lawyer from seeking to avoid appointment "except for good cause, such as: the client or the cause is so repugnant to the lawyer as to be likely to impair the client-lawyer relationship or the lawyer's ability to represent the client." Morris's position on the board of an organization that seeks to prevent teen drug abuse would be good cause for her to avoid representation of a defendant charged with selling drugs to a minor. Although the appointment was made by order of the court, exceptions such as this one exist to negate the order. Further, conflict of interest and financial burden may be considered, but the most reasonable argument to show "good cause" in this situation is the defense of actions that are repugnant to the attorney.

36. C: Model Rule 1.3 requires an attorney to "act with reasonable diligence and promptness in representing a client." Importantly, as stated in Comment 4, "unless the relationship is terminated ... the lawyer should carry to conclusion all matters undertaken for a client." While Moon was waiting for payment, he had not terminated the relationship and was responsible for diligently continuing the representation. This duty of diligence would not be excused merely by leave of court to withdraw and regardless of whether it resulted in harm to the client's case.

37. A: In general, Model Rule 1.7(a) prohibits a lawyer from representing "a client if the representation involves a concurrent conflict of interest." Rule 1.7(b), however, allows the representation if "(1) the lawyer reasonably believes that the lawyer will be able to provide competent and diligent representation to each affected client; (2) the representation is not prohibited by law; (3) the representation does not involve the assertion of a claim by one client against another client represented by the lawyer in the same litigation or other proceeding before a tribunal; and (4) each affected client gives informed consent, confirmed in writing." Walker reasonably believes he is able to competently represent both parties. It is a common (and therefore, presumably legal) practice in his jurisdiction. Hometown Bank and Duncan Development are not making a claim against each other, and both gave informed consent to the representation. This exception is allowed regardless of which party pays the attorney fees and regardless of whether there are competing interests between the parties.

38. D: Model Rule 3.5(b) prohibits an attorney from communicating ex parte with a juror or prospective juror "during the proceeding unless authorized to do so by law or court order." Richardson violated this rule by using an investigator to communicate with potential jurors prior to trial. The rule bars this communication so that the information obtained cannot be used to influence a jury. Even though the communication was voluntary, it could still lead to improper influence. The risk is not overcome by simply disclosing the information to opposing counsel.

39. D: Model Rule 3.9 provides that "a lawyer representing a client before a legislative body or administrative agency in a nonadjudicative proceeding shall disclose that the appearance is in a representative capacity." As Meadows is representing the interests of UHI, she is required to disclose the representation to the Senate. She is not prohibited from payment by UHI. Lawyers frequently serve as paid lobbyists. The Senate would be interested in who is paying her as it could possibly bias her testimony, thus the disclosure requirements set forth in Rule 3.9. The fact that she believes her position is in the best interest of the public does not negate the disclosure requirements.

40. C: Model Rule 3.7(a)(1) prohibits a lawyer from acting "as advocate at a trial in which the lawyer is likely to be a necessary witness unless the testimony relates to an uncontested issue." Since there is no contested issue of fact as to the execution of the will (only the terms of the will itself), Fox is not prohibited from representing the executor in probate, even though he is likely to be a necessary witness. The rule applies without regard for any beneficial interests or possible hardship of the executor.

41. D: Model Rule 1.6(b)(7) permits an attorney to "reveal information relating to the representation of a client to the extent the lawyer reasonably believes necessary to detect and resolve conflicts of interest arising from the lawyer's change of employment." As the information is being used to resolve conflicts of interest arising from Whitten's transition between firms, it is not improper for him to disclose the information. This is an exception to the general rule that an attorney must obtain consent from the client to disclose confidential information. The rule does not limit the scope of disclosure as suggested by Answer B. If the disclosure is for the purpose of detecting conflicts of interest, there is no additional requirement to advise Brown and Associates of the disclosure.

42. D: Model Rule 5.4(a)(4) prohibits an attorney from sharing "legal fees with a nonlawyer, except that: a lawyer may share court-awarded legal fees with a nonprofit organization that employed, retained or recommended employment of the lawyer in the matter." Alliance for Justice retained Jacobs, so he is allowed to share the attorney fees with this nonprofit organization. The rule does not specify how the fees must be divided, regardless of each party's contribution to the case.

43. B: Model Rule 1.5(b) states that "the scope of the representation and the basis or rate of the fee and expenses for which the client will be responsible shall be communicated to the client … any changes in the basis or rate of the fee or expenses shall also be communicated to the client." Although Beta is obligated to pay Simpson for work completed, the company only consented to the original hourly rate outlined in the retainer agreement. Whether the rate is reasonable or not is irrelevant. The agreement may be modified even though it is in writing, but the key issue is Simpson's communication of the changes to Beta.

44. B: Model Rule 1.9(a) states that an attorney "who has formerly represented a client in a matter shall not thereafter represent another person in the same or a substantially related matter in which that person's interests are materially adverse to the interests of the former client unless the former client gives informed consent, confirmed in writing." The key issue in this question is whether the residents' claims are "substantially related" to the rezoning matter. Comment 3 to the rule defines "substantially related" as involving "the same transaction or legal dispute or if there otherwise is a substantial risk that confidential factual information as would normally have been obtained in the prior representation would materially advance the client's position in the subsequent matter." Here, it does not appear that the residents' claims and James's original representation of Summit Development are substantially related. Therefore, there is no conflict of interest and James may represent the residents. Since there is no conflict of interest, then the written informed consent of Summit Development is not required.

45. A: Model Rule 1.1 requires a lawyer to "provide competent representation to a client. Competent representation requires the legal knowledge, skill, thoroughness and preparation reasonably necessary for the representation." Comment 3 to Rule 1.1 states that, "in an emergency a lawyer may give advice or assistance in a matter in which the lawyer does not have the skill ordinarily required where referral to or consultation or association with another lawyer would be impractical. Even in an emergency, however, assistance should be limited to that which is reasonably necessary in the circumstances, for ill-considered action under emergency conditions can jeopardize the client's interest." Cook attempted to refer the case to an estate planning attorney but was unsuccessful. Given the step-aunt's medical condition, it was proper for Cook to draft the will before the step-aunt's imminent death. A familial relationship is not an exception to the requirement of competence in representation. Although Answers C and D are technically correct answers, their descriptions of competence in representation are subject to the emergency exception outlined in Comment 3 to Rule 1.1.

46. D: Restatement of the Law (Third), The Law Governing Lawyers Section 19(1) states that "a client and lawyer may agree to limit a duty that a lawyer would otherwise owe to the client if: (a) the client is adequately informed and consents; and (b) the terms of the limitation are reasonable in the circumstances." Hope advised Mr. Nichols about the limitation on services before beginning representation, and Mr. Nichols consented to the arrangement. It is neither unreasonable nor unethical to request a second attorney under the circumstances. On the contrary, it would be unethical for Hope to agree to perform services he is not competent to perform. Finally, whether a fee is reasonable or sufficient is not determinative of the reasonableness of a limitation of the scope of duties.

47. C: Model Rule 7.2(b) prohibits a lawyer from giving "anything of value to a person for recommending the lawyer's services." Since Mary Lou is receiving valuable advertising space and recommendations, the agreement violates this rule. The issue is not that McLaughlin asked for Mary Lou to display ads for his legal services, but rather that he provided valuable advertising to her business. Although McLaughlin did not pay for the referrals, he provided something of value in the form of free reciprocal advertising. The rule applies regardless of whether the agreement is exclusive or non-exclusive.

48. B: Model Rule 1.8(g) states that an attorney "who represents two or more clients shall not participate in making an aggregate settlement of the claims of or against the clients, or in a criminal case an aggregated agreement as to guilty or nolo contendere pleas, unless each client gives informed consent, in a writing signed by the client." Comment 16 to the rule states that the attorney's disclosure must include "all the material terms of the settlement, including what the other clients will receive or pay if the settlement or plea offer is accepted." Here, Fredrickson failed to tell both of his clients that the plea offer is contingent upon both pleading guilty. Because he did not disclose this, the defendants could not provide informed consent to the offer, and Fredrickson would be subject to discipline.

49. A: Comment 5 to Model Rule 1.6(a) states that "lawyers in a firm may ... disclose to each other information relating to a client of the firm, unless the client has instructed that particular information be confined to specific lawyers." Mr. Hicks told Harrison that he did not want him to reveal confidential information to the former counsel. Harrison disregarded the instruction and is subject to discipline for disclosing the information against the wishes of Mr. Hicks. The rule applies regardless of whether the disclosure is beneficial or detrimental to the client.

50. D: Model Rule 4.2 prohibits an attorney, in the course of representing a client, from communicating "about the subject of the representation with a person the lawyer knows to be represented by another lawyer in the matter, unless the lawyer has the consent of the other lawyer or is authorized to do so by law or a court order." However, Comment 5 to the rule states that "communications authorized by law may also include investigative activities of lawyers representing governmental entities, directly or through investigative agents, prior to the commencement of criminal or civil enforcement proceedings." The mayor had an attorney on retainer and the recorded conversation related to the investigation. Such communication would violate the rule absent the exception for the government attorney or his agent who communicates with a represented person prior to commencing criminal proceedings. A court order was not necessary since the law already permitted the conversation. Therefore, Finley is not subject to discipline.

51. C: Model Rule 7.1 prohibits an attorney from making "a false or misleading communication about the lawyer or the lawyer's services." Nothing in Graves's announcement is false, and it appears the main purpose in sending the announcement is simply to alert members of the community of his return to private practice. Although the information is public, it could still be presented in such a way as to create an improper implication of influence. Here, however, the statement of his service as attorney general does not in and of itself imply an improper influence. Model Rule 7.3 prohibits written contact with non-clients if it "involves coercion, duress or harassment." Graves's announcement appears to do none of these things.

52. C: Model Rule 3.4(b) prohibits an attorney from offering "an inducement to a witness." Comment 3 to the rule, however, states that "it is not improper to pay a witness's expenses or to compensate an expert witness on terms permitted by law. The common law rule in most jurisdictions is that it is improper to pay an occurrence witness any fee for testifying and that it is improper to pay an expert witness a contingent fee." Here, giving the eyewitness a percentage of the damages awarded is an improper payment that could encourage false testimony. The impropriety isn't negated by the fact that the testimony is believed imperative to the client's case.

53. D: Model Rule 3.9 provides that "a lawyer representing a client before a legislative body or administrative agency in a nonadjudicative proceeding shall disclose that the appearance is in a representative capacity." Comment 3 to the rule, however, specifically indicates that filing a tax return on behalf of a client does not fall within the scope of the rule. Because Ms. Joyner did nothing beyond filing Mr. Tripp's tax returns at this point, her activity does not fall within the rule, and she would not be subject to discipline. Ms. Joyner neither advised Mr. Tripp to forego filing tax returns, nor was she representing him or otherwise knowledgeable of his actions at the time. Therefore, she is not subject to discipline for criminal action.

54. C: Model Rule 1.9(a) states that an attorney "who has formerly represented a client in a matter shall not thereafter represent another person in the same or a substantially related matter in which that person's interests are materially adverse to the interests of the former client unless the former client gives informed consent, confirmed in writing." Sutton should not represent Marty in his lawsuit against Rick because he concurrently represented both of them in a substantially related case in which the brothers' interests were materially adverse to each other. The rule still applies even if another lawyer will represent Rick in the new lawsuit. The fact that Sutton did not have knowledge of the missing information in the breach of contract action is not an exception to conflict-of-interest rules. The reasonableness of Marty's belief in a different outcome to the breach of contract action has no impact on the conflict-of-interest issue.

55. A: Model Rule 3.5(c) prohibits an attorney from communicating "with a juror or prospective juror after discharge of the jury if: (1) the communication is prohibited by law or court order; (2) the juror has made known to the lawyer a desire not to communicate; or (3) the communication involves misrepresentation, coercion, duress or harassment." The jury foreman made it clear to Nixon that he did not want to speak to him, so Nixon was prohibited from making further contact.

Additionally, Model Rule 8.4(a) provides that "it is professional misconduct for a lawyer to violate or attempt to violate the Rules of Professional Conduct ... through the acts of another." Nixon used his paralegal to contact the foreman even after he knew the foreman did not want to talk to him. The rules do not absolutely prohibit an attorney from communicating with a juror after dismissal of the jury, but this is subject to the exceptions outlined in Rule 3.5(c). The fact that Nixon refrained from further contact with the foreman does not absolve him of the violation.

56. A: Model Rule 1.1 requires an attorney to "provide competent representation to a client. Competent representation requires the legal knowledge, skill, thoroughness and preparation reasonably necessary for the representation." Even after attempts at study and legal research, Moulder recognizes that he is not competent to represent his client so continuing to do so would be improper. An attorney is not required to become a certified specialist in order to satisfy the rule's requirement of competence. Neither the court appointment nor the defendant's informed consent relieves Moulder from the requirement of competence.

57. B: Model Rule 4.3 provides that when a lawyer is "dealing on behalf of a client with a person who is not represented by counsel, a lawyer shall not state or imply that the lawyer is disinterested. When the lawyer knows or reasonably should know that the unrepresented person misunderstands the lawyer's role in the matter, the lawyer shall make reasonable efforts to correct the misunderstanding." Mead knew that Dr. Jameson was not represented, but he also should have known that Dr. Jameson believed he was being represented by him. As such, he was required to make reasonable efforts to correct the misunderstanding. While informed consent and participating in an investigation of a claim are both appropriate, the issue here is that Dr. Jameson did not understand Mead's limited role, and Mead did not make any effort to correct the misunderstanding.

58. A: Model Rule of Judicial Conduct 2.10 states that "a judge shall not, in connection with cases, controversies, or issues that are likely to come before the court, make pledges, promises, or commitments that are inconsistent with the impartial performance of the adjudicative duties of judicial office." Sealy's statement improperly made an assurance about how he would decide the marijuana issue if it comes before him in the Supreme Court. This is inconsistent with his duty of impartiality in adjudicating issues as a judge. He is not prohibited from discussing the court decision as long as it is in compliance with judicial rules. Sealy's right to free speech is limited by his duty of impartiality. Any immunity defense does not apply to protect the judge from appropriate discipline.

59. B: Model Rule 1.8(d) states that "prior to the conclusion of representation of a client, a lawyer may not make or negotiate an agreement giving the lawyer literary or media rights to a portrayal or account based in substantial part on information relating to the representation." Comment 9 to Rule 1.8 acknowledges that "an agreement by which a lawyer acquires literary or media rights concerning the conduct of the representation creates a conflict between the interests of the client and the personal interests of the lawyer." Cochran may obtain media rights but not until after his representation is concluded. Even if Mac consulted with another lawyer, Cochran could not make this kind of agreement until after the case concludes. The rule is not limited to either a criminal or a civil action.

60. A: Model Rule 7.1 prohibits an attorney from making "a false or misleading communication about the lawyer or the lawyer's services. A communication is false or misleading if it contains a material misrepresentation of fact or law, or omits a fact necessary to make the statement considered as a whole not materially misleading." Osborn's advertisement is misleading because it implies that he has argued a case in court, when he has never actually done so. While the advertisement may create an expectation about results, the greater misleading issue is that he has

actually argued a case in court. The prohibitions outlined in the rule are not overcome by a disclaimer nor by the argument that the communication is merely a dramatization.

How to Overcome Test Anxiety

Just the thought of taking a test is enough to make most people a little nervous. A test is an important event that can have a long-term impact on your future, so it's important to take it seriously and it's natural to feel anxious about performing well. But just because anxiety is normal, that doesn't mean that it's helpful in test taking, or that you should simply accept it as part of your life. Anxiety can have a variety of effects. These effects can be mild, like making you feel slightly nervous, or severe, like blocking your ability to focus or remember even a simple detail.

If you experience test anxiety—whether severe or mild—it's important to know how to beat it. To discover this, first you need to understand what causes test anxiety.

Causes of Test Anxiety

While we often think of anxiety as an uncontrollable emotional state, it can actually be caused by simple, practical things. One of the most common causes of test anxiety is that a person does not feel adequately prepared for their test. This feeling can be the result of many different issues such as poor study habits or lack of organization, but the most common culprit is time management. Starting to study too late, failing to organize your study time to cover all of the material, or being distracted while you study will mean that you're not well prepared for the test. This may lead to cramming the night before, which will cause you to be physically and mentally exhausted for the test. Poor time management also contributes to feelings of stress, fear, and hopelessness as you realize you are not well prepared but don't know what to do about it.

Other times, test anxiety is not related to your preparation for the test but comes from unresolved fear. This may be a past failure on a test, or poor performance on tests in general. It may come from comparing yourself to others who seem to be performing better or from the stress of living up to expectations. Anxiety may be driven by fears of the future—how failure on this test would affect your educational and career goals. These fears are often completely irrational, but they can still negatively impact your test performance.

> **Review Video: <u>3 Reasons You Have Test Anxiety</u>**
> Visit mometrix.com/academy and enter code: 428468

174

Elements of Test Anxiety

As mentioned earlier, test anxiety is considered to be an emotional state, but it has physical and mental components as well. Sometimes you may not even realize that you are suffering from test anxiety until you notice the physical symptoms. These can include trembling hands, rapid heartbeat, sweating, nausea, and tense muscles. Extreme anxiety may lead to fainting or vomiting. Obviously, any of these symptoms can have a negative impact on testing. It is important to recognize them as soon as they begin to occur so that you can address the problem before it damages your performance.

> **Review Video: 3 Ways to Tell You Have Test Anxiety**
> Visit mometrix.com/academy and enter code: 927847

The mental components of test anxiety include trouble focusing and inability to remember learned information. During a test, your mind is on high alert, which can help you recall information and stay focused for an extended period of time. However, anxiety interferes with your mind's natural processes, causing you to blank out, even on the questions you know well. The strain of testing during anxiety makes it difficult to stay focused, especially on a test that may take several hours. Extreme anxiety can take a huge mental toll, making it difficult not only to recall test information but even to understand the test questions or pull your thoughts together.

> **Review Video: How Test Anxiety Affects Memory**
> Visit mometrix.com/academy and enter code: 609003

Effects of Test Anxiety

Test anxiety is like a disease—if left untreated, it will get progressively worse. Anxiety leads to poor performance, and this reinforces the feelings of fear and failure, which in turn lead to poor performances on subsequent tests. It can grow from a mild nervousness to a crippling condition. If allowed to progress, test anxiety can have a big impact on your schooling, and consequently on your future.

Test anxiety can spread to other parts of your life. Anxiety on tests can become anxiety in any stressful situation, and blanking on a test can turn into panicking in a job situation. But fortunately, you don't have to let anxiety rule your testing and determine your grades. There are a number of relatively simple steps you can take to move past anxiety and function normally on a test and in the rest of life.

> **Review Video: How Test Anxiety Impacts Your Grades**
> Visit mometrix.com/academy and enter code: 939819

Physical Steps for Beating Test Anxiety

While test anxiety is a serious problem, the good news is that it can be overcome. It doesn't have to control your ability to think and remember information. While it may take time, you can begin taking steps today to beat anxiety.

Just as your first hint that you may be struggling with anxiety comes from the physical symptoms, the first step to treating it is also physical. Rest is crucial for having a clear, strong mind. If you are tired, it is much easier to give in to anxiety. But if you establish good sleep habits, your body and mind will be ready to perform optimally, without the strain of exhaustion. Additionally, sleeping well helps you to retain information better, so you're more likely to recall the answers when you see the test questions.

Getting good sleep means more than going to bed on time. It's important to allow your brain time to relax. Take study breaks from time to time so it doesn't get overworked, and don't study right before bed. Take time to rest your mind before trying to rest your body, or you may find it difficult to fall asleep.

Review Video: The Importance of Sleep for Your Brain
Visit mometrix.com/academy and enter code: 319338

Along with sleep, other aspects of physical health are important in preparing for a test. Good nutrition is vital for good brain function. Sugary foods and drinks may give a burst of energy but this burst is followed by a crash, both physically and emotionally. Instead, fuel your body with protein and vitamin-rich foods.

Also, drink plenty of water. Dehydration can lead to headaches and exhaustion, especially if your brain is already under stress from the rigors of the test. Particularly if your test is a long one, drink water during the breaks. And if possible, take an energy-boosting snack to eat between sections.

Review Video: How Diet Can Affect your Mood
Visit mometrix.com/academy and enter code: 624317

Along with sleep and diet, a third important part of physical health is exercise. Maintaining a steady workout schedule is helpful, but even taking 5-minute study breaks to walk can help get your blood pumping faster and clear your head. Exercise also releases endorphins, which contribute to a positive feeling and can help combat test anxiety.

When you nurture your physical health, you are also contributing to your mental health. If your body is healthy, your mind is much more likely to be healthy as well. So take time to rest, nourish your body with healthy food and water, and get moving as much as possible. Taking these physical steps will make you stronger and more able to take the mental steps necessary to overcome test anxiety.

Review Video: How to Stay Healthy and Prevent Test Anxiety
Visit mometrix.com/academy and enter code: 877894

Mental Steps for Beating Test Anxiety

Working on the mental side of test anxiety can be more challenging, but as with the physical side, there are clear steps you can take to overcome it. As mentioned earlier, test anxiety often stems from lack of preparation, so the obvious solution is to prepare for the test. Effective studying may be the most important weapon you have for beating test anxiety, but you can and should employ several other mental tools to combat fear.

First, boost your confidence by reminding yourself of past success—tests or projects that you aced. If you're putting as much effort into preparing for this test as you did for those, there's no reason you should expect to fail here. Work hard to prepare; then trust your preparation.

Second, surround yourself with encouraging people. It can be helpful to find a study group, but be sure that the people you're around will encourage a positive attitude. If you spend time with others who are anxious or cynical, this will only contribute to your own anxiety. Look for others who are motivated to study hard from a desire to succeed, not from a fear of failure.

Third, reward yourself. A test is physically and mentally tiring, even without anxiety, and it can be helpful to have something to look forward to. Plan an activity following the test, regardless of the outcome, such as going to a movie or getting ice cream.

When you are taking the test, if you find yourself beginning to feel anxious, remind yourself that you know the material. Visualize successfully completing the test. Then take a few deep, relaxing breaths and return to it. Work through the questions carefully but with confidence, knowing that you are capable of succeeding.

Developing a healthy mental approach to test taking will also aid in other areas of life. Test anxiety affects more than just the actual test—it can be damaging to your mental health and even contribute to depression. It's important to beat test anxiety before it becomes a problem for more than testing.

> **Review Video: Test Anxiety and Depression**
> Visit mometrix.com/academy and enter code: 904704

Study Strategy

Being prepared for the test is necessary to combat anxiety, but what does being prepared look like? You may study for hours on end and still not feel prepared. What you need is a strategy for test prep. The next few pages outline our recommended steps to help you plan out and conquer the challenge of preparation.

STEP 1: SCOPE OUT THE TEST

Learn everything you can about the format (multiple choice, essay, etc.) and what will be on the test. Gather any study materials, course outlines, or sample exams that may be available. Not only will this help you to prepare, but knowing what to expect can help to alleviate test anxiety.

STEP 2: MAP OUT THE MATERIAL

Look through the textbook or study guide and make note of how many chapters or sections it has. Then divide these over the time you have. For example, if a book has 15 chapters and you have five days to study, you need to cover three chapters each day. Even better, if you have the time, leave an extra day at the end for overall review after you have gone through the material in depth.

If time is limited, you may need to prioritize the material. Look through it and make note of which sections you think you already have a good grasp on, and which need review. While you are studying, skim quickly through the familiar sections and take more time on the challenging parts. Write out your plan so you don't get lost as you go. Having a written plan also helps you feel more in control of the study, so anxiety is less likely to arise from feeling overwhelmed at the amount to cover.

STEP 3: GATHER YOUR TOOLS

Decide what study method works best for you. Do you prefer to highlight in the book as you study and then go back over the highlighted portions? Or do you type out notes of the important information? Or is it helpful to make flashcards that you can carry with you? Assemble the pens, index cards, highlighters, post-it notes, and any other materials you may need so you won't be distracted by getting up to find things while you study.

If you're having a hard time retaining the information or organizing your notes, experiment with different methods. For example, try color-coding by subject with colored pens, highlighters, or post-it notes. If you learn better by hearing, try recording yourself reading your notes so you can listen while in the car, working out, or simply sitting at your desk. Ask a friend to quiz you from your flashcards, or try teaching someone the material to solidify it in your mind.

STEP 4: CREATE YOUR ENVIRONMENT

It's important to avoid distractions while you study. This includes both the obvious distractions like visitors and the subtle distractions like an uncomfortable chair (or a too-comfortable couch that makes you want to fall asleep). Set up the best study environment possible: good lighting and a comfortable work area. If background music helps you focus, you may want to turn it on, but otherwise keep the room quiet. If you are using a computer to take notes, be sure you don't have any other windows open, especially applications like social media, games, or anything else that could distract you. Silence your phone and turn off notifications. Be sure to keep water close by so you stay hydrated while you study (but avoid unhealthy drinks and snacks).

Also, take into account the best time of day to study. Are you freshest first thing in the morning? Try to set aside some time then to work through the material. Is your mind clearer in the afternoon or evening? Schedule your study session then. Another method is to study at the same time of day that you will take the test, so that your brain gets used to working on the material at that time and will be ready to focus at test time.

STEP 5: STUDY!

Once you have done all the study preparation, it's time to settle into the actual studying. Sit down, take a few moments to settle your mind so you can focus, and begin to follow your study plan. Don't give in to distractions or let yourself procrastinate. This is your time to prepare so you'll be ready to fearlessly approach the test. Make the most of the time and stay focused.

Of course, you don't want to burn out. If you study too long you may find that you're not retaining the information very well. Take regular study breaks. For example, taking five minutes out of every hour to walk briskly, breathing deeply and swinging your arms, can help your mind stay fresh.

As you get to the end of each chapter or section, it's a good idea to do a quick review. Remind yourself of what you learned and work on any difficult parts. When you feel that you've mastered the material, move on to the next part. At the end of your study session, briefly skim through your notes again.

But while review is helpful, cramming last minute is NOT. If at all possible, work ahead so that you won't need to fit all your study into the last day. Cramming overloads your brain with more information than it can process and retain, and your tired mind may struggle to recall even previously learned information when it is overwhelmed with last-minute study. Also, the urgent nature of cramming and the stress placed on your brain contribute to anxiety. You'll be more likely to go to the test feeling unprepared and having trouble thinking clearly.

So don't cram, and don't stay up late before the test, even just to review your notes at a leisurely pace. Your brain needs rest more than it needs to go over the information again. In fact, plan to finish your studies by noon or early afternoon the day before the test. Give your brain the rest of the day to relax or focus on other things, and get a good night's sleep. Then you will be fresh for the test and better able to recall what you've studied.

STEP 6: TAKE A PRACTICE TEST

Many courses offer sample tests, either online or in the study materials. This is an excellent resource to check whether you have mastered the material, as well as to prepare for the test format and environment.

Check the test format ahead of time: the number of questions, the type (multiple choice, free response, etc.), and the time limit. Then create a plan for working through them. For example, if you have 30 minutes to take a 60-question test, your limit is 30 seconds per question. Spend less time on the questions you know well so that you can take more time on the difficult ones.

If you have time to take several practice tests, take the first one open book, with no time limit. Work through the questions at your own pace and make sure you fully understand them. Gradually work up to taking a test under test conditions: sit at a desk with all study materials put away and set a timer. Pace yourself to make sure you finish the test with time to spare and go back to check your answers if you have time.

After each test, check your answers. On the questions you missed, be sure you understand why you missed them. Did you misread the question (tests can use tricky wording)? Did you forget the information? Or was it something you hadn't learned? Go back and study any shaky areas that the practice tests reveal.

Taking these tests not only helps with your grade, but also aids in combating test anxiety. If you're already used to the test conditions, you're less likely to worry about it, and working through tests until you're scoring well gives you a confidence boost. Go through the practice tests until you feel comfortable, and then you can go into the test knowing that you're ready for it.

Test Tips

On test day, you should be confident, knowing that you've prepared well and are ready to answer the questions. But aside from preparation, there are several test day strategies you can employ to maximize your performance.

First, as stated before, get a good night's sleep the night before the test (and for several nights before that, if possible). Go into the test with a fresh, alert mind rather than staying up late to study.

Try not to change too much about your normal routine on the day of the test. It's important to eat a nutritious breakfast, but if you normally don't eat breakfast at all, consider eating just a protein bar. If you're a coffee drinker, go ahead and have your normal coffee. Just make sure you time it so that the caffeine doesn't wear off right in the middle of your test. Avoid sugary beverages, and drink enough water to stay hydrated but not so much that you need a restroom break 10 minutes into the test. If your test isn't first thing in the morning, consider going for a walk or doing a light workout before the test to get your blood flowing.

Allow yourself enough time to get ready, and leave for the test with plenty of time to spare so you won't have the anxiety of scrambling to arrive in time. Another reason to be early is to select a good seat. It's helpful to sit away from doors and windows, which can be distracting. Find a good seat, get out your supplies, and settle your mind before the test begins.

When the test begins, start by going over the instructions carefully, even if you already know what to expect. Make sure you avoid any careless mistakes by following the directions.

Then begin working through the questions, pacing yourself as you've practiced. If you're not sure on an answer, don't spend too much time on it, and don't let it shake your confidence. Either skip it and come back later, or eliminate as many wrong answers as possible and guess among the remaining ones. Don't dwell on these questions as you continue—put them out of your mind and focus on what lies ahead.

Be sure to read all of the answer choices, even if you're sure the first one is the right answer. Sometimes you'll find a better one if you keep reading. But don't second-guess yourself if you do immediately know the answer. Your gut instinct is usually right. Don't let test anxiety rob you of the information you know.

If you have time at the end of the test (and if the test format allows), go back and review your answers. Be cautious about changing any, since your first instinct tends to be correct, but make sure you didn't misread any of the questions or accidentally mark the wrong answer choice. Look over any you skipped and make an educated guess.

At the end, leave the test feeling confident. You've done your best, so don't waste time worrying about your performance or wishing you could change anything. Instead, celebrate the successful completion of this test. And finally, use this test to learn how to deal with anxiety even better next time.

Important Qualification

Not all anxiety is created equal. If your test anxiety is causing major issues in your life beyond the classroom or testing center, or if you are experiencing troubling physical symptoms related to your anxiety, it may be a sign of a serious physiological or psychological condition. If this sounds like your situation, we strongly encourage you to seek professional help.

Tell Us Your Story

We at Mometrix would like to extend our heartfelt thanks to you for letting us be a part of your journey. It is an honor to serve people from all walks of life, people like you, who are committed to building the best future they can for themselves.

We know that each person's situation is unique. But we also know that, whether you are a young student or a mother of four, you care about working to make your own life and the lives of those around you better.

That's why we want to hear your story.

We want to know why you're taking this test. We want to know about the trials you've gone through to get here. And we want to know about the successes you've experienced after taking and passing your test.

In addition to your story, which can be an inspiration both to us and to others, we value your feedback. We want to know both what you loved about our book and what you think we can improve on.

The team at Mometrix would be absolutely thrilled to hear from you! So please, send us an email at tellusyourstory@mometrix.com or visit us at mometrix.com/tellusyourstory.php and let's stay in touch.

SCAN HERE

Additional Bonus Material

Due to our efforts to try to keep this book to a manageable length, we've created a link that will give you access to all of your additional bonus material.

> Please visit http://www.mometrix.com/bonus948/mpre to access the information.

Made in United States
Orlando, FL
29 July 2023

35571868R00109